CW01095847

The Historical Arthur
and the *Gawain* Poet

STUDIES IN MEDIEVAL LITERATURE

Series Editor: Albrecht Classen, University of Arizona

Advisory Board

Studies in Medieval Literature invites scholars to publish their most powerful, exciting, and forward-looking studies, which will thus become an excellent platform for Medieval Studies at large.

Recent Titles

The Historical Arthur and the Gawain *Poet: Studies on Arthurian and Other Traditions* by Andrew Breeze

The Secret in Medieval Literature: Alternatives World During the Middle Ages by Albrecht Classen

Becoming the Pearl-Poet: Perceptions, Connections, Receptions edited by Jane Beal

Incarceration and Slavery in the Middle Ages and the Early Modern Age Cultural-Historical Investigation of the Dark Side in the Pre-Modern World edited by Albrecht Classen

Dante Satiro: Satire in Dante Alighieri's Comedy and Other Works by Fabian Alfie and Nicolino Applauso

Dante's Comedy and the Ethics of Invective in Medieval Italy: Humor and Evil by Nicolino Applauso

Prostitution in Medieval and Early Modern Literature: The Dark Side of Sex and Love in the Pre-Modern Era by Albrecht Classen

Chaucer's Neoplatonism: Varieties of Love, Friendship, and Community by John M. Hill

The Historical Arthur and the *Gawain* Poet

Studies on Arthurian and Other Traditions

Andrew Breeze

LEXINGTON BOOKS

Lanham • Boulder • New York • London

Published by Lexington Books
An imprint of The Rowman & Littlefield Publishing Group, Inc.
4501 Forbes Boulevard, Suite 200, Lanham, Maryland 20706
www.rowman.com

86-90 Paul Street, London EC2A 4NE

British Library Cataloguing in Publication Information Available

Library of Congress Cataloging-in-Publication Data

Names: Breeze, Andrew, author.
Title: The historical Arthur and the Gawain poet : studies on Arthurian and other
    traditions / Andrew Charles Breeze.
Description: Lanham : Lexington Books, [2023] | Series: Studies in medieval literature |
    Includes bibliographical references and index.
Identifiers: LCCN 2022046820 (print) | LCCN 2022046821 (ebook) |
    ISBN 9781666929546 (cloth) | ISBN 9781666929553 (ebook)
Subjects: LCSH: Arthurian romances—Sources. | Arthur, King. | Britons—Kings and
    rulers—Historiography. | Great Britain—History—To 1066. | Sir Gawain and the
    Green Knight. | Stanley, John, Sir, approximately 1350-1414.
Classification: LCC DA152.5.A7 B74 2023 (print) | LCC DA152.5.A7 (ebook) | DDC
    942.01/4—dc23/eng/20221108
LC record available at https://lccn.loc.gov/2022046820
LC ebook record available at https://lccn.loc.gov/2022046821

To Rosamund Allen of Queen Mary, University of London, and
Rosalind Field of Royal Holloway, University of London

Contents

Preface

In Wilde's *The Importance of Being Earnest*, Gwendolen Fairfax describes her diary as a "sensational" work, suitable for reading on trains. *The Historical Arthur and the* Gawain *Poet* is sensational, too, if in another way. It contains proof for "King" Arthur as a real person, a North British champion killed in 537 at *Camlan* (the fort of Castlesteads on Hadrian's Wall). As if this was not enough, its second part offers proof for the Arthurian romance *Sir Gawain and the Green Knight* as written in 1387 by Sir John Stanley (d. 1414), Cheshire magnate, who (it seems) intended it for Christmas festivities at Chester Castle. Besides this and other poems (*Patience*, *Cleanness*, *Pearl*) of John Stanley are two more, also tales of the supernatural. One is *St. Erkenwald*, perhaps written by his brother Sir William Stanley (of Storeton and Hooton in the Wirral, Cheshire); the other is *The Awntyrs off Arthure*, an alliterative poem in the tradition of *Sir Gawain* (and composed by an unknown Cumbrian cleric in 1424–1425). So, if the above is correct, we settle for all time the question of "King" Arthur's historicity; and introduce John Stanley to the pantheon of England's poets. He there ranks with Chaucer himself, whom he knew, and who in his *Squire's Tale* imitated *Sir Gawain and the Green Knight*.

In the writing of this book, it has been useful to have publications (some penetrating, some colorful and adventurous, but all listed in the bibliography) sent by scholars in the US and elsewhere in Europe. In the foreground here are the London medievalists Rosalind Field and Rosamund Allen. While some material below has appeared in Spanish or North African or US journals (as indicated below), it gained emphatic confirmation in 2022 thanks to these two ladies. It was through them that the author was alerted to Ann Astell's *Political Allegory in Late Medieval England* (1999) and Piero Boitani's *Chaucer and the Italian Trecento* (1983). They are vital to the section on the *Gawain* Poet. Remarks by Ann Astell on lines 678 and 866 of *Sir Gawain and the Green Knight* as mischievous allusions to Robert de Vere (d. 1392), Duke of Ireland, are crucial for dating the poem to 1387, when de Vere spent a flamboyant summer at Chester Castle with John Stanley, his deputy for the government of Ireland. As for the essays edited by Boitani, Wendy Childs there notes how Antonio de Romanis, a Neapolitan physician, was Sir John Stanley's doctor at Chester in 1387. His presence would account for the Italian influences (of Dante, Boccaccio, Jacopo della Lana) on *Pearl* and *St. Erkenwald*. Both poems would be composed for a Cheshire audience. Neither they nor *Sir Gawain and the Green Knight* had a direct link with Richard II's court, despite assertions by Professor Jill Mann (of Cambridge) and others. Hence the dedication of this book to these distinguished scholars of London University. Also to be thanked are the editors of *Revue de Traduction et Langues*, *SELIM*, and *The Journal of Literary Onomastics*, who first published material reproduced in chapters 2, 3, and 7; and the historian Nikolai Tolstoy, to whom the writer owes many kindnesses, and whose *The Quest for King Arthur* (due for publication in 2023) will most certainly provide a stimulating critique of arguments in this book.

PART ONE

Arthur

Chapter One

The Historical Arthur

In 1956, Sir Winston Churchill had a gruff comment on one Arthurian scholar. He could not say whether Arthur fought any of the battles attributed to him, producing the Churchillian riposte, "This is not much to show after so much toil and learning."[1] A few years later, Kenneth Jackson (a great scholar) was not even sure if there ever was such a man as Arthur, declaring that the only honest answer was "We do not know, but he may well have existed."[2]

After such obscurity, we are today in a blaze of light. Arthur existed, and we know much about him. He was a North British commander and raider (not a king), killed near Carlisle in 537. So we can see historians of past and present with new eyes, including Churchill, who comes out of the matter rather well. His discussion shows characteristic impatience (even scorn) for the vagueness of professional historians; a confidence in Arthur as a figure of history, not legend; shrewd comments on the Battle of Mount Badon (a British victory of 493, which yet has no link with Arthur); and (more dubiously) a vision of Arthur as a cavalry officer (like Churchill) who (like Churchill) defended civilization against Germanic barbarism. Sir Winston's views on Arthur are thus no bad place to start a book on this sixth-century hero. Churchill had a mastery of words and no small experience of politics and war. What he said of Arthur has a weight not found in work by the rest of us.

This chapter, then, has three parts. Churchill's account gives us an initial survey; we go on to aspects of Arthur's career; and end with recent commentary. First, Churchill. His pages on Arthur in *A History of the English-Speaking Peoples* show that he had done his homework. He knew that the historian Gildas (493–570, and writing in the year 536), mentioning a British victory at Mount Badon over the English, added that it took place in the year of his birth. Churchill also knew that Gildas left the British leader unnamed, but the ninth-century Latin *Historia Brittonum* (formerly attributed to Nennius) did name him, as Arthur. In Churchill's words, "a great captain gathered the forces of Roman Britain and fought the barbarian invaders to the death. Around him, around his name and his deeds, shine all that romance and

poetry can bestow." The legend of Arthur appealed to the emotional patrio-
tism at the heart of Churchill's being, the tale of Britain through the ages
being (for him) one of unfolding glory.

Churchill still acknowledged the doubts of historians, referring to Arthur's
other battles as "located in scenes untraceable." Better for him was Arthur's
international fame. It possessed "the splendours of feudalism and martial aristocracy" (plus "knights in steel and ladies bewitching"), all due to *Historia
Regum Britanniae*, written by Geoffrey of Monmouth in the 1130s. These
stories, "true or false," had "gained an immortal hold upon the thoughts of
men. It is difficult to believe that it was all an invention of a Welsh writer. If
it was, he must have been a marvellous inventor."

With Churchill in mind, then, we move forwards to updated commentary.
Besides Gildas and British triumph at Mount Badon (in 493, as we now
know), there was the question of other battles listed in the ninth-century
Historia Brittonum or "History of the Britons." The oldest copy, written in
about 1100, is in London, British Library, MS Harley 3859. Its chapter 56 sets
out Arthur's Twelve Battles, which he fought in the company of British kings,
though he himself was not a king, merely *dux bellorum* "leader of battles."
(On what that means, see chapter 2.) These battles are a notorious historical problem. They have obscure and uncouth names. Yet every one of them
can now be placed in southern Scotland or on its border, with the exception
of Badon, fought in the spring or summer of 493 in what is now southern
England, and so nothing to do with Arthur, even though it is described as his
greatest victory. Of the eleven remaining conflicts, seven took place by rivers
or on river-sites called Glein, Douglas, Bassas, or Tryfrwyd. The other four
were at the Caledonian Forest, Guinnion Fort, City of the Legions, and Agned
Hill. But where were they all? And when did they take place?

Crucial here is a paper by David Woods of Cork, who dated the Battle of
Mount Badon to 493. His arguments are rather elegant and run as follows.
Badon is mentioned by the sixth-century writer Gildas, who says that the
conflict occurred forty-three years and a month before his time. Later in
his text, Gildas alludes to a strange dark cloud over the "whole island" of
Britain. Woods proved from these allusions that Gildas wrote in early 536,
when the northern hemisphere was covered by a volcanic cloud (following
a mega-eruption in Central America) which was to produce a catastrophic
dip in temperature, harvest failure, and famine. Gildas, a British Jeremiah, is
yet curiously silent on this catastrophe. He therefore wrote before the effects
of the volcanic winter were evident. This worldwide climatic disaster will
date both Gildas and Badon.[3] Now, 536 minus 43 = 493. If Arthur died near
Carlisle in 537, his career is too late for him to have been at Badon in 493.
So Mount Badon can be detached from his triumphs. The real victor was
presumably the Ambrosius Aurelianus praised by Gildas, whose family had

associations with the Gloucester-Cirencester area, his grandsons being mentioned (in negative terms) by Gildas.

As for locations, light is shed by a thirteenth battle. According to the Welsh annals, Arthur died a soldier's death in 537 at *Camlan*. The archaeologist O. G. S. Crawford argued in 1935 that *Camlan* was *Camboglanna*, a fort on Hadrian's Wall. Modern researchers identify it as Castlesteads, near Carlisle. It is evidence for Arthur as a North Briton, perhaps from Strathclyde, which for centuries was an independent British kingdom. It also puts him in the 530s. On all twelve battles proper, work with maps fills in the picture. The River "Glein" is the Northumberland Glen; the Douglas is near Lanark, in south-west Scotland; "Bassas" is a corrupt form related either to Cars*tairs*, or else to *Tarras* Water, also in southern Scotland (the former southeast of Glasgow, the latter near the border with Cumbria); "Tryfrwyd" is apparently Dreva, a small place on the River Tweed, near Peebles. Scholars accept the Caledonian Forest as the wilderness around Beattock, between Glasgow and Carlisle; Guinnion Fort was identified by Dr. Tim Clarkson (of Manchester) as Carwinning, near Lochwinnoch (not far from Dalry, north Ayrshire). As for the names of Legion City, Agned Hill, and Mount Badon, all three are corrupt. Medieval documents let us take the first as a location on the Antonine Wall near Bo'ness, West Lothian; the second as a spot south of Hawick, and so again in southern Scotland; and the third (nothing to do with Arthur) as a hillfort above *Braydon* Forest, northwest of Swindon, in the English county of Wiltshire.[4]

What is the upshot? It is startling. It means that Arthur can be identified as a warrior of the 530s, defeating enemies in what are now Scotland and its borders. We can end this first part with a series of Arthurian truths, to be distinguished from Arthurian myths.

1. We can be sure that Arthur really existed. The Welsh annal for 537 on his death in battle at *Camlan* can be accepted as fact. It shows Arthur as a North Briton, the archaeologist O. G. S. Crawford having (as noted) in 1935 located *Camlan* at the fort of *Camboglanna* on Hadrian's Wall, a few miles north of Carlisle in what is now northern England.

2. We also know that his name is of Latin origin, from *Artorius*. It does not derive from Celtic. The historical Arthur of North Britain was not a Roman, but displayed influence from Rome's four-hundred-year occupation of Britain. No doubt he spoke Latin as well as British (= ancestor language of modern Welsh, Cornish, and Breton).

3. As for the twelve battles listed in *Historia Brittonum*, they can all be placed and (with the exception of Mount Badon) ascribed to Arthur. Detailed arguments being in papers cited here, we need not go into detail. What matters is that, except for one, they can all be placed in

southern Scotland or northern England. The four battles on the Douglas will have been southeast of Glasgow, on the River Douglas near the modern town of Lanark. The conflict in the Caledonian Forest was certainly in Scotland, in the rugged mountain country between Glasgow and Carlisle. As for the River Glen, this has long been accepted as the Glen of north Northumberland, not far from the modern Scottish border. The picture that emerges is not of Arthur fighting English invaders up and down Britain, but of Arthur in conflict with other North Britons. The implication is not only that he was a North Briton, but that he was from the Glasgow region; that he attacked the Britons of Edinburgh, of the Tweed valley, and of Carlisle and the rest of Cumbria; but also defended Strathclyde against counterattack, as (for example) in the four engagements on the Douglas, near Lanark.

4. One battle which he did not fight is that of Mount Badon. Its name is Celtic, but makes no sense as it stands. If we emend the text of Gildas and read *Bradon*, understanding dawns. We can then identify the "mount" as a hill above Braydon Forest, northwest of Swindon, a summit crowned by the Iron Age hillfort of Ringsbury. It is only a few miles northwest of the Badbury mentioned by Churchill, whose strategic understanding of the campaign was sound. Its location far from Arthur's genuine battles in North Britain, and the fact that early Welsh native tradition, while saying much of Camlan, never mentions Badon, explain why Gildas speaks of it without reference to Arthur. It had no connection whatever with the British hero.

As regards Churchill's account of Arthur, then, on some matters his judgment was well-founded. On others, he was misled by professional historians. On one great point he was completely right, in believing that Arthur existed, that he was as historical as Oliver Cromwell or Abraham Lincoln. Churchill can be vindicated against those who in the 1970s pulled out a new red herring for writers on the past, maintaining that there was no historical evidence for Arthur and making him out as legendary, a figure of mythology or folklore.

There is a more general point. It is always (as Dr. Johnson remarked) easy to be negative. Here we come back to that Churchillian gruffness; for he went on to speak of the timidity of scholars (timidity was not a Churchillian defect), among whom a "fear of being contradicted leads the writer to strip himself of almost all sense and meaning," so that he quoted a passage from one (unnamed) historian, who suggested that Arthur may have existed as a "petty chieftain" (probably "in South Wales"); that he could have had "some military command uniting" forces of the Britons against "raiders and invaders" (not necessarily the Anglo-Saxons); and that he perhaps fought all the battles attributed to him, although "the attribution may belong to a later date."

Hence Churchill's brusque "not much to show." All the same, the words quoted by him have some truth. Notions of South Wales, or Arthur as petty chieftain and defender against English invaders, can alike be rejected. The real Arthur was a North Briton, commander of a war-band, raiding British neighbors and defending his territory again their attacks. It is also true that he fought the battles ascribed to him, excepting Mount Badon, where the attribution really does "belong to a later date."

Now for Churchill's further and emphatic remark, "It is all true, or it ought to be; and more and better besides." And he went on rhetorically to declare how "Arthur and his noble knights, guarding the Sacred Flame of Christianity and the theme of a world order, sustained by valour, physical strength, and good horses and armour, slaughtered innumerable hosts of foul barbarians and set decent people an example for all time." It is a revealing comment, especially on Churchill. His romanticism, insouciance, bluffness, humor, gift for rhetoric, and practical military sense are all there. Still, the Arthur of history certainly possessed strength and valor. Those who lack prowess are rarely the stuff of legend. Like Churchill (an ex-cavalryman), Arthur would have been expert on horses, weapons, strategy, planning, and the like. Comparison between an ancient British hero and a modern one is not empty.

Churchill ended his discussion with statements on the ninth-century *Historia Brittonum*. Arthur appears in it not as king but *dux bellorum*. Again, this must be correct. No early source claims Arthur as a king, merely as a very successful general, who fought his battles in alliance with princes whose rank was superior to his own. But Churchill's belief that the title made Arthur out as a "new Count of Britain," the "commander of a mobile field army, moving from one part of the country to another," depends on wild speculations by the Oxford historian R. G. Collingwood (1889–1943). They must be dropped. One sees how Collingwood's Arthur (a cavalryman) had fatal allure for Churchill (a proficient horseman), so that he warmed to the idea. He had arguments to support it, because "the fourth century witnessed the rise of cavalry to the dominant position on the battlefield." Against Saxon infantry, "a small force of ordinary Roman cavalry might well prove invincible." And Churchill proceeded to quote Collingwood on Arthur as "last of the Romans," the last to understand Roman ideas and use them for the good of the British people.

Such ideas must, alas, collapse for two reasons. First, there is not the slightest reason to think that *dux bellorum* denoted a general in charge of cavalry squadrons capable of rapid deployment. It makes better sense as a Dark Age Welshman's rendering of the native term *penteulu*, the commander of a royal warband. Second, the locating of Arthur's battles in the North (and not all over Britain) demolishes any need for highly-mobile units of horsemen to fight them.

Finally, the great victory of Mount Badon. Churchill here admitted defeat. All efforts to fix its site "have failed. A hundred learned investigations have brought no results." Yet the darkness was not total. It seems clear that "it was fought in the Debatable Land to check the advance from the East," so that the "best claimant" here is Liddington Camp, an ancient hillfort looking down on Badbury, near Swindon in southern England. Churchill's sense of strategy was correct. We can put Mount Badon to within a few miles of the very place that he thought likely. He noted further that we can be fairly sure on the date. Gildas spoke of it as taking place forty-three years and a month from when he was writing. Now, Gildas launched his invective against British tyrants of his day, including Maelgwn Gwynedd, ruler of northwest Wales. Maelgwn died in 547. The Battle of Mount Badon therefore took place no later than 503. Because Irish annals give 570 as when Gildas died, he would hardly have been born much earlier than 490. Churchill hence concluded that "the date of the battle seems fixed between 490 and 503." Timing and location are fundamental to commanders and historians. In his historical writings Churchill neglected neither. On both, he was to the point.

Not only can we locate Mount Badon or Bradon, but we can say even more precisely than Churchill did when it was fought. We have mentioned David Woods and his paper of 2010, drawing attention to Gildas's chapter 93 and a "certain thick mist and black night" sitting "upon the whole island" of Britain. Because Gildas says nothing of the famine which resulted from this cloud of volcanic ash and dust, even though Welsh and Irish annals refer to "dearth of bread" (as does the Byzantine historian Procopius), we can be certain that Gildas wrote after the cloud had appeared, but before it began to destroy harvests. His book will date from the summer of 536; the Battle of Mount Badon will have been in the spring or summer of 493, forty-three years and a month previous, and long before Arthur was active.

What Arthur did was to fight other North Britons. He did not fight the English invader, as the compiler of *Historia Brittonum* wrongly assumed. The circumstances of 536–537 even suggest why he was leading attacks on his British neighbors, and defending Strathclyde (as it seems) against counterattack. His people were facing starvation. Early Welsh and Irish poems and sagas have much on cattle-raiding, a prerogative of lords and princes.[5] It is likely that Arthur brought back cattle to feed his people with such success that he was first a hero, then a legend. The last is implied by British princes of the late sixth century who were called after him, like the Artúr (grandson of Aedán) dealt with below. Arthur's victories for a while gave his name prestige. It was fit for those of royal blood.

To sum up, then, we can say that Arthur really existed. He was not a Welshman or Cornishman, but a North Briton, a British Celt living in what is now southern Scotland. Second, he was a supreme warrior, who fought other British tribes or peoples, and not the English (who were nowhere near Scotland in his day). Third, he died in 537 at "Camlan" or *Camboglanna*, the fort of Castlesteads on Hadrian's Wall, now within England. Fourth, he lived in a time of crisis. The volcanic winter of 536–537 brought starvation to northern Europe, including Britain and Ireland. Famine is mentioned in annals from both countries. So Arthur probably engaged in cattle-raids on other North Britons. Hence his "battles." His success in obtaining food for his people was to bring him legendary fame. Fifth, he would have spoken British (the Celtic language which developed into Welsh and Cornish) and Latin. Sixth, he had a name of classical (not Celtic) origin, from Latin *Artorius*. Even though he lived outside the long-term bounds of the Roman Empire, he had a debt to Roman culture, including being a Christian (and no pagan). He was not a Roman cavalry officer, as Churchill imagined. Early Welsh poetry, such as Aneirin's *Gododdin* (perhaps of the year 603, when Northumbrians crushed Celtic attacks on their territory), demonstrates how Britons of the Dark Ages fought their battles on foot. When British armies were on the march, the officers had steeds. On reaching the scene of conflict, they dismounted. Horses as chargers in battle are never mentioned.

The result of the above is that analysis of place-names and other evidence for Arthur proves Churchill right in several aspects. He was right in his confidence that Arthur was a man of flesh and blood (and not a myth). He was right as well in locating Mount Badon near Swindon and dating it to between 490 and 503. Where we disagree with him, and with R. G. Collingwood, whose speculations he took too much on board, is on Arthur as a Roman cavalry commander fighting all over Britain. The use of horses in war, a pride in empire, the defence of Britain again barbaric Germanic invaders, were all subjects on which Churchill knew much. His experience naturally colored his views of the past, so that his Arthur comes out as a sixth-century Churchill. Nevertheless, his knowledge of warfare kept his comments within the realm of the realistic. So an account of Churchill on Arthur reveals things to be accepted and others to be rejected. But it also tells us about the contrasts of romantic and sharply realistic within Churchill himself.

Now for our second part. Those involved in historical research soon discover the perennial truth that All New Ideas Meet Resistence. Solution: stick to your guns, and you will be certain to win through. This brings us to a wager. In June 2018 the amateur Scottish historian David Carroll offered a prize (equivalent to $50,000) to whoever disproved his identification of the "real" King Arthur. In his Kindle book, *Arturius: A Quest for Camelot*, Mr. Carroll maintained that the Arthur of history was Artúr (d. 596), grandson of the Scottish warrior-king Aedán (d. 608), son of Gabrán. David Carroll, confident that he will keep his money, presents six statements on Artúr as proof for his case.

Whether anyone challenged Mr. Carroll with success and became some $50,000 richer is unclear. Perhaps, whatever was said, no money changed hands. All the same, no harm in itemizing the no-sense in Mr. Carroll's case. If there are those who wish to use what follows and find themselves $50,000 better off, they have the writer's blessing. Here, then, are his six pieces of evidence and why collectively they fall down. The conditions are these. To disprove what David Carroll says on Artúr, grandson of Aedán, claimants must find another fighting man who:

a. was called Arthur
b. was active in the sixth century
c. had a sister called Morgan
d. died in battle against the Picts
e. was a Christian, and
f. fought alongside Urien and other British kings.

Let us take the points one by one, presenting the evidence as simply as we can.

(a) The name of Arthur. Mr. Carroll's Artúr is well known to historians. He is mentioned in a Latin life of St. Columba (d. 597). It survives in a seventh-century copy in Switzerland (where Mr. Carroll went to look at it). The life tells how Artúr, grandson of the renowned King Aedán (d. 608), was butchered in a battle against the Miathi, a Pictish people located between Stirling and the Mounth. So this Artúr lived in the sixth century, in Scotland, and died in 596.

The problem here is in Welsh sources that mention another Arthur, who also fought battles in the North during the sixth century, but earlier than Artúr. Latin annals from Wales have a laconic entry for 537 on how this Arthur fell in combat at Camlan. The entry (as we know) refers in addition to famine in Britain and Ireland, which is known of from other sources and was due to the volcanic winter of 536–537. The date of the famine being historical fact, Arthur's death at Camlan in 537 is also surely factual. Yet this Camlan had nothing to do with the Picts. It will be *Camboglanna* on Hadrian's Wall, the fort at Castlesteads not far from Carlisle, Cumbria. It was not in Pictland, the region north of the Rivers Clyde and Forth.

Conclusion: the real Arthur was not the Gaelic-speaking Artúr of the 590s, but a warrior of the 530s, campaigning in and around Strathclyde, and speaking a language akin to Welsh or Cornish.

(b) The sixth century. It is clear from the above that the hero of Welsh tradition was called Arthur, died in 537, and was active in North Britain, not Wales. One might think that the case for him as the Arthur of history was already strong, particularly as no early writer refers to him as of royal blood (unlike Artúr). In the ninth-century *Historia Brittonum*, a Latin text from northwest Wales, Arthur is merely a "captain in battles" (*dux bellorum*) who fought alongside British princes. So what is going on?

Conclusion: the earlier Arthur, active in the North Britain of the 530s, was so famous that his name (not Celtic but Latin, deriving from *Artorius*) could be given to a Gaelic prince like Artúr. In 1893 the German scholar Heinrich Zimmer pointed out that the prestige of Arthur's name among Celts of the later sixth century was evidence for an earlier historical Arthur. The royal Artúr killed in 596 would be called after the non-royal Arthur killed in 537.

(c) Arthur's sister Morgan. This lady is also thought of as a goddess or witch. The twelfth-century Latin writer Geoffrey of Monmouth mentions her in his *Life of Merlin*, where she appears as one of nine sisters welcoming the dying Arthur to an isle of healing. As "Morgne la Faye" she is also the wicked fairy of the Arthurian poem *Sir Gawain and the Green Knight* (discussed in this volume). Being a goddess with supernatural powers of healing and unhealing, she was hardly a sixth-century Scot. She is not historical. Nor does early Celtic tradition ever link her with Arthur.

Conclusion: as regards Arthur and sixth-century Scotland, Morgan the *femme fatale* is irrelevant. Skilled in magical blessings and curses, this Celtic immortal has nothing to do with Arthur the sixth-century British warrior.

(d) Death in battle against the Picts. Here is more historical spoon-bending. Everyone agrees that Artúr, grandson of King Aedán, died in 596 or so in an expensive victory over the Miathi, a Pictish people. But nothing else in early sources for Arthur shows that he fought the Picts. *Historia Brittonum*'s twelve battles won by Arthur are (with one interpolated exception) all in southern Scotland and northern England. Nothing to do with Picts, their lands north of the Firth of Forth. Of the eleven genuine Arthurian battles, one obviously in Scotland was that of the "Caledonian Forest" (near Beattock in the Southern Uplands, because Welsh sources consistently show the place as within reach of both Glasgow and Carlisle). Another of these eleven was at the mouth of the Glen, the River Glen of Northumberland. But none of them was against Picts. The Firth of Forth and the ancient morass on the Forth west of Stirling were effective barriers between Picts and North Britons. Hence the importance of the ford at Stirling, and the stronghold on the rock above it (as Scottish history books make clear). Arthur's raids for cattle would be against the Gododdin of southeast Scotland and the people of Rheged in east Cumbria. Swamps on the upper Forth ruled out any attempt to steal lowing Pictish heifers.

Conclusion: the Picts, like the goddess Morgan, have nothing to do with Arthur. Annals and chronicle records from Wales prove that his battles were against other North Britons, not Picts.

(e) Arthur's Christianity. Mr Carroll is perfectly correct to take Arthur as a Christian. Yet this applies to the North British Arthur who died a soldier's death near Carlisle in 537, as well as to the Artúr of 596. Writing in 536, the British historian Gildas tells how the Britons formerly worshipped the pagan divinities of hills and rivers and springs, but do so no longer. For him, the Britons are a Christian people. What he says is confirmed by inscriptions of this period from Whithorn and Kirkmadrine and Yarrow in southern Scotland (where they are among the few sources for sixth-century North Britain, the genuine "Age of Arthur").

Conclusion: like the Artúr killed in 596, the Arthur who perished in 537 worshipped the Christian God. For him, Lug and Taranis and the rest of the Celtic pantheon were dead.

(f) Fighting alongside Urien and other British kings. This puts cart before horse. Artúr was a contemporary of the British ruler Urien, who in the late sixth century governed Rheged, with his court near Penrith (in modern Cumbria), but with power over territory as far north as the River Ayr in Scotland, where he fought Strathclyders. Almost all knowledge of Urien comes from poems of the bard Taliesin, containing much on his defiance of English and Strathclyder enemies, yet never mentioning Arthur. There is another strange silence in *Historia Brittonum*. It has much on Urien and Arthur, but never associates the two, even though Mr. Carroll maintains that they fought side by side. What has happened?

Conclusion: no early source relates Arthur to Urien or his contemporaries of the 590s. So he was hardly their ally. The kings who accompanied the real Arthur were of the 530s, not the 590s.

Hence, after going through Mr. Carroll's six points, we can end positively. Artúr grandson of Aedán was not the real Arthur. The authentic hero was a brave North Briton and, it seems, a Strathclyder, who saved his people by raids for food during the great famine of 536–537. He is part of history. If he was not Artúr (named in his honor), neither was he (as argued from the 1970s onward) a mythical being, like the Fingal of Fingal's Cave. Nor had he anything to do with Wales or Cornwall. His links with them are romances spread by the twelfth-century romancer Geoffrey of Monmouth. Nor was he a king. The oldest sources are clear on his being merely a great warrior or commander. Also ready for a bonfire of the vanities is apocryphal lore on the Sword in the Stone, Camelot, the Round Table, and the Lady in the Lake. There is in particular no reason to think that Camelot, first mentioned by a twelfth-century French poet, was anything but imaginary. This section therefore ends with fighting talk on Arthur as a fighting man of North Britain, a sixth-century hero and then a legend, whose fame spread to Wales and thereafter the whole world.

Now for a third and final part, on academic reception since the mid-2010s of ideas on Arthur and Scotland in the 530s. One sees from it how fresh thinking always has to make its way through a kind of psychological treacle. Eleven books are involved. Most of their authors think Arthur legendary; a few regard him as perhaps historical; several do not mention recent discussion at all; but one independent writer now comes down for him as a "real person" (so that, if some of these eleven items tell us little about sixth-century Britain, they are still highly informative on modern academic politics).

The issue was soon taken up by Tim Clarkson (of Manchester), with a complete chapter on Arthuriana, a map of Arthur's conflicts between Forth and Tyne, and varied opinions on historicity, yet tending to scepticism, on the grounds that Gildas and Bede never mention him (despite his being "so important"). That "he did not exist" will hence be the preferred answer.[6] (Answer: he did exist, but was less significant than later generations thought him, as Sir Frank Stenton observed in 1943.) The Twelve Engagements are also dealt with by Nick Higham, again with scepticism. His is an excellent book. Not a word, however, in its 380 pages to indicate belief in Arthur as a historical figure, like Henry V or Robert E. Lee. This may, alas, in Churchill's pithy utterance, be due to a "fear of being contradicted" which "leads the writer to strip himself of almost all sense and meaning." An instance of this corrosive pusillanimity is Professor Higham's remark on the Welsh annals as unable to bear "much historical or chronological weight."[7] Why? The famine mentioned for 537 is factual enough; so too is the bald statement on Arthur's fall at Camlan, a real place with obvious strategic and tactical significance. These are facts as concrete as anything in a military gazette.

Resolute investigators, who have the courage to learn Welsh, will find much of value in a translation of Gildas, even though the translator puts the British victory of Mount Badon not in 493 but 665, with the Latin text here allegedly dating from 708, not 536.[8] His verdict creates grave problems. If a however, a modern Welshman can be misled by authorities, so may a Cornishman. An admirable account of Cornwall's later medieval gentry has frequent comments on Arthur, the duchy's greatest glory. He was "the legendary figure who most caught the Cornish imagination."[9] Alas, the author is hoodwinked by his advisers on Celtic tradition; he seems quite unaware of published proof for Arthur as not "legendary" at all.

There is a similar attitude for Wales. A reference book has allusion to "early Welsh tradition of Arthur" in poems of the thirteenth-century Black Book of Carmarthen.[10] Never a word in its 825 pages on Arthur as a real man, though. Compare another large book. Although entirely about Arthur, its editors declare that "a putative historical Arthur is not the concern of this volume."[11] In its 407 pages, not once will readers find anything on a Northern hero of the 530s. His actual existence was not thought worth mentioning.

Thereafter appeared the writer's *British Battles 493–937*, its first chapter on Badon or Bradon or Braydon in 493 (when Arthur was unborn), its second on Camlan in 537 (when Arthur, who lived like a hero, died like one).[12] In the same year came out a very different book with this sentence, on British dreams of a national *reconquista*:

"A parallel tradition among the British, glimpsed early in Gildas's reference to a significant defeat of the Saxons at the siege of Mount Badon, *c*. 500, cast resistance to the tide of conquest in terms of increasingly legendary battles and the growing figure of Arthur, whom 'Nennius' had fight twelve great engagements, while the Welsh *Armes Prydien* [*sic*] *Fawr* (The Great Prophecy of Britain), composed *c*. 927–950, looked to a great battle in which the Cymry would drive" the English out of Britain.[13]

Here are six historical errors or misconceptions. First, nothing on Badon as at Braydon and occurring in 493. Second, nothing on Gildas as writing in 536, as proved in 2010 by David Woods. Third, the conflicts of *Historia Brittonum* were not "legendary": Badon was won and lost in 493, in Wiltshire; the other eleven combats are of 536–537 and took place between Forth and Tyne. Fourth, even though the twelve conflicts appear in *Historia Brittonum* as fought against the English, all (Badon excepted) would be against other North British peoples. Fifth, those eleven were victories of Arthur, a northern commander slain in 537 at Camlan. Sixth, *Armes Prydein* dates from late 940, following West Saxon capitulation that year to the Vikings at *Lego* or Leicester, which the bard mentions in his text, a propaganda call for annihilation of the English, to be achieved in the campaigning season of 941. In short, the sentence casts a dismal light on a dismal book. No better is an account of the "storytelling pizzazz" of Geoffrey of Monmouth in the twelfth century, and how he put Arthur "firmly on the historiographical radar (though whether Arthur deserves to be there is another matter)" with no mention of proof for the historical Arthur, champion of Strathclyde.[14]

Fortunately, we end with a fanfare and a salute; for genuine enlightenment comes now from Peter Field of Bangor, North Wales. Tim Clarkson and Nick Higham think Arthur legendary; Professor Field's opinion is other. "The early evidence suggests that Arthur was a real person" is more than a phrase. It is a towering landmark in the whole course of British historical investigation.[15] With it, a centuries-old problem on Britain's past can be laid to rest.

However, to remind us how in such writing (and other things) change comes footing slow, two final books. Deficient here is a study of Gildas, where the author (disastrously unaware of David Woods's article on 493 and 536), comments on how his subject's reputation "continues to 'languish'" from attempts to "historicize King Arthur."[16] This is wrong-headed. Gildas spoke the truth on Badon in 536. It was not his fault that scribes miscopied

Bradonici as "Badonici"; or that ninth-century Welshmen foisted the triumph of 493 on an Arthur active four decades later. Implication: on events of his time Gildas knew what he was talking about. Of higher quality is a monograph on Welsh historical tradition from Gildas (493–570) to Bishop Asser (d. 909).[17] But it has nothing on Arthur (and also requires corrections on dates and place-names).

To end. Surveys of what has been said on any issue are always rewarding. They soon bring out the difference between the visionary and the myopic; and how putting money on the latter is a wonderful way to lose it.

NOTES

1. Churchill, *The History of the English-Speaking Peoples*, 60.
2. K. H. Jackson, "The Arthur of History," 1–11.
3. Woods, "Gildas and the Mystery Cloud of 536–537," 246–34.
4. Breeze, "The Historical Arthur," 58–81.
5. Breeze, "Arthur's Battles," 161–72.
6. Clarkson, *Scotland's Merlin*, 110.
7. Higham, *King Arthur: The Making of the Legend*, 225.
8. Daniel, *Llythyr Gildas a Dinistr Prydain*, 101, 373.
9. Drake, *Cornwall*, 58.
10. Fulton, "Britons and Saxons," 28.
11. Lloyd-Morgan and Poppe, "Introduction," 6.
12. Breeze, *British Battles 493–937*, 1–24.
13. Strickland, "Undying Glory," 52.
14. Naismith, *Early Medieval Britain*, 89.
15. Peter Field, "King Arthur," 9.
16. Joyce, *The Legacy of Gildas*, 5.
17. Rebecca Thomas, *History and Identity in Early Medieval Wales*.

Chapter Two

Arthur *Dux Bellorum* and Welsh *Penteulu* "Chief of the Royal Warband"

Even though the North British hero Arthur (d. 537) is in medieval romance styled a king, he is not so termed in the earliest documents relating to him. The ninth-century *Historia Brittonum* states merely that he fought *cum regibus Brittonum* ("alongside kings of the Britons"), but was himself merely *dux bellorum*. What this means has been long disputed. It has been taken to represent a senior rank in the Roman army, with Arthur as a commander of cavalry forces fighting up and down Britain. Closer analysis shows this as a fantasy. Comparison with medieval Welsh texts indicates that *dux bellorum* instead corresponds to Welsh *penteulu* ("captain of the bodyguard, chief of the royal host"). As commander of the king's bodyguard, the *penteulu* was the most important of the twenty-four officers of the court. He had a position of supreme trust, invariably being the ruler's own son or nephew or another man of rank. Setting out his income and status (which included the right to praise by the official poet of the bodyguard), medieval Welsh legal and other sources are thus the most reliable sources of information on what the Arthur of history was and was not.

So we start our survey thus. Arthur, too easily thought of as a king, was not so regarded during the ninth century. In *Historia Brittonum* he is called *dux bellorum* (usually understood as "leader of battles"). In this chapter we shall, then, look at what previous writers have made of the phrase, and go on to compare it with its closest equivalent in Welsh sources, *penteulu* or "captain of the bodyguard" (the élite corps who were a Welsh king's strength and protection). If *dux bellorum* has no exact equivalent elsewhere in Latin, native Welsh sources tell us much of the *penteulu* and the *teulu* or warband which he commanded. It should make the figure of Arthur intelligible. It is also revealing on what historians professional or amateur have made of Arthur.

A preface to the subject was offered by Sir John Rhŷs (1840–1915). Problems of security in fourth-century Britain led to the appointment of a *Dux Britanniarum* "Commander of the Britains" (the provinces into which Roman Britain was divided), and a "Count of the Saxon Shore" or *Comes Litoris Saxonici*. They were no petty people, the latter having authority over a chain of forts from Brancaster (in Norfolk) to Portchester (in Hampshire). Rhŷs thought that the office of these generalissimos continued with that of the Welsh *gwledig* "ruler, prince" because, "with the exception of Arthur, those who seem to have succeeded to supreme power here when the Romans left are always styled in Welsh literature *gwledig*" (and not "emperor" or "king").[1] The word is used in the *Mabinogion* tale of Magnus Maximus or Macsen Wledig (d. 388), a Spaniard who usurped power in Britain and beyond, and in *Historia Brittonum* of the British leader Ambrosius Aurelianus (apparently the victor at Mount Badon in 493). But it was, we note, never used of Arthur. This has not stopped writers from glamourizing him with the dignity of a Roman *dux*, and so trailing a glory that he neither possessed nor claimed. It contrasts with the plain translation by Hugh Williams (1843–1911) of Bala, who took Arthur as fighting the Saxons of Kent as the "leader in the wars" (if aided by the kings of Britain).[2]

Our survey proper begins with Sir Edmund Chambers (1866–1954), who supplied (after Theodor Mommsen) the relevant passage from *Historia Brittonum* and a translation of it. Having heard of Vortigern and how the Saxons grew in power, we learn that Hengist's son Octha established a realm in Kent. "Of him sprang the kings of the Kentishmen. Then Arthur fought against them in those days with the kings of the Britons, and it was he who led their battles." Or, *Tunc Arthur pugnabat contra illos in illis diebus cum regibus Brittonum, sed ipse dux erat bellorum* (the notorious list of those twelve battles coming after that).[3] By using a paraphrase, Chambers ducked the question of whether *dux bellorum* was or was not a title.

A pregnant remark was thereafter made by the Chadwicks, that the source of this passage was "in all probability to be sought in a catalogue poem" which resembled other vernacular ones (still surviving) on the campaigns and triumphs of Welsh rulers.[4] The point is crucial. If the source was of native origin, it makes a world of difference. It implies that *dux bellorum* renders a North British or Welsh expression and is nothing to do with Rome. The observation in mind, we turn to Robin Collingwood (1889–1943), whose writings so brilliantly mix gold and dross. Collingwood was sure "that Arthur really lived" (as did Alexander, Aristotle, Vergil, or Roland, likewise transmuted into legend). Collingwood was here wiser than more recent critics. He added (also correctly) that Arthur's name is of Latin origin, from *Artorius*, but that "he was not a king, still less king over all the kings of Britain" (again, correct). After this, Collingwood lurched into error. The phrase *dux bellorum* implies two things: first, "the governments of his day entrusted him with a special military command"; second, the expression "he fought 'with the kings of the Britons' implies that this commission was valid all over the country" and so "not in any one kingdom or region, but wherever he was wanted" as the commander of a mobile field army. Arthur was, in short, "a new count of Britain."[5] These bold assertions have sown confusion. Despite the scepticism of Kenneth Jackson (1909–1991) and others, few have escaped their spell.

An early comment came from Albert Williams. Collingwood's "rather ingenious explanation of the Arthurian legend" represents Arthur as a sixth-century equivalent to the fifth-century Count of Britain, dealing (like him) with "the barbarian menace" and with an army modeled on those of the Romans after "after the disaster of Adrianople in 378, when an effective cavalry force" put their infantry to flight. Arthur was not only thoroughly Roman, but (as Collingwood put it) "the last of the Romans."[6] Churchill responded on similar lines, as we saw in chapter 1.

Yet Jackson saw Collingwood with a colder eye. The British struggle with the Saxons "seems to have been carried on by the shadowy figure of Arthur" as "a leader of the official Roman kind" (a view "ably" defended by Collingwood) or as "another 'tyrant' like Vortigern"; but "we cannot really know" which, and "nothing useful can be said" further. Jackson went on to locate the victory of "Badon" near Swindon; the British leader "may or may not have been" Arthur.[7] We agree in part. Although Arthur was neither a Roman commander nor a local Celtic ruler, but a captain of fighting men, "Badon" was indeed a victory of Britons over Saxons of the southeast, and was won near Swindon (at the hillfort east of Braydon Forest), but had no link with Arthur. Jackson's caution was justified.

Although Jackson's pupil Rachel Bromwich (1915–2010) lacked his incisive intellect and style, she was nearer the truth on Arthur than he was. For her, Arthur was a Northern warrior who perhaps fought some of his battles "against rival British factions" (not the Saxons) "within the northern area," as one might gather from the very obscurity of the toponyms. She yet cited (as "indirect evidence which points to his having been a great leader of the Britons during the chaotic period which followed the break-up of Roman rule") the passage of Collingwood on how Arthur as *dux bellorum* "commanded a cavalry force whose mobility enabled it to pass rapidly from one area of Britain to another, opposing external invaders wherever the need was greatest."[8] In other words, she wanted to have it both ways: Arthur as Northern warrior and as Roman cavalry commander. Jackson's hostility to the Northern Arthur and to his battles as northern ones is clear from his acid (but mistaken) remark that "the philological evidence relied on by the proponents of this view does little to support it."[9] In this debate, the significance of *dux bellorum* is vital.

So much appears from Geoffrey Ashe. Rhŷs and Collingwood had explained the form as an "old Roman military title" granted to high-ranking officials, and then retained by the Britons. Ashe hence portrayed Arthur in flattering terms. He was a "Roman-blooded aristocrat born about 470"; the leader of "a picked company" and an expert in "cavalry fighting." Arthur (having "taught the smiths to forge armour and the troops to manage their horses") set off with "a mobile squadron that could hurtle from place to place carrying all before it."[10] Fortunately, Ashe later retreated from these fantasies, as we shall see.

This was wise, given further comments from Jackson. He doubted that Arthur was granted any supreme Roman rank as *Dux Bellorum* (with appropriate capitals). It corresponded to nothing in Rome or elsewhere. Bede in one of his minor works referred to St Germanus as *dux belli* and was here echoed by the Vatican recension of *Historia Brittorum*. Yet the phrase is merely descriptive. It was not a formal title. Jackson thus rendered *dux bellorum* as no more than "commander in the battle." On Collingwood he was terse. Jackson dismissed him as urging "an argument which it would be an understatement to call 'imaginative.'"[11] Jackson's reasoning on *dux bellorum* is, however, not as compelling as one might think. It does not account for the emphasis put upon the expression in *Historia Brittonum*'s Latin, which is clumsy, but still indicates a contrast between Arthur's rank and that of the kings who were his allies or opponents.

In his account of Arthur's twelve battles, Count Tolstoy was not primarily concerned with Arthur's identity.[12] He yet reminds us that the questions of who Arthur was and where he fought are inseparable. On the background to that we at this point make a digression. Jackson, in a lecture not directly concerned with Arthur, described a monument which brings us close to him. It stands at Yarrowkirk in Selkirkshire/Borders, and bears the inscription HIC MEMORIA PERPETUA / IN LOCO INSIGNISIMI PRINCIPES NUDI DUMNOGENI / HIC IACENT IN TUMULO DUO FILII LIBERALI. "This is the eternal memorial: in this place lie the most illustrious princes Nudus and Dumnogenus. Here lie in the grave the two sons of Liberalis."[13] It tells us more than one might think. The lettering dates it to the early sixth century, and so to the genuine "Age of Arthur." It shows the blend of Celtic and Roman in the culture of these chiefs (otherwise unknown), who were his contemporaries and neighbours. They lived beyond the Empire, but naturally wrote in Latin. Liberalis had a Latin name, his sons had Celtic ones. They were also Christians. Their epitaphs parallel those on similar monuments from Wales, Cornwall, and beyond. These people were in contact with the wider world. The household of Liberalis might have been provincial and lacking in polish: but it still looked to Rome, even though southern Scotland had lain beyond the Empire since the late second century.

After this encounter with epigraphical fact, a return to standard histories. Sheppard Frere commented on Arthur as perhaps succeeding Ambrosius, continuing his governance of the Britons with a title going back to the late Empire, and leading "mounted forces" in "some sort of unified command arranged between several petty kingdoms."[14] But by 1968 Geoffrey Ashe was acknowledging the "grave criticism" against such views. Such aspects of Roman rule would hardly have survived into sixth-century Britain. At the same time, rather than giving short shrift to Collingwood's notions, he half-believed them, with Arthur adopting "a remembered title and organized cavalry of a sort."[15] Error is always long a-dying. It here extended into the 1970s. On breathing its last, it was succeeded by a new error (itself dispatched after forty years).

The last years of the Collingwoodian heresy are hence of interest. Leslie Alcock, despite reviewing military senses of the word *dux*, moved in the right direction by proposing *dux bellorum* as translating a Welsh (or Cumbric) bardic expression, and so in no way a Roman "formal rank or title." Yet he did not follow the idea through in further remarks on Arthur. He was perhaps not a "territorial ruler"; he might thus have been a "freelance who offered the services of himself and a band of followers to whatever king would pay best" (= a mercenary) or else "an overall commander appointed collectively by the kings of the Britons" (= the wraith of Collingwood's "new count of Britain"). Having it both ways, Alcock went on to devise a Latin formula for the second position, meaning "General Officer Commanding British Land Forces."[16] Despite rejecting *dux bellorum* as indicating an Imperial role for Arthur, Alcock still treated him as a supremo, on the shaky grounds of battles supposedly won throughout the length of Britain. This despite Gildas's failure to mention Arthur, a silence suggesting that "the Arthur of history was a less imposing figure than the Arthur of legend."[17]

Charles Thomas (1928–2016) also moved in the right direction. He correctly saw the earliest references to Arthur as "categorically northern." The "British tribes in what is now southern Scotland may have formed his native background." Thomas could do this on the basis of arguments advanced by O. G. S. Crawford in 1935 for Arthur's final battle of Camlan as at *Camboglanna* on Hadrian's Wall, and of Jackson's 1969 translation of the seventh-century *Gododdin*, a Northern poem mentioning Arthur as a historical figure (not a legendary one). As regards *dux bellorum*, Thomas alluded to "the disruptive quarrels of *duces*, war-leaders and would-be Arthurs connected with the network of native principalities to the west and north."[18] In shunning all imperial echoes, Thomas here likewise approached the truth.

Now advancing in the opposite direction, geographically and otherwise, was Leslie Alcock. His attempts to associate Arthur (on the basis of pseudo-etymology and post-medieval folklore) with the hillfort at South

Cadbury, Somerset, was one of the twentieth century's archaeological blunders, a blemish on what excavation actually revealed of the place. Alcock admitted to a disappointed public that they had disclosed no relic of Arthur, but still took him as "leader of battles" on "behalf of several kingdoms" and so the "direct successor to Ambrosius Aurelianus" (foe of the Anglo-Saxons) and commander of British forces "owing general allegiance to an overlord or high king." Alcock went further. Arthur's army might have had a thousand men, and Cadbury was "a suitable base for such a body." The place being refortified in the 470s or later, "this date would fit Arthur, especially if we put his victory at Badon in AD 490 or 499."[19] For all that, Alcock's investigations will have new significance if we locate the victory of "Badon" at Braydon in Wiltshire, and in the spring or early summer of 493. Refortification at South Cadbury may prove that Britons of the southwest had stiffened their resolve. Anglo-Saxon aggressors met a new spirit of resistance. The initiative behind that did not come from Arthur. But it may have come from Ambrosius Aurelianus.

Alcock's defects were yet white as snow compared with the scarletry of John Morris (d. 1977). If "Arthurian" Cadbury was an archaeological charade, Morris's "imperial" Arthur was a historical one, even if endowed with the brilliance and vision of a poet in prose. Behind it is the notion of the *dux*. In the fifth century, the Britons had "repelled their enemies with outstanding success" because "the *dux*, the *comes*, and the civil government worked together." Their successor was Arthur, "the supreme commander who defeated the English" and "who long maintained in years of peace the empire of Britain" which "his arms had recovered and restored."[20] For page after page we see Morris wafted upwards by balloons of stately fantasy. A needle to prick them was soon produced in a famous paper, if with a smokescreen of historical negativism dispelled only now.[21]

In the meantime we find older and better counsels repeated. Hunter Blair, not given to hyperbole, regarded Arthur's part in Badon as unproven. He still thought Arthur historical, "for Arthur's fame was great in the sixth century, though we do not know why."[22] Hunter Blair was aware (after Heinrich Zimmer in 1893) that sixth-century northern and other princes were named "Arthur"; a circumstance not explained by those who dismiss Arthur as a Celtic myth. He said nothing on *dux bellorum*. Nor did Rachel Bromwich, who yet noted how the "oldest allusions to Arthur associate him with North Britain."[23] In a useful student edition, Morris himself rendered *dux bellorum* as "leader in battle" and no more.[24] Here no imperial overtones to the expression.

Morris's romantic extravaganzas and the reactions to them by Dumville and others left commentators in disarray. One spoke of how modern speculation had alighted on Arthur as leader of the Britons, when others denied his very existence.[25] Another remarked that conclusions on him, not least his association with "actual places" including South Cadbury, should be "held in abeyance" pending thorough examination of the texts.[26] (That examination is what the reader is getting in this book.) Charles Thomas turned 180 degrees, being now convinced (after Dumville) of there being "no historical evidence about Arthur."[27] Over in Oxford, James Campbell understood *dux bellorum* as "commander in wars" and further remarked on how some had regarded Arthur as "the last of the emperors of Roman Britain, or as the commander of the field army for such an emperor." Perhaps "there were such emperors" or "such an army"; yet nothing was proven.[28]

None of this was heard by Morris, who died in 1977. But his ghost thereafter sidled into the scholarly uproar. In a posthumous book it proclaimed how Arthur "fought for the preservation of Roman Britain" and thus became "emperor, the last Roman emperor in Britain" and heir to those enthroned there since 410. This he related to the *duces* "military commanders" mentioned by Gildas, who "grew to manhood under Arthur's government." The *duces* had by then made themselves petty kings and tyrants; but their name demonstrated the survival of some "semblance of a Roman government."[29] From wisps of evidence, Morris created a hallucinatory Imperial Britain. But it was doomed to vanish. A lay writer made the obvious objection. In "the years after Badon, Arthur may have risen to be emperor over the shades of Roman Britain. If so, it is strange that Gildas does not mention him, for Gildas was writing less than half a century after these events."[30] Ian Wood makes the further point that *dux* at this time was used "without military connotations" at all.[31]

By the 1990s, the rout of the Morrisians was complete. Dumville's critique of the "no smoke without fire" approach to sources (which for the most part allegedly show Arthur as "a figure of legend") was quoted with approval.[32] Oliver Padel (b. 1948), thus represented Arthur as purely legendary, like the Irish folklore hero Fionn mac Cumhaill.[33] He glossed over the questions of *dux bellorum* and the identity of Arthur's battles. Alcock (as already noted) observed that the "Arthur/Camelot attribution seemed a reasonable inference" for South Cadbury until the late 1970s, when attacks began on Arthur's historicity.[34] Dr. Padel translates *dux bellorum* as "war-leader" and asserts that the battles attributed to Arthur "cannot be identified" (i.e., cannot be identified by him, Dr. Oliver Padel).[35] Ken Dark likewise starts with Dumville's denial of historical evidence for Arthur, yet makes a pointed objection. If Arthur was a mere folklore or legendary entity, why was his name given to northern princes in the late sixth century, but not thereafter?[36]

Dark's paper was, however, ignored by most later writers. The received view of Arthur as non-historical appears in a well-known booklet. Its treatment of *dux bellorum* is revealing. It says this. "Arthur is depicted as the great military leader (*dux bellorum*) who led the British kings against the second generation of English settlers"; but the context "seems to imply that Arthur was not regarded as a king himself."[37] Within "great military leader" is still the phantom of Arthur as supremo. Let us exorcize it. Since we can be sure that Arthur did not fight the English, *dux bellorum* will have no implications for him as a "great" national commander. We can also be certain that he was not a king. No early source calls him that. What we are left with is *dux bellorum* as indicating a status different from (*sed*) and inferior to that of kings. There is no reason to take *dux bellorum* as a supra-regal title.

This ground cleared, we turn to Nick Higham. If Dr. Padel sees Arthur as a British Fionn mac Cumhaill, Professor Higham sees him as a British Joshua, with the author of *Historia Brittonum* presenting him on the strength of "his own reading of Deuteronomy" (and other Old Testament books) as a doughty smiter of foes. At the same time Arthur appears too in *Historia Brittonum* as "a pan-British war-leader, a veritable *dux bellorum*."[38] There are three things to say here. The supposed parallel with Joshua is not made in *Historia Brittonum*, which never actually mentions Joshua. Second, the notion of Arthur as a "pan-British" leader is due to mislocating his battles all over Britain, from Wessex to Scotland. Third, the rhetoric of "veritable" attributes to *dux bellorum* a grandeur that it hardly possessed. Such are the dangers of imposing meanings on a document which will not bear them. Better, if in merely taking the text *au pie de la lettre*, is Martin Aurell. He tells how Arthur, was "chef de guerre (*dux bellorum*) luttant auprès des rois des Bretons et remportant douze batailles."[39] Less desirable, one fears, is the Welsh Academy encyclopaedia. On the *dux Britanniarum* (who from the early fourth century led "a mobile army based at York"), it adds that "Arthur was possibly a commander in the same tradition a century after the title had ceased to exist."[40] This is a last and faint echo of what Collingwood and Morris spoke loud between 1936 and 1982. It should fade entirely.

More up-to-date are Higham's observations on the passage as a whole. Its 186 words are "embedded" within an account of the Germanic invasions of Britain (making up the "filling of this Saxon sandwich"). Higham reasonably regards its inclusion as due to *Historia Brittonum*'s compiler (and not from "some pre-existing source"). He thinks that the feats of this "invariably successful Christian soldier" within the dismal record of the Loss of Britain made him "a warrior type of the Messiah for his people" as "a product of Biblical metaphor."[41] One need not believe all that to see how Arthurian traditions served to bolster up Welsh morale. More significant is this inference. The Arthurian source had no original link with those on the English settlement of Kent. It is here as a more or less arbitrary interpolation. So we need not imagine that Arthur lived at the time of Hengest's son Octha. Higham provides another wedge to crack the graven image of Arthur, vanquisher of the Saxons.

The most recent comments are varied. In a glossy volume with sensational illustrations, a consultant endocrinologist in Udine asks "è Artù un soprannome guerriero veneto? La risposta è sì, in forza di tutte le evidenze elencate."[42] Professor Halsall of York takes seriously (but should not) the notion of how "'leader of battles' (*dux bellorum*) refers to a title, possibly a corruption of *dux britanniarum* (Duke of the Britains), one of the late Roman military commanders in Britain."[43] Dr. Padel, who assures himself that "further work has not significantly affected the conclusions" given in his book, said the same on *dux bellorum* in 2013 as he did in 2000.[44]

New insights come from archaeology. There are important remarks by Rob Collins of Newcastle on papers of the 1990s by Ken and Petra Dark. These demonstrated post-Roman garrisoning of forts on Hadrian's Wall, the evidence consisting of earth defences with stone or timber revetments, burials, British artifacts, or early Christian inscribed stones, including one (it seems) from Castlesteads itself.[45] That Camlan or Castlesteads was occupied by Britons in the years about 500 sheds a most interesting light on the death there of Arthur in 537. The papers by the Darks are further cited by John Koch.[46] Flint Johnson similarly notes how forts on Hadrian's Wall "were either reoccupied or refortified in the fifth or sixth century" and that they should "inexplicably come into use around 500" is "an anomaly for post-Roman Britain." Conventional accounts cannot explain it. Yet he relates this to "a powerful kingdom in this area" and to what he calls "the office of the *dux brittonum* during the late Roman period."[47] We develop the comments of Collins, Koch, and Johnson. O. G. S. Crawford in 1935 took the Camlan where Arthur fell as *Camboglanna*, now understood as Castlesteads, a fort near Carlisle reoccupied in around 500. Archaeological evidence for sixth-century reuse of forts on Hadrian's Wall hence accords with Crawford's observation. They will have been garrisoned and reinforced because of fighting between the North British peoples of Strathclyde, Gododdin, and Rheged. Finds from excavations at Castlesteads tally in a striking way with the record of Arthur's death there in 537, surely in a raid on Rheged. They provide real evidence for Arthur, as South Cadbury and Tintagel do not. An astute tourist-board might promote Castlesteads as the site of Arthur's last battle.

Tim Clarkson of Manchester gives *dux bellorum* as "leader in battle."[48] He says nothing on it as a supposed Roman military title; which is progress. In a book neatly printed and with many maps and illustrations, Kurt Liebhard of Waiblingen renders the *Historia Brittonum* sentence as "Der grossmütige Arthur kämpfte mit all den Königen und militärischer Gewalt von Grossbritannien gengen die Sachsen."[49] So *dux bellorum* is here taken as reflecting an Imperial office. Finally, Dr. Favero (whom the writer thanks for gifts of his books). In the English version of his original text (also provided with new illustrations), he does not comment directly on *dux bellorum*, but reposes confidence in Arthur as coming from Venedotia or Gwynedd (= northwest Wales), and thus being linked with the Veneti of Venice and northeast Italy. "Venedotia is known as the land of the Venedoti and is connected with the dynasty of King Arthur, so the association between the Veneti and the Arthurian myth is clear."[50] His study may be commended for its startling and entertaining comments on Arthur and the ancient world alike.

As often in Celtic Studies, generations of comment have seen little advance. Scholars have merely repeated statements by other scholars. There has been (to adapt a phrase of Yeats) much coughing in ink. Let us now say something new. Because we can be certain that Arthur was a North British warrior, brought up beyond the bounds of Empire and fighting his battles there, we shall find evidence for his status not in the Roman army but in native tradition. Here Welsh *penteulu* "head of the retinue of a court, captain of the bodyguard" will help us. In the modern language, *teulu* means "family"; in the laws and heroic poetry, however, it has the further sense "comitatus, bodyguard, household troops, war-band": the picked warriors who were the commandos of early and medieval warfare. Their leader had to have the sovereign's implicit trust. It seems evident that *dux bellorum* in *Historia Brittonum*'s version of an Old Welsh poem of battles is a fumbling attempt to render "chief of the royal warband" or *penteulu*. This officer having received much attention, we are thus in a position to say a great deal on the historical Arthur, his likely status and activity.

Welsh law, surviving in manuscripts of the twelfth century onward, and hence evidence for the *penteulu* in the later period, gives pride of place to this man. He comes first of the officers of the court. Mistranslation of *teulu* as "household" (by earlier writers) still led to absurdities. This position is reserved solely for "a son of the king, or a nephew" or one of similar rank. Among the many details of his rights are some gory ones. For medical treatment, his doctor gets nothing from him except "his bloody clothes"; unless he have "a stroke on the head penetrating to the brain; a stroke in the body penetrating to the bowels; or the breaking of one of the four limbs."[51] As soon as one sees him as no chamberlain but a military man, the above need for trust and the dangers of his profession will make sense. He was not telling cooks and footmen what to do.

The *penteulu* was mentioned in passing by Sir John Lloyd (1861–1947). He made this point. In Welsh law, the monarch's successor was the *edling* (a term borrowed from Old English), who might succeed "by election" (rather than "mere right of birth"). Election was, however, weakened by the existence of the *penteulu*, responsible for "the military needs of the tribe" and so with obvious political implications. If a British *edling* felt more at home in council than at the head of his troops, it mattered less than it would elsewhere, for he had the *penteulu* to look after defence. As *penteulu*, Arthur would thus not have been first in line to rule, even if princes were to bear his name. Despite changes over the centuries for the office of *edling*, it is unlikely that Arthur would ever have been "King" Arthur. Lloyd had further comments on the *teulu*. Its literal sense is not the modern one "family" but "house-host, house-troop"; it had nothing to do with the ruler's kin, although the *penteulu* himself "was always a near relative of the reigning chief" (for obvious reasons). It might have as many as 120 members; Gruffydd ap Llywelyn in 1047 had a warband of 140. Desertion of its lord was accounted a disgrace. It maintained order within a petty kingdom and defended it. During the fighting season, the *teulu* might attack the realms of distant rulers for the sake of plunder. Welsh law gives "minute directions" for how the booty was divided when the warriors came home. It consisted for the most part of cattle.[52] Working from the laws, Lloyd provided an illuminating picture of the number and nature of the forces seemingly led by Arthur, including their function as raiders. The earlier evidence cited below tends to confirm what he said.

Misunderstanding *teulu* as "household" (and *penteulu* as "chief of the household"), Rees viewed this officer as a kind of steward.[53] He thus misinterpreted references in the laws on the substantial recompense which the *penteulu* received as being due to maintaining order in the hall, or on where he sat with his men. The *teulu* comprised not servitors but professional fighting men, who on occasion might throw their weight about. Hence the respectful consideration given to them in the laws, and to the *penteulu* responsible for their discipline. A *penteulu* did not come cheap.

The twelfth-century *Four Branches of the Mabinogi* have more on the *teulu*, regularly to be found at the court of a prince or king as its household guard. Sir Ifor Williams (1881–1965) set out its context and gave its exact Old Irish cognate as *teglach* "household troops" (showing it as an ancient institution).[54] Deriving from a Common Celtic original, *teulu* and *teglach* are words for an entity going back to pre-Christian times. No surprise that *teulu* should occur too in the seventh-century *Gododdin*, itself significantly alluding to Arthur as a ferocious man of war, who might glut crows with human carrion (though he was evidently not a man of the Gododdin in southeast Scotland).[55] The duties and rights of the *penteulu* appear again in a legal treatise edited by Stephen Williams (1896–1992) of Swansea and the young Enoch Powell, English politician.[56] (A translation of the passage is quoted below.)

A further indication of the *teulu*'s antiquity comes from stray verses in the margin of a Cambridge manuscript. They are in a ninth-century hand, and begin:

I shall not talk even for one hour tonight;
My retinue (*telu*) is not very large:
I and my Frank, round our cauldron.

Sir Ifor Williams regarded the speaker as a chieftain in low spirits. "He has lost all his war-band, or retinue, in battle probably, except one foreign merce-nary, whom he calls his Frank. His hall this night is empty, desolate." There is no "merry host of noble youths to share the feast" or drink mead from the bowl.[57] Williams's brilliant interpretation of the lines, composed within three centuries of Arthur's *floruit*, gives us a snapshot of the *teulu*'s mess life in good times and bad.

A later *penteulu* appears in the thirteenth-century *Mabinogion* tale of Rhonabwy's Dream, outlining difficulties of the Powys ruler Madog ap Maredudd (d. 1160) with his violent brother, Iorwerth. Given the position of *penteulu*, and so possessing a status equal to Madog himself, Iorwerth is kept busy by a grant of land near Oswestry (now in Shropshire). If a man did not succeed with a war-band there (says the storyteller), he would not succeed anywhere else in Powys. The implication is clear. As the region of Powys closest to England, it was liable to attack.[58] In the Book of Blegywryd, the passage on the *penteulu* (older and less developed than the thirteenth-century version translated in *The Myvyrian Archaiology*) has rights including those for booty. He receives "the share of two men if he be with them, and any animal which he shall chose from the share of the king." He is, of course, to be "a son of the king or his nephew."[59] Comparison of what the various recensions of Welsh law declare of the *penteulu* is a rewarding exercise. His rights become more elaborate. In the latest version, on the three great feasts of the year he hands the harp to the *bardd teulu* or poet of the warband, and has a right to a song from this bard whenever he wishes.[60] Pen and sword had struck an alliance.

T. Jones Pierce (1905–1964) noted how in the last years of Welsh indepen-dence the position of *penteulu* was supplanted by that of "constable"; while the *teulu*'s custom of making a "circuit" independent of the prince figures in thirteenth-century records of the lordship of Denbigh. Its inhabitants were liable for "the entertainment of a fixed number of men and the provisioning of a fixed number of horses and dogs each year."[61] A visit from the brutal and licentious soldiery was doubtless a memorable experience for local communi-ties, especially when they had to billet that animating rabble.

Kenneth Jackson had, as one might expect, lucid remarks on the *teulu* in the earliest poetry, together with a wondrously mistaken comment on Arthur. He doubted that the three hundred warriors whom the *Gododdin* poet describes as sent from Edinburgh (in 603 CE?) to fight at Catterick (in North Yorkshire) were a *teulu*. The *teulu* made up the "life guard" of a monarch, attending upon him constantly. They "were not at all the same as a whole royal army"; nor did Jackson think of the early *teulu* as using cavalry to attack enemy infantry. Material set out by Jackson is precious evidence for warfare in early Britain. His translation of verses on the warrior Tudfwlch, praised in his *teulu*, shows it as war to the death. With "bloodstained blades covering the ground, the hero red in his fury" was "a man-slaying champion" and "joyful like a wolf at his post." Before he was slain, Tudfwlch was "the forceful in slaughter, the barrier of the fortress." Following this are lines on the fighting man Gwawrddur, who "stabbed over three hundred of the finest" and glutted "black ravens on the rampart of the stronghold, though he was no Arthur." Jackson observed that, if this passage belongs to the original poem, it dates from a time when people who remembered Arthur "would still be alive"; he then made a final swipe at his ex-pupil Rachel Bromwich, asserting that because Arthur was the national hero of Britons from Scotland to Brittany, "there is therefore no logic whatever in the idea" of Arthur as "a Northern leader."[62] Jackson was usually right. But, when he was wrong, he was very wrong.

Ifor Williams's edition of the Juvencus verses (written down in "the early ninth century") is now to be had in English.[63] It demonstrates what the *teulu* did in the hall and on the field of battle, with its potential for dramatic monologue. Nicolas Jacobs discusses the Anglo-Saxon *comitatus*, mentioning Professor Eric Hamp of Chicago for Celtic-Germanic links here.[64] The *teulu* long predated Arthur, originating among the Continental Celts. Hence, as noted above, Old Irish *teglach* as the exact cognate of *teulu*.

As for the *bardd teulu* "poet of the warband" (who, according to the Welsh laws, would sing a war song to the king's warriors as they prepared for battle), his status was second to that of the *prydydd*.[65] The *prydydd* was the highest grade of poet, and the word for him means "shaper, maker" (and so "poet"). He was craftsman and artist in one.

Praising Madog ap Maredudd (d. 1160), whom we encountered above as the Powys ruler with a troublesome brother, the master-poet Cynddelw likened his warband to that of Arthur (*teulu Arthur*).[66] Even when Geoffrey of Monmouth's tamperings with the past were beginning to distort Welsh tradition, Cynddelw still thought of Arthur as leader of a band of warriors. What they might do is shown by Wendy Davies, whose dry-eyed comments on them, derived in part from her knowledge of saints' lives and Book of Llandaff charters, repay study. She remarks on how from "the sixth to the eleventh centuries, kings moved about with soldiers (*milites*); we might term this a warband, a military retinue, a band of thugs, a bodyguard, depending upon our own perspective or that of the recording source." These individuals had "easy recourse to violence"; and she quotes a sixth-century poem by Taliesin on "Eight herds alike of calves and cattle" plundered from a neighbor, and the eleventh-century life of St. Cadog on a raid by Gwynedd men on Gorfynydd (the area around Bridgend, Glamorgan), where local people fled and hid themselves "in woods and thickets and holes and caves of the earth"; which prompts her crisp conclusion. "Kings had force, and used it."[67] The Juvencus verses of about 800 on one such warlord (who bit off more than he could chew) are again translated by Jenny Rowland.[68]

In the context of Arthur as *penteulu*, a leader of men whom some regarded as Patriot Heroes and others as Licensed Brigands, comments of Rachel Bromwich are revealing. She noted that the eleventh-century life of St Cadog styles Arthur as "king of Britain"; verses on Geraint (written about 800?) in the Black Book of Carmarthen call him "emperor"; while, in the tale of Culhwch, Arthur is "Chief of Princes of this Island" (where everyone owns his sway). The porter Glewlwyd lists places even beyond Britain where Arthur rules; these have confused scholars, but can be identified as Mediterranean and Oriental locations (indicating the tale's author as surely a cleric) known from Orosius's History. (They contast with older material in the ninth-century *Historia Brittonum*, stating that Arthur was not a king.) With characteristic wordiness and lack of logic, Rachel Bromwich commented on how "it is not easy to discount the likelihood that these allusions to Arthur's far-flung conquests owe something to the exalted status accorded to him" by Geoffrey of Monmouth and his Welsh translators. (Not so. Texts written before 1100 can owe nothing to those written from the 1130s onward.) Better is her remark on how popular and learned sources alike present Arthur as "defender of his country" against danger, whether in the form of foreign enemies, giants, witches, monsters, or dragons. He is also a "releaser of prisoners": an interesting observation. Citing the Dutch philologist A. G. van Hamel, she made Arthur out as a British peer of the mythical Irish champion Fionn mac Cumhaill (with both as "defenders, hunters, and slayers of monsters"). She concluded that (whatever his "ultimate origins") Arthur in the early texts belongs to "the realm of mythology rather than that of history."[69]

Another interpretation is, however, more compelling. The role of a *penteulu* in attack (for plunder, especially cattle) and defence (against those seeking plunder) has been made evident. No surprise that Arthur should be remembered as both saviour of his country and as a huntsman. Even his links with Northern rulers may account for his apotheosis in legend. He acted in concert with British kings; his name was given to early princes; he was no rebel. The comment on Arthur as "releaser of prisoners" may indicate how, in raids on other peoples, Arthur did just that, rescuing hostages taken by neighbouring kings, and thereby producing sagas of him as Liberator. What early Welsh accounts leave no space for is Arthur as a Romanized calvary commander. He will instead have been a native British warrior, albeit with a Latin name, from *Artorius* (a fact inconvenient for Dr. Padel and others who depict Arthur as a Celtic sprite). As with Roland, whose legends preserve a historical core (on death in a Navarrese mountain-pass), or El Cid (on ascendancy in Iberian conflicts of Moor and Christian), so with Arthur, traditions of whom grew naturally out of genuine sixth-century events and show traces of their origin.

On those events, Ken Dark of Reading designates a task for researchers. He does not mention Arthur. But he does set out a problem on the warbands which he would have led: did British kings preserve their "own type of warrior entourage" from pre-Roman times? Or were such retinues "organized by the Britons according to Roman military styles"? For the latter he refers to Latin borrowings in early Welsh. He also deals with the mixed evidence for Roman features (as against native ones) in Dark Age warfare, including its economic basis as discussed by Leslie Alcock.[70] A full answer to the question would make a big book; yet one may point out that *teulu* as a purely Celtic word tilts the argument toward the nativists. There is a sidelight here from the *meddyg teulu* ("the warband's physician"). His status is revealing. Named in the earliest laws as near the end of the list of court officials, he ranked far lower than the *penteulu* whom he sat next to at feasts. Later laws (of Gwynedd) give him a higher status (in twelfth place) and state that he accompanies the warband on expeditions. He was entitled to the use of a horse. Details of his rights to compensation (six head of cattle and six score pence) are also those of a junior official.[71] This British army doctor sounds less of a professional than a modern medical officer (or his equivalent in the Roman military). How much, one wonders, did his stitching-up of troopers owe to Galen? Just as we seek to disengage what is Celtic from what is Roman for Arthur, we may do the same for the physician who treated the wounded. Most recently, a comprehensive study says nothing on the *teulu*, *penteulu*, or the historical Arthur; it nevertheless has perceptive analysis of the warrior ethos of the age as represented in Aneirin's *Gododdin*.[72] It brings us close to what drove Arthur's men into attack.

Early Celtic sources in Latin and the vernacular provide abundant material on the *teulu* and *penteulu*. There were (of course) changes between the sixth century and the twelfth, when surviving copies of the Welsh laws first appear, so that scholars can exercise their wits on distinguishing the archaic from the innovative in their account of the *teulu*. Despite that, these and other sources allow conclusions on what Arthur as *dux bellorum* would have done. He was no Roman cavalry general or chivalrous sovereign of romance. First is the interpretation of *dux bellorum* as *penteulu* or "commander of the royal warband." Celtic records name no other office which in any way corresponds to what the *dux bellorum* would be. Second is the *penteulu*'s high status and crucial importance, with the post normally entrusted to an immediate relation of the king. We do not know the name of Arthur's father. But his position implies that he was of exalted birth. He did not rise from the people. In third place are the functions (not always noble) of the warband. A principal one was cattle-reaving, whereby Celtic chieftains exacted plunder from less fortunate neighbours. Arthur was a sort of land-pirate, lauded by his own, loathed by others. Fourth is the origin of his position. *Teulu* being a purely Celtic form (like *penteulu*), whatever his forces owed to Roman arms and tactics, the institution was an old one, going back to the earliest Celtic period. In this the best evidence is to be found in the poems of Taliesin and Aneirin's slightly later *Gododdin*, both surely composed (despite the doubts of some) within living memory of Arthur's raids in the 530s. Finally come many details, of which each would make a study in its own right. Welsh laws give an indication on the protocol and privileges appertaining to the *dux bellorum/penteulu*: where he sat in hall, his entitlement to mead, his salary, share of the loot, role in disputes, horse, *sarhad* or compensation for insult (related to the Roman law of *iniuria*), lodging, share of fines paid, linen and woollen garments, dogs, hawks, arms, horseshoes from the smith, presiding at court in the king's absence, and medical treatment. The laws tell of his right to hand the bard his harp at the three great feasts of the year, and a song from the bard whenever he wishes. They mention how his cook and other servants may demand the hides, tallow, and guts of beasts slaughtered on his official progress (after Christmas) through the king's realms. The legalistic elaboration of all this is medieval, and does not go back to the sixth century. But the office does, and so will various of its powers and dues. One of these will be a bard's obligation to sing the *penteulu*'s praises, thereby promoting his honour and fame. Gildas (writing in 536) knew of Maelgwn Gwynedd's bards, whom he dismissed as "gaolbirds" (*furciferi*). If Maelgwn had official flatterers, Arthur might have one too, which brings us back to the lost poem on his battles. It may be the oldest Welsh or Cumbric or Brittonic poem to survive in any form. It could go back in some form to the 530s and been heard by Arthur himself.

Accounts of the *penteulu* in any case leave no doubt that it was a position occupied by formidable men, not to be trifled with. As *dux bellorum* or *penteulu*, Arthur held a position which was second only to that of a king, and was Celtic (not Roman) in its duties, rights, and perquisites. The thought opens doors. The more we understand Welsh law and heroic poetry, the better we shall envisage a sixth-century *penteulu*, as also the numbers, equipment, and strategies of the *teulu* under his command.

The above in effect reproduces an article published (with admirable dispatch) in 2019 from the University of Oran.[73] Since then, the most significant advance has been a chapter (already mentioned) by Peter Field of Bangor.[74] It shows progress. It should be read. Yet it still needs correction. So this section on the Arthur of history ends with a score of comments on Professor Field's work. For the most part, the following glosses are mere restatements of what is already in print. But readers will see again how understanding of the past will dawn again and again as soon as we stop believing that medieval scribes were infallible and always copied place-names perfectly.

a. Peter Field's claim that the "Arthurian legend appeared in Britain" perhaps in the "fifth" century CE is impossible. Not so. Arthur belongs to the early sixth century.

b. Arthur was not "invented by the Britons to console themselves" for defeat by English invaders. His battles were against other Britons, not the English.

c. Nor was he "the first and most successful" of British leaders who resisted the English, like Ambrosius Aurelianus in 493 or Cadwallon of Gwynedd in 633–634. We say again that Arthur in the 530s was not fighting the English.

d. He is thus not a "mythological character who has acquired some historical characteristics"; better is Field's alternative view of him as a "historical figure whose story has attracted mythological and folktale elements."

e. Yet Professor Field correctly derives Arthur from Latin *Artorius*, and recognizes it as evidence for historicity.

f. The year of Gildas's birth and the Siege of Mount Badon was not "in the late 490s." It was 493, as independently stated by Bede, and forty-three years before 536, when the whole island of Britain was covered by (in the words of Gildas) the "thick mist and dark night" of a volcanic cloud.

g. Professor rightly sees "Badon" as of British origin, but stumbles in thinking that the spot may "have an Anglo-Saxon place-name now." Knowing nothing of the Celtic languages, he does not grasp that "Badon" is corrupt; it must be emended to *Bradon*; and this will be Braydon, near Swindon, Wiltshire. This place still has its Celtic name and Iron Age hillfort fifteen centuries after Gildas alluded to them.

h. Peter Field is yet very probably right in regarding the Britons at that conflict as the besieged and the English as the besiegers. Britons were expert on fortification. The English replied on "speed of movement and ferocity of attack." His observation points to a foiled Saxon attack on Cirencester, the British capital in what is now Gloucestershire, north of Wiltshire.

i. Of prime importance is his remark on the vanquished leader at Badon as perhaps Ælle, founder of the dynasty of Sussex. Bede refers to this king as *bretwalda* or "ruler of many kingdoms"; in 491 he wiped out the British garrison in the Roman fort of Pevensey, near Hastings; he then disappears from the records. If in 493 he advanced on Cirencester, but died in action, it would explain much.

j. Professor Field correctly takes as historical an allusion to Arthur in the *Gododdin*, a series of elegies for North British heroes massacred in an attack on the English at Catterick (in Yorkshire), perhaps in 603.

k. However, on the claim of Arthur as probably "the victor of the Battle of Bradon" we utter a loud Not So. The conflict is in the wrong place at the wrong time. A siege in Wiltshire in 493 has no link with a North British warrior of 536–537.

l. On the twelve Arthurian battles in *Historia Brittonum*, that of *urbs legionis* "legion town" is rightly doubted as being Chester. But claims of York as instead a "thoroughly plausible location" may be dismissed. York was never known by this name. Nor was Arthur fighting the English there in about 500 CE. The place is more probably the *Karig Lion* or "legion rock" recorded by Willem Blaeu (d. 1638) at the east end of the Antonine Wall, Scotland. Welsh scribes, not being faultless geniuses, yet unfortunately knowing of Caerleon "legion fortress" or Chester, corrupted this obscure northern toponym via confusion of *karig* with Welsh *caer* (= fortress, walled town) into *urbs legionis*; an idea wrong, but easy to grasp (like many wrong ideas). No conflict at York, then.

m. Now for *dux bellorum*. Field claims that all explanations fail, because in this period "several kings" never jointly "delegated their military authority" to a non-king. This is too subtle. The clumsy phrase *cum regibus Brittonum* "with kings of the Britons" does not mean that they were all brothers-in-arms. The sense is that Arthur fought on behalf of one king (of Strathclyde) against other kings (of Rheged and the Gododdin). Interpretation of *dux bellorum* as "chief of the royal warband" may stand.

n. Now for the list of battles, which are all real (and not "completely fictional" as stated by one unintelligent observer), starting with that of Glen. Field makes difficulties for *ostium* "river-mouth, estuary" as applied to the Glen of Northumberland, which is a mere tributary. Yet Welsh and Cumbric *aber* "confluence" is used of points inland (as with remote Aberlosk, in the Southern Uplands of Scotland) and removes difficulties here. The North British context shows that Arthur's Glen was not the southern one, in Lincolnshire.

o. Also not in Lincolnshire were conflicts on the *Dubglas* or Douglas, as Professor Field wrongly thinks. He fails to notice (in the works that he quotes) this textual emendation. *Linnuis* in *Historia Brittonum* is certainly the Lincolnshire district of Lindsey; which yet has no River Douglas. Emend to Old Welsh *Clutuis* or (in modern spelling) *Cludwys* "people of (the River) Clyde, Strathclyders" and sense appears; for in their territory, near Lanark, was the River Douglas, vital for their security. Professor Field's observations on Arthur's "multiple battles" near Lincoln can be set aside. Arthur fought those four battles in what is now Scotland.

p. As for the River "Bassas" (which he thinks "completely unknown"), a suggested emendation has once more escaped him. "Bassas" being an impossible form, we emended in previous publications to *Tarras*, either the stream which gave its name to Cars*tairs*, southeast of Glasgow, or Tarras Water, near Langholm in southern Scotland, near the border with Cumbria.

q. While Field's "Guinnion Fort" as "Binchester in County Durham" at first seems persuasive, a look at the sources rules it out. The British-Latin name of this Roman stronghold was *Vinovia* or *Vinovium*. Old Welsh *Guinnion* would not derive from that. The place will (as argued by Tim Clarkson) be Carwinning, a small hillfort near old quarries two miles north of Dalry, Ayrshire.

r. The tenth battle at the strand of Tryfrwyd is stated as at "an unknown place"; it was yet not far from Edinburgh, and might thus be Dreva, on the Upper Tweed in the Borders region of Scotland.

s. Similarly, the conflict as "Mount Agned" (not too far from High Rochester, Northumberland, as Professor Field rightly says), may (with a textual emendation) be taken as Pennango, found on today's maps as Newmill, on the A7 trunk road southwest of Hawick, in southern Scotland.

t. On the basis of the above, Peter Field's statement on eight of the engagements as locatable in "what is now northeast England" can be squashed. One of them was there, that on the Glen. Ten others can be placed north of the Border and south of the Clyde-Forth line; non-Arthurian "Mount Badon" of 493 is rightly put by Field in "southern England" (in modern Wiltshire).

To sum up, then, while Peter Field's acceptance of Arthur as a historical figure is an advance, we must (a) chuck out fables on him as a Roman-style leader fighting the English, and (b) take on board what the art of textual criticism tells us about ancient toponyms. Comparison with early Welsh texts shows this *dux bellorum* as a *penteulu*, a "captain of the royal host": not a king, but the trusted commander of Strathclyde forces attacking other North British peoples to seize their herds and flocks.

NOTES

1. Rhys, *Celtic Britain*, 104.

2. Hugh Williams, *Christianity in Early Britain*, 350.

3. Chambers, *Arthur of Britain*, 1, 238.

4. Chadwick and Chadwick, *The Growth of Literature: The Ancient Literatures of Europe*, 155.

5. Collingwood and Myers, *Roman Britain and the English Settlements*, 321–22.

6. A. H. Williams, *An Introduction to the History of Wales: Prehistoric Times to 1063*, 73.

7. K. H. Jackson, *Language and History in Early Britain*, 116, 199.

8. Bromwich, "The Character of the Early Welsh Tradition," 124–25.

9. K. H. Jackson, "The Britons in Southern Scotland," 81.

10. Ashe, *King Arthur's Avalon*, 75–76.

11. K. H. Jackson, "The Arthur of History," 8–9.

12. Tolstoy, "Nennius, Chapter Fifty-Six," 118–62.

13. K. H. Jackson, "Angles and Britons," 63–64.

14. Frere, *Britannia*, 382.

15. Ashe, "The Arthurian Fact," 53

16. Alcock, *Arthur's Britain*, 60–61, 86–87, 358.

17. Stenton, *Anglo-Saxon England*, 3.

18. Thomas, *Britain and Ireland*, 38–42.

19. Alcock, *"By South Cadbury is That Camelot . . . ": Excavations*, 193–94.

20. Morris, *Age of Arthur*, 54, 116–41.

21. Dumville, "Sub-Roman Britain."

22. Hunter Blair, *An Introduction to Anglo-Saxon England*, 30.

23. Bromwich, *Trioedd Ynys Prydein*, 275.

24. Morris, *British History*, 35.

25. Stephen Johnson, *Later Roman Britain*, 123.

26. Salway, *Roman Britain*, 485, 501.

27. Thomas, *Christianity in Roman Britain*, 245.

28. Campbell, "The Lost Centuries," 27.

29. Morris, *Londinium*, 340–41.

30. Robert Jackson, *Dark-Age Britain*, 49.

31. Wood, "The End of Roman Britain," 11.

32. Cummins, *King Arthur's Place in Prehistory*, 8.

33. Padel, "The Nature of Arthur," 19.

34. Alcock, *Cadbury Castle*, 6.

35. Padel, "Arthur," 48.

36. Dark, "A Famous Arthur in the Sixth Century?" 77.

37. Padel, *Arthur*, 3.

38. Higham, *King Arthur*, 143, 148.

39. Aurell, *La Légende du roi Arthur*, 83.

40. Anon., "Dux Britanniarum," 227.

41. Higham, "Chroniclers," 12, 14, 16.

42. Favero, *La Dea Veneta*, 169.

43. Halsall, *Worlds of Arthur*, 20.

44. Padel, *Arthur*, 2nd edn, 1.

45. Collins, "Military Communities," 22–25.

46. Koch, "Waiting," 189.

47. Flint Johnson, *Evidence,* 127–32.

48. Clarkson, *Scotland's Merlin,* 107.

49. Liebhard, *Suche nach dem historischen Arthur,* 62.

50. Favero, *King Arthur's Tribe,* 43.

51. Owen Jones et al., *Myvyrian Archaiology,* 1015–16.

52. J. E. Lloyd, *A History of Wales,* 310, 316–18.

53. William Rees, *South Wales and the March, 4,* 208.

54. Ifor Williams, *Pedeir Keinc y Mabinogi,* 107–8.

55. Ifor Williams, *Canu Aneirin,* 263, 343.

56. S. J. Williams and J. Enoch Powell, *Cyfreithiau Hywel Dda,* 10–11.

57. Ifor Williams, *Lectures,* 29.

58. Melville Richards, *Breudwyt Ronabwy,* 1–2, 25–26, 28.

59. Melville Richards, *The Laws of Hywel Dda,* 30.

60. Aled Rhys Wiliam, *Llyfr Iorwerth,* 4–5.

61. Jones Pierce, *Medieval Welsh Society,* 34, 116, 320.

62. K. H. Jackson, *Gododdin,* 16–18, 84–86, 111, 112.

63. Ifor Williams, *Beginnings,* 95.

64. Jacobs, "Y Traddodiad Arwrol Hen Saesneg," 178 n. 22.

65. Mac Cana, *The Learned Tales of Medieval Ireland,* 27, 135, 138.

66. Jarman, *Llyfr Du Caerfyrddin,* 77.

67. Wendy Davies, *Wales in the Early Middle Ages,* 51, 68–70, 127.

68. Rowland, *Early Welsh Saga Poetry,* 389, 510.

69. Bromwich and Evans, *Culhwch and Olwen,* xxvii–xxix.

70. Dark, *Civitas,* 189–91, 197–200.

71. Morfydd E. Owen, "Some Points of Comparison," 184.

72. Charles-Edwards, *Wales and the Britons,* 350–1064, 377.

73. Breeze, "King Arthur *Dux Bellorum,*" 51–76.

74. Field, "King Arthur."

PART TWO

The *Gawain* Poet and His School

Chapter Three

Was Sir John Stanley (d. 1414) the *Gawain* Poet?

The *Gawain* Poet was the author of *Sir Gawain and the Green Knight*, a fourteenth-century Arthurian romance, and perhaps the greatest poem ever written in Northern England. Its anonymous creator ranks with Marvell, Wordsworth, and the Brontës as among the North's supreme literary artists. The question naturally arises as to who he was. In 2004 the present writer gave an answer, publishing (in the US journal *Arthuriana*) an analysis of the poem and its associated works *Pearl*, *Cleanness*, and *Patience*. He there proposed that the unknown poet was Sir John Stanley (*c*. 1350–1414), the evidence including dialect, topography, and verbal parallels between the four texts and Stanley's correspondence. What follows offers a revised survey of publications before and after 2004, examining whether they strengthen the case for Stanley as the *Gawain* Poet, weaken it, or demolish it completely.

Questions of authorship aside, John Stanley is well known. The son of a minor landowner, he rose in a spectacular way through his own skills and marriage to an heiress. He became a provincial magnate, a courtier to Richard II, and the founder of the Stanley dynasty, with the present Earls of Derby as his descendants. He ended his days as Knight of the Garter, Lieutenant of Ireland, and King of the Isle of Man. He was also an expert hunter, responsible for the royal forests of Macclesfield, Delamere, and Wirral. If, in addition, this remarkable man wrote some of the finest poems in the English language, it will draw further attention to him and to the Lancashire and Cheshire of his time, where his estates were located and (it appears) his poems of love, adventure, chivalry, and religion were composed. It will be proof of the sophisticated literary, courtly, and religious civilization which Northern England possessed in the later middle ages.

It is true that, despite its far-reaching implications, the *Arthuriana* paper has not been much noticed. Hence this paper, with its material in two sections. In the first we survey comments on who the *Gawain* Poet was; in the second, we look at what is known of Sir John Stanley, particularly as regards his language. We start with some facts on *Sir Gawain and the Green Knight* and its related poems. It appears solely in London, British Library, MS Cotton Nero A.x, in a hand of about 1400. The manuscript, with some inferior illustrations, is undistinguished. But the four poems in it are the very opposite. The most important of them tells this story.

It begins at the court of Arthur, where a New Year's feast is interrupted by a green horseman with an axe, who challenges the guests to a beheading contest. Gawain accepts the offer and decapitates the stranger. What follows is unexpected. The trunk runs forward and snatches up its head, which opens its eyes and commands Gawain to meet him in a year's time for a return blow at the "Green Chapel"; head in hand, the body thereafter gets back in the saddle: horse and rider then hasten off through the door. The months pass. Gawain begins his journey and, after various adventures (including bedroom ones, where he politely evades an attractive chatelaine's attempts to seduce him), arrives at the Green Chapel for a second encounter with the Green Knight (and the axe). He survives with no more than a nick on his neck, and to his amazement and chagrin discovers that the challenger is none other than his host, whose young wife tested his chastity. (Had he succumbed to her, he would surely have lost his head.) Gawain returns mortally discomfited to Camelot, where the other knights regard his trials as a huge joke. In the same dialect and manuscript as *Sir Gawain and the Green Knight* are *Pearl*, *Patience*, and *Cleanness*. The first is an allegory wherein the speaker tells of losing a precious pearl (interpreted as a deceased infant daughter); he thereafter falls asleep to find himself in a garden of exotic beauty, there meeting a mysterious girl in white, who from beyond an uncrossable river speaks to him words of religious consolation. *Pearl* is accompanied by the Scriptural poems *Patience* and *Cleanness*, setting out respectively the stories of Jonah and those of Noah's Flood, the Destruction of Sodom, and Belshazzer's Feast. These texts were effectively unknown until modern times, with an edition of *Sir Gawain and the Green Knight* in 1839 and of all four poems in 1864.[1]

In commentary since then one hears diverse opinions. Some show sense on what they say of the poet; others, less so; but critical fashion and personal impulse are frequent. Kenneth Sisam observed on the romance of Gawain that the "descriptions of nature, of armour and dresses, the hunting scenes, and the love-making, are all excellently done"; while the author has "a quiet humour that recalls Chaucer." *Pearl*, on the other hand, is "almost overwrought"; it has a richness and luxuriance that at first "seem scarcely English" together with alliteration and rhyme of such intricacy that one wonders how the author sustained "his marvellous technique without completely sacrificing poetry to metrical gymnastics."[2]

Another writer maintained that the castle where Gawain stayed was based on Clitheroe Castle, belonging to John of Gaunt.[3] But no one accepts that. Better was his later praise of the author, whose "remarkable attitude to nature" reveals "rare gifts" for literary creation, as do his powers of description, whether of the arming of a knight, the pinnacles of a fortress, the hunting of hart, boar, or fox, or "the cutting up of a beast."[4] He rightly stressed the poet's pride in hunting and butchery (routinely ignored by critics), which does not flinch from details of a slaughtered deer's windpipe and guts (line 1336). Yet Oakden was modestly silent on the fur coat (trimmed "ful fyne with felles" or pelts) worn next to the skin of Gawain's chatelaine, who (her throat "all naked" and "brest bare before") enters the knight's bedroom (closing the door behind her) early in the morning, while her husband is away hunting on the moors (lines 1733–49). Whether presenting an animal's innards or the blandishments of a *femme fatale*, the poet demonstrates remarkable powers of observation, as well as easy familiarity with the life of lords and ladies.

Sir Israel Gollancz (1863–1930) made unconvincing proposals on the Gawain poem as written for an audience in North Wales, and a better one for the Green Chapel as in the rugged country of northwest Staffordshire.[5] This area of the Peak District was in the Forest of Macclesfield. We shall use this as a clue to authorship. Gervase Mathew (1905–1976) had careful remarks on the manuscript. It belonged to Henry Savile (1568–1617) of Bank, near Halifax in West Yorkshire, indicating a northern province; two annotations in fifteenth-century hands suggest that its previous ownership was secular, not monastic. On authorship, Mathew took similarities between the four poems as pointing to "a single author or a single redactor, perhaps a clerk or esquire in some household" (others will now reject "redactor" and its implications of multiple authorship). The manuscript itself is a professional but clumsy effort, the dialect forms perhaps indicating a scribe from Chester (later dialectologists would modify this to "south-east Cheshire or north-west Staffordshire"), whose copy-text had deluxe illustrations and was probably "commissioned by a magnate of wealth not much before 1390" and his household possibly at "the Earl of Arundel's castle of Holt" near Wrexham, Wales. Mathew also provided analysis of the knightly virtues implicit in the text, with "prowess and loyalty" here being paramount. There are two points here.[6] Mathew's study of the poet's chivalric values is now little read, but deserves attention. Mathew was a Dominican friar, and so knew much about the religious life. He did not think that *Sir Gawain* was the work of a cleric, his preference being for a layman in a great household.

Despite concentrating on poem rather than poet, George Kane referred to the latter's eye for "gold and silver and the filigree of both, and precious stones, against backgrounds of rich Eastern stuffs"; they contrast with "the driving sleet on Gawain's journey, the fatigue of his charger, the misery of sleeping out in armour, the brightness of blood on snow"; with the last being at Gawain's ordeal by axe.[7] The writer had a genius for detail. E. V. Gordon had comments of a different kind. Although "a man of education" the writer made less parade of learning than did Chaucer, Gower, or Langland. He had "less interest in philosophy" than they did, and more in "the arts and the aristocratic activities of his day." He may "have had a monastic education" but was hardly "himself a monk." He might have been "a chaplain in an aristocratic household." (Given his tenderness for a lost daughter, zest for killing animals, and awareness of sexual attraction in near-adultery, "chaplain" here makes little sense.) Gordon yet admitted that the poet's interest in theology might be that of a "pious layman."[8]

Dorothy Everett (1894–1953) of Oxford had interesting observations. The four poems (which she put in "the last quarter of the fourteenth century") have "obvious links" with each other in vocabulary, phrasing, and (*Pearl* excepted) metre, as well as less obvious ones in "the doctrine of the Beatific Vision" and "the pearl as a symbol of perfection." They point to a single author for all, because two or more writers would hardly possess "this rare and, one would think, inimitable quality." The poet read widely: in French, the *Roman de la Rose* and some Arthurian romances; in English, alliterative poetry; in Italian (most unusually) Dante's *Divine Comedy*; in Latin, Boccaccio's *Olympia*, as also the Bible with its commentaries and interpretations, the latter perhaps indicating "an ecclesiastical education. If so, his independence of mind is the more remarkable." She quoted Menner's 1920 edition of *Cleanness* on his unfettered attitude to "theological doctrine and conventional interpretation," while "in *Pearl* he employs both in a manner still more individual." He was yet "sufficiently at home in courtly, or at least aristocratic, society to be able to depict with fidelity its manners, pastimes, and setting," including details of dress, armor, architecture, and sport.[9] For the poet, religion and the worldly met in unusual combination.

Her remarks are more thoughtful and helpful than those of John Speirs (d. 1979), observing that *Sir Gawain and the Green Knight* "is of course a Christian poem. But it is Christian rather as some of the medieval Christmas carols are, as Christmas itself is; Christian in harmony with pre-Christian nature belief and ritual."[10] This 1950s venture into lay anthropology says much about Speirs, little about the poet. Preferable are comments of Laura Loomis. "Was he a monk, a minstrel, a learned clerk, an official in some lordly household, or himself a man of rank and wealth? In any case he wrote as one familiar with courtly life, its pleasures, luxuries, arts, and ways."[11] Reflection on the poems will rule out most of these. It is the "man of rank and wealth" whose face we perceive in these texts: a religious man, but with the confidence and independence that status and income supply. Laura

Loomis deserves full credit as the first to regard *Gawain* as the work of a provincial magnate.

What she said tallies with perceptions of John H. Fisher on the social views of Ricardian writers. The *Gawain* poet "wrote about and for the aristocracy"; he had none of the "overt questioning of the social changes that troubled Langland and Gower"; despite supposed criticism of kingship in his calling Arthur *sumwhat child-gered* (line 86) or "boyish, merry," this "does not mean that the author questioned the aristocratic system"; his "choice of garden paradise or castle put his pieces in the context of the agrarian aristocracy" (unlike Langland's London settings, at a far lower social level). The garden of *Pearl* is not that of Eden, with "no lords or ladies" (and so a "nascent primitivism" producing "Wyclif's communism"), but that of love, where "everyone is a lord or lady." Hence the "courtly maiden" and "humbly suppliant lover." As for the parable of the vineyard, it contains "the notion of arbitrary authority in the familiar context of lord and laborer"; while the maiden's "explanation of her state in paradise evidently recognizes grades in the hierarchy of heaven," together with a "heavenly state of equality impossible of attainment in mortal society" owing to man's sinful nature.[12] In short, the poet's attitude to aristocracy is unquestioning and profoundly conservative, even reactionary. Fisher's insights are of the first importance. They deserve notice, despite his strange view of the author as a "writer with predominantly theological interests," glossing over what he says on feasts, jewels, furs, armour, horses, hunts, and illicit love.

C. S. Lewis dealt firmly with the observations of Speirs on supposed pre-Christian elements in *Sir Gawain and the Green Knight*.[13] Not much has been heard of them since. They led nowhere, unlike the enquiries of John Dodgson, place-name scholar. He cited R. W. V. Elliott on the landscape of the Castle and Chapel as like that "around Swythamley in northeast Staffordshire, near the Cheshire border and in the southwestern hills of the Peak district," the poet perhaps actually living at Swythamley, "a grange of Dielacres Abbey, near Leak, Staffordshire." (Yet Elliott's belief that the poet was perhaps a monk on a monastic estate must be rejected. There is nothing monastic in the four poems attributed to him.) Together with Dodgson's words on the wild country of the Peak are comments on the "Holy Hede" from which Gawain, having traveled through North Wales, crosses into the "wyldrenesse of Wyrale" (lines 700–1), where the first can be linked with Holywell, Flintshire, and where allusion to the Wirral Peninsula of Cheshire indicates a region known to the poet and his audience.[14] He made clear the poet's knowledge of northeast Wales, Cheshire, and the Peak.

A different approach to the poem was made by the Polish-American Marxist, Margaret Schlauch. The text is a "society romance" showing "an exceptional talent for descriptions of nature" and for dialogue between the

characters. Readers know no more about Gawain's situation or "the true relationship among the characters" than Gawain does himself, a technique antici-
pating the "unity of point of view" employed by Henry James and others.
The text nevertheless had no influence on later English fiction. For historians
of the modern novel, its interest is "largely antiquarian."[15] Her somewhat
perfunctory comments keep the poet at a distance. Fisher had had compelling
remarks on him as a social arch-conservative, wedded to the cause of aristocracy. If Schlauch had developed Fisher's ideas on classic Marxist lines, she
would have provided a study with real insights.

Dodgson's views on topography were treated positively by John Burrow.
He observed how "the original audience of *Sir Gawain*, in Cheshire perhaps, or Lancashire," would know Holywell as the shrine of St Gwenfrewi
or Winifred, whose legend tells how a local tyrant had her decapitated, her
head being miraculously restored.[16] Topographical allusions show the poem
as a Cheshire one. Derek Brewer (1923–2008) offered reflections on the poet
and courtesy, which he interpreted as a religious entity relating to personal
integrity, beauty, politeness, honour, self-control, courage, and cleanliness. It
did not include asceticism, *fin amour*, or (for example) almsgiving.[17] Brewer
again removed the quartet of poems from a monastic milieu. Like the analyses of Mathew and Fisher, his essay is now little read.

There are acid lessons on how not to read *Gawain* in a paper by Heinrich
Zimmer (1851–1910) of Berlin. Zimmer was a respected Celticist, advancing
sound arguments on the British hero Arthur (d. 537) as a historical figure. But
he was also a Jungian, believing in the "mythological archetypes" of the col-
lective unconscious. He thus saw Gawain as going through a valley of death
to "the aloof and lonely sanctuary of life renewed" where he is duly reborn,
having encountered the Green Knight, who is Death, and his wife, who is
Life, "traditionally Death's bride." Even Zimmer, recognizing that the poem
does not really bear out this interpretation, concluded that its author was
unaware of "the meaning that inevitably emerges."[18] But some may hold that,
when what we find does not fit the theory, the latter has to go. Zimmer was
neither the first nor the last to write absurdities on *Sir Gawain*. In a different
vein was Patricia Kean, here as cautious as Zimmer was not. Although her
study of *Pearl* has much of interest (as on the poet's apparent knowledge of
Dante), she describes the "old controversy" on whether the text is "biographi-
cal or allegorical" as hardly "relevant to the real purpose of the poem." Her
conclusion is that the author was "essentially, a Christian."[19] This does not
help us much.

The standard Oxford edition of *Sir Gawain* has more perceptive comments,
on the poet's consistent "theological concern" and "moral seriousness"
(despite this poem's "surface lightheartedness"). He knew much of "the life
and etiquette of noble households"; possessed "a detailed, even technical,

knowledge of hunting, of castle architecture, and of the armor and gear of a knight. In *Patience* he uses with an air of assurance the right terms for the parts of a ship." He was deeply read in the Vulgate Bible; *Pearl* implies some knowledge of patristic theology. He had read widely in French romance. His language (although "strongly provincial") is yet sophisticated, courtly, and elegant. He had interest in neither "astrology and its associated sciences" nor the "Boethian problems of foreknowledge and free will" (unlike Chaucer). On date and provenance, the editors are circumspect; more so than Dorothy Everett, whom they quote. The text "cannot be dated precisely"; but must be earlier than the manuscript, itself hardly later than 1400. Emphasis on display may "imply a date towards the end of the century"; while dialect and allusions to North Wales and the Wirral suggest that the poet "was writing not far" from them.[20]

So: the poet was familiar with courts, hunting, horses, castles, arms and armor, ships, French romance, the Bible, and theology. He had no interest in philosophy, science, astrology, or astronomy. He did not read the Latin classics, unlike Chaucer. He did, however, know French and perhaps even Italian literature of his time. He was not university-trained and lacked Chaucer's wide intellectual interests, but had practical experience of foreign travel and military life. His confidence on such matters (as also, we recall from Fisher, the administration of justice) points less to Laura Loomis's "official in some lordly household" than to her "man of rank and wealth"; a devout individual, at ease in the court, on the bench, and on campaign, but not an urban intellectual.

With this, contrast views offered by Larry Benson. He regarded *Sir Gawain* as proof of "the scrutiny that older values were undergoing as the middle ages came to an end." It was a century when "crusades" had "nothing but the name in common" with previous ones; when the "examples of chivalric conduct" admired by Froissart are "glaring exceptions in his chronicles of a cruel and greedy era"; when "peasants were asserting themselves in a way that showed clearly that the old feudal order was dying"; when "the Great Schism and the rise of heresy showed that even the Church was not as secure" as supposed; and when "plague and famine threatened the existence even of society itself."[21] True, of course. The *Gawain* poet certainly knew about atrocities, peasant revolts, schism, and epidemics, especially the last, one of which perhaps killed his daughter (as argued below). Yet *Sir Gawain* is no polemic on obsolete institutions and beliefs. While Benson saw the poet as a doubter, Fisher and Brewer regarded him as subscribing to the values of medieval chivalry and Christianity, even to the point of reaction. The point is fundamental.

In a studious account, Ian Bishop (1927–1990) of Bristol favoured an autobiographical approach to *Pearl* (while dismissing the extravagances of some critics), quoting Norman Davis on the line "In Crystes dere blessyng and myne" near its close as "an epistolary formula" then "used almost exclusively by parents addressing their children."[22] The phrase expresses tender love. With it, a father might bid everlasting farewell to an infant daughter. A mere allegorist would feel no such emotion, one imagines. In the same year Gervase Mathew published a book which abounds in insights on the English nobility at the time when *Sir Gawain* was written. He thus mentioned Henry of Grosmont (1299?–1361), whose daughter married John of Gaunt. Henry, Duke of Lancaster, was an unexpected combination of soldier, magnate, and author, whose *Livre de Seyntz Medecines* of 1354 is a volume of frank confessions. From this and other sources we find in him a man of piety, chivalry, courage, and sexual frailty, who craved honour but also had an "itch to possess more lands." He was not alone as a devout warrior-nobleman who valued books. Thomas of Woodstock (1355–1397), Duke of Gloucester, showed "rash courage in the French wars"; but also founded a college of priests at Pleshy (his seat in Essex) and possessed a magnificent library (with an English Bible still extant). Mathew showed how military courage, wealth, religious fervor, and a love of books might at this date co-exist in one man. He made a further comment of far-reaching importance. It is this. "I have a theory that Sir John Stanley was the patron of the *Gawain* poet. The poem ends 'Hony Soyt qui mal pence,' and this suggests that it was written for a knight of the Garter; the dialect suggests that it was written in south-west Lancashire, and at this period Sir John Stanley was the only knight of the Garter in south-west Lancashire. It is also possibly relevant that he was hereditary forester of Wirral and had links with the North."[23] Another aspect of the poet was investigated by James Oakden, tracing the influence of the liturgy on *Pearl*.[24]

There is an insight (its context unexpected) from Rosemary Woolf. She distinguished between "naturally anonymous and accidentally anonymous" texts. Most medieval English lyrics, romances, and mystery plays have a "self-effacing style." Even if we knew who wrote them, it would be "unimportant," arousing neither "curiosity or excitement." But *Pearl* and *Sir Gawain* gain from being read in conjunction, "so that here knowledge of authorship would be very valuable." She cited an instance in lines 345–46 of the former, where the maiden tells the narrator how, even if he should writhe like a doe (*daunce as any do*), and struggle and bray (*braundysch and bray*) out his agonies, he is trapped and must endure what happens. The image is of a deer at bay, exhausted and at the mercy of hounds.[25] It is not the only hunting metaphor in *Pearl*. When the narrator first encounters the Maiden, he takes her (line 185) as a spiritual *purpose*, which has been understood as "quarry, object of a pursuit." An exquisite sensibility notwithstanding, the poet referred naturally to the ungentle business of tearing animals to bits. He rejoiced in hunting.

In his edition of *Patience*, John Anderson of Manchester noted the "sixteen lines of narrative" where the poet described "in generous detail" the preparation of a ship for sea. He gave its date as perhaps after 1357 and before 1390, and possibly before the completion in about 1379 of the B-text of Langland's *Piers Plowman*, which apparently alludes to *Patience*. On provenance he cited a famous 1963 paper by Angus McIntosh of Edinburgh, which allocated the dialect of the MS Cotton Nero A.x scribe (not that of the poet) to "south-east Cheshire or north-east Staffordshire."[26] If there are references to hunting in Cheshire forests or on Staffordshire moor, others point to experience of shipping on the Dee or Mersey.

Although Basil Cottle (1917–1994) of Bristol is another scholar now little read, he had illuminating remarks on the poet. He gave a picture of a "well-off provincial society, with its classes happily dovetailed and bestowing service and patronage," which possessed "a noble court of great luxury and taste," where "due order was observed but nobody groused." The ritual arming of a knight engaged his attention; so, too, did heraldry (in nearly fifty lines). He said much on courtesy, and not merely of "refined and privileged equals": the porter is polite to Gawain and is "thanked for his services"; grooms are "thanked for stabling Gawain's horse"; the boorish intruder at Camelot is addressed as if he had been invited; Gawain and his host dispute whose presence grants more honor; there are no hard words from the temptress, "even when the seduction fails"; and Cottle then analyses at length the poet's scrupulous use of familiar "thee" and formal "you" in the dialogues.[27] So the poet was an expert observer, who saw society from above and not from below. He could be affable, but in no way questioned established order. The point on heraldry is underlined by the Scrope-Grosvenor case of 1386, routinely cited in biographies of Chaucer. Scrope and Grosvenor took to law their quarrel about a certain coat of arms. Chaucer, despite giving testimony in court, in his verse gave no space to blazon. The subject did not interest him (just as it interests hardly any modern critic). But it very much interested the *Gawain* poet. It is yet more evidence for him as a provincial grandee.

Tony Spearing in 1970 provided a book-length study of the poet, following Gordon in dating him to 1360–1395, and Angus McIntosh on the dialect of MS Cotton Nero A.x as that of a scribe from south-east Cheshire or north-east Staffordshire, differing little from the poet's own dialect. Yet Spearing, despite copious remarks on the author's attitude to feasting, hunting, court life, the Bible, French and Latin poetry, and the mystical theology of his day, shied away from defining his identity or social status.[28] Despite its title, his book says almost nothing about the poet. His face or image is left blurred or indistinct. In the same year D. J. Williams published an able (if conservative) account. Stating that there is "no proof that these four poems were written by one man" (which he yet thought probable), he offered no proposals on what kind of person he was. All the same, he had interesting remarks on *Sir Gawain* and Chaucer's tale of the Knight, especially their contrasts. Both narratives are serious and sophisticated, but are "informed by a different spirit." The former is closer to the twelfth-century romances of Chrétien de Troyes and is "a more highly developed work." It was "written to entertain an aristocratic circle"; it embodies "courtly ideals" similar to Chrétien's, but "under a closer critical scrutiny," although they are not "under fire." The ambivalence here is paralleled by that of Jonah's "escapade in the whale" in *Patience*.[29]

John Burrow pointed out the accidents of time. If Chester and not London had been England's capital, the *Gawain* poet would "immediately have been acknowledged a national classic, and a north-western Caxton would have rushed his work into print." Instead, he was forgotten for three centuries. His work influenced later alliterative writers (including the author of *The Awntyrs off Arthure*, composed in 1425 or so at Carlisle or thereabouts) and was still read in the Cheshire-Lancashire region into the sixteenth century. After that, oblivion, until Thomas Warton (1728–1790) showed interest in the texts, to be followed by Madden in 1839 and Richard Morris in 1864. Burrow deals more with the poems than the poet, but quotes a 1966 essay by Spearing on how all four of them set out "a confrontation between a human being and some more than human power," the protagonist in each case emerging "humbled by the confrontation."[30] The texts all possess the hand and voice of one author. It is good to be certain of this when reading interpretations of *Pearl*, with the pearl identified as a eucharistic symbol, a believer's soul, the Blessed Virgin, and so on.[31]

Such plurality is welcomely absent from a paper with thorough and decisive views on authorship. While the poet's "analogous phrases, paraphrases for God, methods of introducing a story, stating that something is difficult to describe, and endings that echo beginnings" are elements found in other medieval poems, their frequency in these four poems makes the statistical case for common authorship "overwhelming." Still more important than these five categories are imagery and diction. Identical words, often "in special senses that are uniquely the same," are used to describe the same scenes. Above all is the thematic unity of the poems. Patience, humility, and purity are the subject of the two homiletic texts: they dominate the two others. "The pearl-maiden, a symbol of purity, teaches the dreamer the lesson of resignation. Gawain, the 'perle of prys,' is not perfect" and returns to Arthur's court a humbler knight, having failed the test of loyalty.[32]

Awareness of the above puts into context comments by Charles Muscatine on the author as "a surprisingly uncomplicated moralist, and a conservative one as well"; although he surely noticed the troubles of his time, his response is "oblique," any crisis being "completely absorbed in his art," itself perhaps "a defense against crisis."[33] Spearing likewise comments on the poet's belief in breeding and *cortaysye*, the values of an aristocratic elite.[34] They are yet supplemented by other remarks on how in *Sir Gawain* the courtly world of France or "heraldry and books of romance" or pinnacled castles is combined with that "of a countryman from the borders of Staffordshire and Cheshire, speaking a rough dialect and accustomed to listening to heroic stories."[35] The word "countryman" is too hard. Nor was the dialect "rough" to those who spoke it. Better to speak of a poet "widely read in the most sophisticated literature of the age": religious, secular, English, French, Latin, or even Italian. He was a provincial with "an intimate knowledge of aristocratic life, architecture, etiquette, hunting, feasting, dress and armour, and the terms of courtly conversation" (as also heraldry). He may have been a "secretary or chaplain" in one of John of Gaunt's castles in Lancashire, Staffordshire, or Derbyshire. He was in any case most certainly "a writer of genius."[36]

Here correct observations have an illogical conclusion. A chaplain would not know much about flirting or the chase. The poet's familiarity with all the above, including expensive literature in modern languages, indicates an aristocrat with the appropriate income. Compare again remarks on the poet as "a man of learning, a superb craftsman with a delight in the world of the senses, and a man with a keen and subtle sense of humour."[37] All of this is true, but still (to labor the point) neglects his social conservatism, adherence to chivalric values, profound Christian faith, and zeal for hunting.

Sir Gawain was (?) surely known (despite the doubts of some) to the author of *The Awntyrs off Arthure*, perhaps by a Carlisle cleric writing in 1425 or 1426.[38] At the other end of England was Chaucer, whose *Prologue to The Legend of Good Women* implies (in Tony Spearing's opinion) that he had read *Pearl*, and the opening to *The Squire's Tale* that he had read *Sir Gawain*.[39] (The second is correct, the first is the wrong way round.) Their author evidently possessed exalted rank and social connections in London. Yet Anderson would not go beyond the view that the MS Cotton Nero A.x texts were probably by the same man, who presumably lived in the northwest and read *Mandeville's Travels*, written about 1357. Anderson thought that any attempt to narrow the dating within the limits of 1357 to 1400 "must be speculative."[40] Derek Pearsall, making no reference to Vantuomo's paper of 1971, similarly asserted that we know nothing of the four poems' authorship, "though it has become habitual to attribute them to the same poet."[41] Elsewhere is the comment that the audience for alliterative poetry tended to include gentry, knights, franklins, and the clergy rather than "members of the higher nobility."[42] The critic has not realized that we hear more of the latter (such as the fifteenth-century Yorkshire squire Robert Thornton, who owned

a copy of *The Awntyrs off Arthure* and other romances) because they out-
numbered the nobles, especially in the North. Yet the MS Cotton Nero A.x's
illustrations reproduce those of a deluxe original entirely beyond the means
of any local landowner or country parson.

Although the editors of a standard edition comment on the "subjective
element" in "judgements of similarity of thought and attitude," they come
down all the same for common authorship, seeing the poet's art as combin-
ing "orthodox medieval Christianity" with the "chivalric social morality of
the High Middle Ages."[43] That is surely right. Even in Davenport's study it is
not, however, stressed as it should be. Despite admission of how the *Gawain*
poet's works possess "a range and quality comparable to those of Chaucer,"
when Davenport comments on the northern writer as not "particularly intellectual," but having "a liking for 'university wit'" in word-play and metrical
numerology, he diminishes his subject.[44] The poet was no mere wordsmith;
and "university" is here irrelevant. His education was not scholastic.

New attitudes to *Sir Gawain* were noted and mocked by Derek Brewer.
He ridiculed the view that the poet treated Christmas at Camelot with "ironi-
cally sarcastic criticism of its childishness and irresponsibility," and how
Arthur should instead "be at his desk getting on governing the country." In
his opinion, the author says what he means.[45] His realism was genuine, and
his social and religious values were conservative ones (like those of Derek
Brewer himself).

Now for a digression on clothes. A rare analysis of the Green Knight's
attire (down to his "mantle lined with ermine") provides the conclusion
that his tight tunic was all the rage in 1365, going out by 1370, and *passé*
by 1380.[46] The implications for dating are novel. Taken as they stand, they
torpedo the case presented here. John Stanley was born, it seems, in about
1350. A date of composition in the 1360s would create insuperable obstacles.
Yet there is a way around them. Because nothing else puts *Sir Gawain* before
the late 1380s or 1390s, it may be that the author deliberately provided the
Green Knight with attire that was good but outmoded. The parallel would be
with the time lords or Transylvanian counts of modern entertainment. They
dress well, but not in today's fashions, thereby acquiring a curious authority.
If there is an equivalent for this in *Sir Gawain*, we have a further glimpse
of the writer's skill. (See now, however, chapter 4 on the poem as of 1387.)

Brewer's attitude to the poem would have been contested by Ray Barron.
He found in it "a complex of interrelating ambiguities which challenge the
reader's judgement of meaning and theme and provide a seedbed for ironies
which expose chivalric values to his critical scrutiny," as in the Exchange of
Winnings, wherein Gawain fails to surrender the girdle won from the lady.[47]
Many see the author as conservative. Barron took him as a radical. The latter

may be doubted. Comparison with the genuine article brings this out. The real literature of complaint brims with anti-clericalism, pacifism, attacks on government advisers, condemnation of a corrupt knighthood, and criticism of the wealthy, as is demonstrated by one left-wing historian. But nothing of that in *Sir Gawain*, "written for a local magnate with a family and manor in south-west Lancashire." We agree, noting her further comment on a 1978 paper by George Kane, with "an amusing summary of the variety of interpretations" of *Sir Gawain*.[48] Conservative and Marxian critics hence agree on the poem's ambience as a lay one in England's northwest.

Derek Brewer gave the poet's home as "the hills and moors of Derbyshire in the North Midlands."[49] "Derbyshire" is a slip for "Staffordshire." No dialectal or topographical evidence links the writer with Derbyshire. Nor would he have lived among those hills and moors, though he certainly hunted on them (see Turville-Petre's 2008 paper on the Green Chapel and Ludchurch, in Staffordshire's northern tip). His residence will have been a great hall in the lowlands of the northwest, as indicated by Janet Coleman. (Specifically, as we argue below, Chester Castle.) As for his values, anachronistic attitudes to them are identified by John Burrow in an essay on honour and shame. He observes that, while *Sir Gawain* is not actually about these qualities, it takes them for granted. It displays "an ingrained familiarity with principles which are, at best, strange to the modern reader, and at worst thoroughly objectionable"; which makes it hard for such readers to appreciate how Gawain's moral self-scrutiny slept until it was woken by a fellow knight's reproaches.[50] Further misunderstanding comes in a comment on the unknown "craftsman who produced these four remarkable texts."[51] Yet the poet was more than a craftsman. He was a supreme artist. As for where he lived, Silverstein cited R. W. V. Elliott on the relation of "the Green Chapel to the valley of the River Dane" in north-west Staffordshire.[52]

In a chapter on the MS Cotton Nero poems which abounds with insights, Jack Bennett (1911–1981) echoed Stephen Medcalf on the contrast between "rich feasts, a castle built in the latest style," ornamented armour, fashionable furnishings, polite and elegant conversation, elaborate laws and customs of the chase, as also the international French "terms of art that were current at the court of Richard II and in the households of his nobility" and, on the other hand, "wild and rugged country, winter and rough weather, boisterous humour with some grim touches" and "plain-spoken comment." A singular combination. Vantuomo's paper notwithstanding, Bennett yet opined that common authorship of the four poems could not "be conclusively proved."[53] There are implications here. The familiarity with a king's household indicates a context for the poems altogether grander than a Cheshire or Lancashire manor-house; on the other hand, no evidence has ever been produced to show that the four poems are not by one man.

Paul Strohm, expert on medieval literary sociology, offers more doubts. He followed Spearing (at a distance) on the opening of Chaucer's *Squire's Tale* as perhaps showing knowledge of *Sir Gawain*. If so, it suggests a writer with metropolitan contacts. As for his audience, Strohm attempts to trash critics who locate it "with equal plausibility in baronial courts, among the country gentry, amongst Cheshire servants of Richard II, and in the monastic houses of the south-west Midlands."[54] Yet some of these views are more equal than others, even if Strohm failed to notice. Hunting and attempted seduction are strange fare for the cloister; and the writer evidently walked not with mere gentry, but with magnates and kings. So "Cheshire servants of Richard II" may be rather near the mark. Despite their interest, further chapters by Tony Spearing on *Sir Gawain* and *Cleanness* shed no light on their author.[55]

Felicity Riddy repeats the unlikely suggestion that the poet was a "probably a cleric" and perhaps in the employ of a "secular household."[56] This despite the goings-on in *Sir Gawain*, the expressions in *Pearl* of a father's tender love for a child, and (most startling) the enthusiastic praise in *Cleanness* (lines 703–4, here quoted after Anderson's edition of 1977) of sex:

Bitwene a male and his make [=*mate*] suche mirthe should come,
Wel neghe pure Paradise myght preve no better.

The writer does not sound like a priest. He sounds like a layman, happily married and with children. As for where he wrote, Lee Patterson (with a nod to Fisher's paper of 1961) has a penetrating aside. *Sir Gawain* "is structured by the relationship between a royal and provincial courts. It may even be that the representation of the 'child-gered' [having a child's ways] Arthur," presiding "over an elegantly gamesome court, is meant to reflect Richard."[57] Patterson's remark is casual but arresting. Because Richard II was born in 1367 and died in 1400, this would put the poem between 1382 (when Richard married and attained his majority) and 1400, and no doubt early in that period, when Richard was still youthful. Patterson's suggestion accords with evidence elsewhere for *Sir Gawain* as of 1387. It really is (as the phrase goes) Ricardian Poetry.

Derek Pearsall remarked acutely on hunting as a barrier between us and our ancestors even greater than rhetoric (as C. S. Lewis thought). When the *Gawain* Poet chose to "parade its language of technical expertise," hardly any reader today can respond.[58] This is well said. Because canon law barred clerics from blood sports, the poet's obsession with hunting indicates a lay author. His knowledge of it was authoritative, as shown by his delight in its rituals and protocol. As for what he wrote, scholars who believe in common authorship of the MS Cotton Nero poems are cited against splitters who believe in multiple authorship.[59] Wrangles continue on the integrity of his work, quite unnecessarily.

In a paper which repays careful reading, John Bowyers of Nevada follows Michael Bennett on political links between Cheshire and the court of Richard II. Despite being "agnostic" on whether the MS Cotton Nero texts are by one poet or not, he feels some certainty on the date of *Pearl*. He locates it within the mid-1390s, some ten years after *Sir Gawain*. Composition about 1395 would come after Richard II's "seven quiet years" (in Harold Hutchison's phrase) of 1389–1396, when English politics were relatively stable.[60] We shall see how a paper of 2014, written independently of Bowyers, suggests a date of 1390 on quite different grounds.

As for who the poet was, this brings us to Ad Putter, who combines wise remarks with ones more contentious. He says this. The poet has long been related to "a small baronial household, hostile to King Richard II's absolutist tendencies and his francophile court." Against this we might say that the original deluxe copy of the poems does not indicate a "small" household; nor are francophobia or hostility to absolutism at all obvious in *Sir Gawain*. Putter is, nevertheless, correct is dismissing the negative aspects of "provincial" as applied to the writer. Next is his reference to Michael Bennett's speculation on how, lacking a patron in the northwest, the poet went south in hope of "prospects of patronage by the king" or a Cheshire magnate at his court. The lost luxury manuscript is certainly evidence for a "wealthy" patron. Against that is the argument that, if the poet were himself a magnate, as shown by his effortless allusions to the ostentation and ceremonies of court life, he needed no patron. He could pay for his own manuscripts. Next is the dubious case, after Jill Mann, for *Sir Gawain* as appealing to "'an audience of sophisticated and wealthy merchants and knights' most easily found in London." Against that are its allusions to North Wales, the Wirral, and Green Chapel, of faint interest to those on Cheapside or in Whitehall. The poem's Cheshire associations stare one in the face. Also feeble are the suggestions that the poet's knowledge of Italian literature indicates a London base; that "the Greene Knight" in an inventory of the younger Sir John Paston was *Sir Gawain*, so that the poet probably worked in London; and that, because Richard II understood his Cheshire archers, therefore he would have understood and relished the language of the romance. (Against that, a critic cited below observed that Richard had no known interest in alliterative poetry.) Further unconvincing statements come in the propositions that, while the sources of the poems "suggest a clerical background" (even if their author "does not address his audience as a cleric"), his "ethics of conscientious worldliness" indicates links with merchants. Representing the interests of clerics, knights, and merchants, *Gawain* may thus be related to London, "where people from different backgrounds" made up "a textual community" with "the broad social appeal" to be found in *Sir Gawain*.[61] One fears that this is not compelling. While the poet surely knew London's sophistication and luxuries, his heart belonged to Cheshire and its borders. He placed there the main action of his greatest poem. As for his social views, we observe again how Fisher (whose 1961 paper is not mentioned by Putter) typified them as aristocratic to the point of reaction. Nothing to attract, one might think, the London merchant class.

One finds contrasts to the poet's politics in *The Awntyrs off Arthure*, perhaps written in about 1425 by a Carlisle cleric, and associated with the Neville dynasty. Its author probably knew *Sir Gawain*, but offered a picture of "the instability of power and wealth" which suits a preacher.[62] The later work underlines the point that, while *Gawain*'s London connections are weak (except as regards Chaucer), its northern ones are strong, like those of its surviving manuscript. They are further developed by Michael Bennett, taking up Gervase Mathew's 1968 proposal of a link between *Sir Gawain* and Sir John Stanley (*c.* 1350–1414). His family in the 1370s built the hall at Storeton in the Wirral, a region mentioned in the poem; he himself, "a successful career-soldier," built a stronghold (demolished in 1819) by the quay at Liverpool. In 1389–1391 he was Justiciar of Ireland, acting regularly thereafter as negotiator and raiser of troops for Richard II. So he knew the court well, and Bennett cites Mathew and Edward Wilson for him as perhaps the patron of the poet. Stanley survived political transition to become a Knight of the Garter in 1405, the only one in Cheshire or south Lancashire.[63] He died in 1414 (in Ireland) as King of the Isle of Man.

Ray Barron, observing that the "enigma of author and audience remains unresolved," had comments on the latter. It is hard "to believe that such a sophisticated text" as *Sir Gawain* "could have been produced for provincial gentry," despite the rather scanty evidence for them and "the rising bourgeoisie" as an "audience for romance in English." The poet was obviously a prodigy. He had an intimate knowledge of literary French, law, theology, dialectic, armour, fortification, architecture, fashion, textiles, and "the refined etiquette of court and hunting field."[64] Who could this provincial phenomenon be? One might take his references to royal luxury to show him as (in Lady Bracknell's phrase) evidently a man of some wealth. His social background was utterly unlike that of any other English romance writer.

On the grounds of his sophistication and range of allusion, Sheila Fisher of Connecticut associates the *Gawain* poet "with one of the country courts of Edward III or John of Gaunt" in the northwest Midlands, a speculation traceable to 1930 and J. P. Oakden, who is not here mentioned.[65] Citing Pearsall and Hanna on the Scriptural poems *Pearl*, *Cleanness*, and *Patience*, David Lawton notes that, although "most recent suggestions have focused on the monasteries" for their social context, *Patience*'s story of Jonah "was a favourite of lay and extra-regular readers well into the Reformation."[66] In contrast is James Simpson, uttering 1990s critical fashions, who states that there is no reason why *Sir Gawain* "should not have London or Westminster connections," even though the poem refers to neither place. He adds that the "Stanley family in particular at that time constituted the dominant power in Lancashire and had close contacts with court," without saying what this might mean for the MS Cotton Nero texts.[67] Readers must find bewildering these contrasting backgrounds of court and cloister. All but one of them must be dropped. In a lucid survey of *Gawain*'s ambiguities, Derek Pearsall avoids saying whether our quartet of poems are by one man, but rightly declares him "one of the greatest poets of the English language" whose sole provinciality was his dialect, and assuredly not his "understanding of courtly culture or the conventions of romance."[68]

In 2004 the present writer published a paper taking up the links with Sir John Stanley indicated by Mathew in 1968. He suggested that the *Gawain* Poet was not some clerk or chaplain employed by Stanley, but Stanley himself. Hence the confident familiarity with court life and luxury or the rituals of hunting and love, as also the interest in heraldry, armor, military architecture, French romance; the layman's point of view in matters of religion, the love of children (Stanley had many), the praise of married love; the practical understanding of shipping; the lack of interest in science, philosophy, or scholasticism; and the reactionary politics. Documents by Stanley survive, including a letter in French of 1405 to Henry IV, using words characteristic of MS Cotton Nero poems, including *honor*, *comfort*, *haste*, *gracious*, *joie*, *access*, and *fortune*.[69]

Naturally, papers of this kind take a while to be noticed. In the meantime, John Anderson dealt with Noah's Flood and the Destruction of Sodom and Gomorrah in *Cleanness*. He disagreed with Muscatine's opinion of 1972 on the writer as "completely absorbed in his art" and indifferent to events in the wider world. *Cleanness*, like *Patience*, is about suffering, and in fourteenth-century England there was plenty of that. (It included plague in 1390–1393.) Yet Anderson did not think this the end of the story. The three shorter poems indicate how "God's love is present" in the world, even if the writer "shows no confidence that people can grasp it."[70] On another matter we find Tony Spearing denying Italian influence on *Pearl*, stating that "evidence is lacking" for the poet's knowledge of Dante.[71]

An important paper on the dialect of the MS Cotton Nero texts casts doubt on the famous conclusion in Angus Macintosh's paper of 1963 that the scribe came from "a very small area either in south-east Cheshire or just over the border in north-east Staffordshire"; its authors, for precise linguistic and metrical reasons, would put both scribe and poet "somewhat north of Staffordshire."[72] They thereby reinforce the Cheshire connections to be inferred from place-names in *Sir Gawain*.

Helen Cooper is cautious and negative. Noting how Sir John Stanley has "increasingly been canvassed" as the *Gawain* Poet's patron, she yet finds objections. Events which might link Stanley with these texts (including "the foresterships in 1403" and "incorporation into the Order of the Garter in 1405") occurred "after the composition of the poems."[73] Professor Cooper has not reflected that Stanley, brought up in the Forest of Wirral (and son of a man who in 1346 claimed its Forestership), knew about forests long before 1403. Nor would he have been granted authority over forests if he had never felled a tree or killed a stag. Nor has she noticed Gollancz's view that the Garter motto seems to be a later addition to MS Cotton Nero A.x. Her objections may be put aside.

A different argument for the poet as a man of Cheshire comes from nautical terms. One writer refers to "the extraordinarily meticulous description of the ship's parts" (as also a storm) in *Patience*, here citing Robin M. Ward's 1991 Keele MA thesis on maritime passages in alliterative poetry, where it is taken as showing first-hand experience of navigation.[74] The poet had gone to sea and knew much about it. He knew the gear and tackle and trim of ports and sailors. He did not spend his life in an inland county.

After mariners, hunters. Thorlac Turville-Petre, after noting *Patience*'s factual and specific description of a whale's innards (animal guts figure as well in *Sir Gawain*), discusses Ludchurch, a Peak District ravine east of the Staffordshire-Cheshire border, and identified by R. W. V. Elliott as the "Green Chapel" where Gawain met his axeman.[75] The chasm is remote. Yet it lay in the royal forest of the Peak, bordering the royal forest of Macclesfield. Those who hunted there would know it.

As for Sir John Stanley, he continues to gain notice. A study of early Cheshire writing has a chapter on him and his family, together with another on *Sir Gawain*, although at no point suggesting a direct connection between the two.[76] Another volume, on the landscape and politics of the poem, refers to him as perhaps its patron.[77] Laura Ashe regards the author of *Sir Gawain* as one who exploited romance in order to "betray it"; he "deconstructs the ideology of chivalry from within" so as "to expose the absurdity of its inherited ideals."[78] Her reading of the work is in flat opposition to that of John Fisher (whom she does not mention) in 1961. Fisher thought the poet a reactionary, Laura Ashe a subversive. They cannot both be right. Nor does she suggest what magnate would finance a work which must (on her reading) have mocked his most cherished beliefs, before paying a scribe to copy it into a sumptuous, illuminated manuscript. Preferable, in returning us to reality, is Lee Patterson's perception (in a revised version of his 1992 article) of *Sir Gawain* as juxtaposing "monarch and nobleman, metropolis and hinterland"; Sir Bertilak's court is thus depicted as superior to Arthur's, whether in love, honour, courtesy, or hunting. Bertilak "understands the meaning of court practices more profoundly than the royal court that thinks itself to be the center of fashion." Patterson considers that such loyalty to the provincial, with scepticism on urban values, together fit well with "origins in the Cheshire-Shropshire region" (where "Shropshire" must be a slip), Cheshire being a county palatine that had "very close relations" with Richard II from 1385 onward. Patterson, who cites with approval Fisher's paper of 1961, goes on to reject (on the grounds of the poem's "social meaning and lack of royal interest in alliterative poetry") Michael Bennett's proposal of one of Richard II's "household clerks" as author.[79] Everything in the poem points to a Cheshire patriot as its author. Despite knowing about life at court, he regarded Cheshire as in no way inferior to London, especially on courtly values. With that, the case for an audience of London merchants and the like presented by Jill Mann and Ad Putter must collapse.

In the same year, Thorlac Turville-Petre republished his conclusions on the Green Chapel's whereabouts.[80] Thereafter came further notice of the Stanley family's literary interests, and even how "Andrew Breeze goes so far as to suggest that Sir John Stanley, rather than being simply the patron, might have been the *Gawain* Poet himself."[81] The present writer thereafter developed ideas of Jean-Paul Friedl (d. 2002) as set out by his research supervisor, Ian Kirby of Lausanne. Friedl, noticing the curious repeated use in *Pearl* of the word *spot* "blemish," offered a reason for it: that the maiden died of plague. We can go further. In fourteenth-century England there were five great outbreaks of plague, the last two being in the late 1370s and between 1390 and 1393. We can also say that, if the maiden died (aged under two) of plague, it would have been the bubonic kind, which leaves marks on the skin, and not the more deadly pneumonic variety, which does not. Friedl's suggestion hence allows us to place *Pearl* in the early 1390s (and possibly 1390 itself): the monument of a grieving father to a lost infant child, perhaps called Margaret ("pearl").[82]

In 2014 the "sensational claim" of the *Arthuriana* paper of 2004 was noticed again, this time by Michael Johnston of Purdue University. He admitted its possible truth, but did not consider the subject worth further attention, despite attention to a law suit involving Sir John Stanley.[83] Johnston shines, however, in comparison with Kristina Pérez, who (not having noticed how the destruction of Sodom in *Cleanness* shows the poet's views on homosexuality; or that Gawain and the lady do not commit adultery) opines that the "homosexual kisses between Gawain and the lord are pitted against the heterosexual adultery of Gawain and the Lady of Hautdesert."[84] Johnston is also in advance of Putter and Myres. In a major edition, for all the poet's unclerical interest in armor, attempted seduction, court etiquette, fashion, fatherhood, heraldry, hunting, jewelery, married love, military architecture, and seafaring, they still think him perhaps "a cleric who could not progress beyond minor orders."[85]

A century after we began with John Wells of Beloit, Wisconsin, we end with Walter Wadiak of Lafayette College, Pennsylvania. In a study citing David Aers, Georges Bataille, Pierre Bourdieu, Helen Cooper, Andrew Cowell, Jacques Derrida, Frederic Jameson, Stephen Knight, Jacques Lacan, Jill Mann, Karl Marx, Marcel Mauss, James Simpson, and A. C. Spearing, he agrees with Muscatine in regarding *Sir Gawain* as "a response to chivalric decline." But he does not follow Fisher (who is never mentioned) in styling the poet's social attitudes as reactionary. Wadiak instead offers, after P. B. Taylor, the "Marxist view that what the poem is really about is commerce," as "refined by Jill Mann, who saw the poem's focus on the value of *trewthe* [troth, pledged word] as directed towards a mercantile audience concerned with that virtue's role in underwriting financial transactions," the girdle given by the Lady to Gawain being "a sign of the relativity and arbitrariness that attaches to any kind of value in a commercial world," like money itself.[86] Such opinions do Marxism no good. They ignore Fisher's conclusion, demonstrated by detailed citation of the texts, that the poet's politics were the outdated ones of a landed ruling class; they ignore Lee Patterson's view that *Sir Gawain* has nothing to do with a London audience, courtly or bourgeois, and that its loving representation of life at Hautdesert exalts provincial values against London ones. The poet had the robust right-wing religious and social beliefs of a provincial magnate. For that and other reasons, the recent case for links with the merchant class of London (or anywhere else) cannot be taken seriously. Subsequent to this is David Coley, who on the matter of authorship quotes Derek Pearsall's somewhat disobliging remark that they "are based on such naive and improbable assumptions concerning what constitutes evidence as to bring the study of attribution into disrepute."[87]

With that, we bring to a close the first part of this paper. Commentary over a hundred years demonstrates how some opinions fade, such as the author's being a monk; others replace them, such as his writing for the mercantile class; others again obstinately refuses to go, such as his being a clerk or cleric. There is not a shred of evidence for the last. The poet will instead have been a man of wealth and power with superlative social contacts, as proposed by Laura Loomis as far ago as 1959. One observes a further and general aspect of the above: how time has eroded the influence of careful studies by (for example) Mathew, Fisher, Brewer, or Bennett. One remembers John Burrow's comment on how the questions of honor or religious belief analyzed therein now bewilder younger readers. If changes in mentality poison our comprehension of the past, scholarship will suffer; although there will always be a few perceptive critics, whose work will last.

Laura Loomis, as noted, thought the poet perhaps a man of wealth and power. Her comment in mind, we move to our last part, looking at the life and times of Sir John Stanley in the light of the above. Because they have been set out in the *Arthuriana* paper, using Barry Coward's study of the Stanley family and other sources, we need not go into detail. But we shall add references to three books not at hand in 2004. Stanley was born, it seems, in about 1350 (not 1340). He was brought up at Storeton in the Wirral; his father, William de Stanleigh (1311–1360), had in 1346 claimed Forestership of the Wirral. He was a younger son with miserable prospects, as Coward makes clear. He inherited from his father nothing but a farm at Newton, a hamlet now swallowed up in Macclesfield. (It was, however, only eight miles from the gorge of Ludchurch, the supposed Green Chapel.) As with Malory, John Stanley's early life included crime. In 1369 he was convicted of having attacked Thurstaston Hall, Cheshire; in 1378 he was found guilty of murdering his second cousin, obtaining a pardon only on condition of joining the king's army in Aquitaine. In 1385 his fortunes improved dramatically on his marriage to Isabel Lathom, heiress to Lancashire estates at Knowsley and Lathom. He thereby acquired power and wealth. The next year he was deputy in Ireland for Robert de Vere, the beginning of a long association with Irish wars, politics, and financial crisis. Among the sweeteners coming from his new status was a collar of precious metal given to him in 1387–1388 by the future Henry IV. It perhaps resembled another collar decorated "with scrolls and a swan in the tiret" for which Henry paid over 23 pounds sterling in 1391–1392.[88]John Stanley was now clearly accustomed to the favor of the mighty and the good things which they could grant. He became controller of the wardrobe and a trusted member of Richard II's Cheshire affinity, there perhaps being in (or addressing?) "the primary audience" of *Sir Gawain and the Green Knight*.[89] In 1405, after receiving many offices, he became King of the Isle of Man. In January 1414 he died in Ireland; his body was brought back for burial at Burscough Priory, near Lathom. Storeton Hall, where he was brought up, is now a farmhouse, having come down in the world.[90] But the Stanleys, Earls of Derby and still in possession of lands acquired by him as their ancestor, have most certainly come up in it.

Sir John Stanley thus figures in the documents as a housebreaker, murderer, soldier, colonial administrator, politician, master forester, justice (in 1395, of Chester), courtier, builder, magnate, ancestor, and king. It is an astonishing story, even if one easily recalls others in history who have risen from obscurity to the heights. To his varied qualities can we therefore add that of littérateur and poet of genius? Proof of this is, of course, not possible in our present state of knowledge. But a strong case can be made for it. Since it is already rehearsed in the *Arthuriana* paper, we need present a summary only of the factors, some of them linguistic or topographical, some (the more important) involving the point of view which the four poems display.

1. The dialect found in the Cotton Nero manuscript can be accepted as that of Cheshire, that of the scribe differing little from that of the author.
2. *Sir Gawain* contains allusions to places in North Wales, Wirral, and (as regards Ludchurch) Staffordshire. The viewpoint is a Cheshire one.
3. More subtly, Hautdesert is presented to its advantage against the court of Arthur in south Britain. A provincial author felt in no way inferior in matters of personal integrity or status to those in the metropolis. Their mores are indirectly criticized in the person of Gawain.
4. The author had an expert confidence on matters of castle architecture, etiquette, hunting, luxury items, riding, seafaring, sophisticated flirtation, and war.
5. His politics were resolutely conservative; he was neither a subversive nor anticlerical.
6. MS Cotton Nero A.x is a copy of an original prepared at considerable expense.
7. It bears the motto of the Garter, of which John Stanley (from 1405) was the sole northwestern member at this date.
8. The author complains (*Patience*, lines 34, 46, 528) of poverty. Stanley was a younger son, due to inherit little or nothing; a circumstance which, it seems, dates *Patience* to before 1385.
9. There are strong parallels between the vocabulary of the poems and that of Stanley's letter of July 30, 1405 to Henry IV.
10. The poet knew French and French romance well. Stanley in the 1380s did military service in Aquitaine, with opportunities to learn French well.
11. *Pearl* is most simply read as a father's elegy for a daughter who died before her second birthday. References therein to spots "rashes, blemishes" may indicate the cause as bubonic plague, of which there was an epidemic from 1390 to 1393. Marrying in 1385, the Stanleys might be expected to have had a daughter by them.
12. The allusion to a daughter counts against identification of the poet as a cleric. So, too, do references (*Pearl* 1210, *Patience* 9) to himself not as celebrating mass, but as in the congregation.
13. Approving remarks from the mouth of God on the delights of married love (*Cleanness*, lines 697–704) are secular in tone, not clerical. The same is true for the attempted seductions in *Gawain*.
14. There is no evidence for the poems as the work of a professional clerk or scribe.

The upshot of the above will be to make the author out as a Cheshire and Lancashire magnifico, with important positions at court and in local administration, who had done military service in France; a religious man, happily married and with children. It also places the poems within a relatively short time span. *Sir Gawain* could not predate 1385; if its Arthur represents Richard II (1367–1400), it may be of the later 1380s or early 1390s. *Pearl* on this basis would be of the very early 1390s. (In other chapters is now the case for the former as of 1387, the latter as of 1390.)

If, of course, either poem could be shown as of before 1386, they could not be by Stanley. If critics could prove that they were, the above case would, naturally, collapse. There are other ways in which they could do this, besides that of dating. If Stanley could be proved as having anti-clerical or Wycliffite opinions, as with the "Lollard Knights" of the Oxford historian Bruce McFarlane (1903–1966), this could not be reconciled with the full-blown sacramental Catholicism of *Pearl*. Again, if a document by him in English could be found, proving his dialect as unlike that of the poet, we must also rule him out. If family records indicate that he never had a daughter (called Margaret?) who died in infancy, it would likewise be conclusive.

If, however, there is cogency in the above, we may look on Sir John Stanley as a newcomer to England's literary pantheon. He will join the Earl of Rochester and Lord Byron in the (small) band of English aristocratic poets. As the King of Man, he could even be included in a still smaller one of those who wore crowns, like James I (1394–1437) of Scotland and *The Kingis Quair*. If, on the other hand, critics can prove the case set out here to be ill-judged, baseless, or false, it will offer a permanent lesson on the perils of literary and historical interpretation.

NOTES

1. Wells, *Manual*, 54–57, 578–85, 770.
2. Sisam, *Fourteenth-Century Verse and Prose*, 45, 58–59.
3. Oakden, *Alliterative Poetry in Middle English: The Dialectal and Metrical Survey*, 257–61.
4. Oakden, *Alliterative Poetry in Middle English: A Survey of the Traditions*, 47.
5. Gollancz, *Sir Gawain and the Green Knight*, xviii–xx.
6. Mathew, "Ideals of Knighthood," 354–62.
7. Kane, *Middle English Literature*, 76.
8. Gordon, *Pearl*, xlii.
9. Everett, *Essays*, 69.
10. Speirs, *Medieval English Poetry*, 221–22.
11. Loomis, "*Sir Gawain and the Green Knight*," 528–40.

12. John Fisher, "Wyclif, Langland, Gower, and the *Pearl* Poet on the Subject of Aristocracy," 139–57.

13. Lewis, "The Anthropological Approach," 219–30.

14. Dodgson, "Sir Gawain's Arrival in Wirral," 19–25.

15. Schlauch, *Antecedents*, 23–28.

16. Burrow, *A Reading*, 193.

17. Brewer, "Courtesy and the *Gawain*-Poet," 54–85.

18. Moorman, "Myth and Mediaeval Literature," 209–35.

19. Kean, *The Pearl*, 241–42.

20. Tolkien and Gordon, *Sir Gawain and the Green Knight*, xxiv–xxvii.

21. Benson. "Art and Tradition," 23–34.

22. Bishop, *Pearl in its Setting*, 8, 131.

23. Mathew, *The Court of Richard II*, 109–10, 166.

24. Oakden, "The Liturgical Influence in *Pearl*," 337–53.

25. Woolf, *The English Religious Lyric in the Middle Ages*, 5, 262.

26. Anderson, *Patience*, 11, 20–23.

27. Cottle, *The Triumph of English*, 279–80.

28. Spearing, *The "Gawain" Poet*, 2–18.

29. Williams, "Alliterative Poetry," 107–58.

30. Burrow, *Ricardian Poetry*, 4–5, 102–23.

31. Gradon, *Form and Style in Early English Literature*, 192–211.

32. Vantuono, "*Patience, Cleanness, Pearl*, and *Gawain*: The Case for Common Authorship," 37–69.

33. Muscatine, *Poetry and Crisis in the Age of Chaucer*, 37, 69.

34. Spearing, *Criticism and Medieval Poetry*, 28–50.

35. Medcalf, "*Piers Plowman* and the Ricardian Age in Literature," 643–96.

36. Barron, *Sir Gawain and the Green Knight*, 3, 4.

37. Spearing and Spearing, *Poetry of the Age of Chaucer*, 81.

38. Hanna, *The Awntyrs off Arthure at the Terne Wathelyn*, 38.

39. Spearing, *Medieval Dream Poetry*, 111.

40. Anderson, *Cleanness*, 1.

41. Pearsall, *Old English and Middle English Poetry*, 186.

42. Turville-Petre, *The Alliterative Revival*, 35, 47.

43. Andrew and Waldron, *The Poems of the Pearl Manuscript*, 16.

44. Davenport, *The Art of the Gawain-Poet*, 2, 216.

45. D. S. Brewer, *Symbolic Stories*, 73.

46. Newton, *Fashion in the Age of the Black Prince*, 64.

47. Barron, "Knighthood on Trial: The Acid Test of Irony," 89–105.

48. Coleman, *English Literature in History 1350–1400*, 44, 309.

49. D. S. Brewer, *English Gothic Literature*, 155.

50. Burrow, *Essays on Medieval Literature*, 130.

51. Fowler, *The Bible in Middle English Literature*, 171.

52. Silverstein, *Sir Gawain and the Green Knight*, 17.

53. J. A. W. Bennett, *Middle English Literature*, 202.

54. Strohm, "The Social and Literary Scene in England," 1–18.

55. Spearing, *Readings in Medieval Poetry*, 173–215.

56. Alexander and Riddy, *Macmillan Anthologies of English Literature: The Middle Ages*, 268.

57. Patterson, "Court Politics and the Invention of Literature," 7–41.

58. Pearsall, *The Life of Geoffrey Chaucer*, 57.

59. Blanch and Wasserman, *From Pearl to Gawain*, 150.

60. Bowyers, "*Pearl* in its Royal Setting," 111–55.

61. Putter, *"Sir Gawain and the Green Knight" and French Arthurian Romance*, 191–96.

62. Allen, *"The Awntyrs off Arthure,"* 129–42.

63. M. J. Bennett, "The Historical Background," 71–101.

64. Barron, *"Sir Gawain and the Green Knight,"* 164–83.

65. S. Fisher, "Women and Men in Late Medieval English Romance," 150–64.

66. Lawton, "Englishing the Bible 1066–1549," 454–87.

67. Simpson, "Contemporary English Writers," 114–32.

68. Pearsall, *Arthurian Romance*, 75.

69. Breeze, "Sir John Stanley (*c.* 1350–1414) and the *Gawain*-Poet," 15–30.

70. Anderson, *Language and Imagination in the Gawain-Poems*, 238.

71. Spearing, *Textual Subjectivity*, 172.

72. Putter and Stokes, "The Linguistic Atlas and the Dialect of the *Gawain*-Poems," 468–91.

73. Cooper, "Introduction: The Poet," ix–xviii.

74. Sobecki, *The Sea and Medieval English Literature*, 124.

75. Turville-Petre, "The Green Chapel," 320–29.

76. Barrett, *Against All England*, 133–206.

77. Hill, *Looking Westward*, 168 n. 53.

78. Ashe, "*Sir Gawain and the Green Knight* and the Limits of Chivalry," 159–72.

79. Patterson, *Acts of Recognition*, 71–72, 282.

80. Turville-Petre, "Places of the Imagination," 594–608.

81. Su Fang Ng and Hodges, "Saint George, Islam, and Regional Audiences," 257–94.

82. Breeze, "*Pearl* and the Plague of 1390–1393," 337–41.

83. Johnston, "Romance and the Gentry in Late Medieval England," 33–34, 216–20.

84. Pérez, *The Myth of Morgan la Fey*, 121.

85. Putter and Stokes, *The Works of the Gawain Poet*, xv.

86. Wadiak, *Savage Economy*, 90.

87. Coley, *Death and the Pearl-Maiden*, 16.

88. Fletcher, "The Lancastrian Collar of Essex," 191–204.

89. M. J. Bennett, *Richard II and the Revolution of 1399*, 113.

90. Harding, *Viking Mersey*, 194.

Chapter Four

1387, Year of *Sir Gawain* and the Green Knight

By now, readers will know that the author of four unsigned poems (*Sir Gawain and the Green Knight*, *Pearl*, *Cleanness*, *Patience*) in a British Library manuscript is known as the *Gawain* Poet, and that the poems, in the same West Midlands dialect and dated to the late fourteenth century, show links with the Cheshire region of northwest England. In what follows, possible allusions in *Sir Gawain and the Green Knight* to Robert de Vere (1362–1392), Earl of Oxford, are used to give closer dating. They suggest that the text is no earlier than October 13, 1386, when Robert became Duke of Ireland, and no later than December 20, 1387, when he met his downfall at the Battle of Radcot Bridge. If so, there are three conclusions. One is that *Sir Gawain and the Green Knight* was surely written in 1387, perhaps for Christmas celebrations that year (probably at Chester Castle, when de Vere was expected to far be away in London, with King Richard. But by Christmas 1387 de Vere was a defeated fugitive). Second is a stronger case for identifying the author as Sir John Stanley (d. 1414), who in 1386–1387 was de Vere's administrative deputy in Ireland. Third is that *Sir Gawain* predates *Pearl*, an admired elegy (by the same poet) for an infant daughter who died (it seems) of plague in 1390, during the epidemic of 1390–1393.

Sir Gawain and the Green Knight is a romance with a romantic history. This literary masterpiece was effectively unknown from the fifteenth century until its *editio princeps* appeared in 1839. In 1925 it was co-edited by J. R. R. Tolkien; translations of it include one in Spanish (with an introduction by Jacobo Fitz-James Stuart, son of the late Cayetana, Duquesa de Alba). It has even reached cinema (*The Green Knight*). Yet problems remain, especially for dating. On this there are, however, two clues. One is in line 678, with praise of Gawain as he sets off in the quest of the Green Knight: *And have dight yonder dere a duk to have worthed* or "And have had the worthy one yonder made a duke." Gawain's courage deserved the highest rank of nobility. The other is in line 866: *The ver by his uisage verayly hit semed* or "Verily by his appearance it seemed vernal to all." In the latter, Gawain is putting on magnificent new clothes, resembling the flowers of *ver* or spring. There is something odd about each phrase. But the mystery will evaporate if both allude to Robert de Vere (1362–1392), Earl of Oxford and favourite of Richard II. On October 13, he was made Duke of Ireland, the first non-royal person in England ever to have this rank. As for the second, it will be another sly dig at de Vere, whose sartorial flamboyance was notorious. Together, they allow a dating for *Sir Gawain* to between October 1386, when the making of dukes became topical, and December 1387, when the new Duke of Ireland lost everything except life. An exile in the Low Countries, he no longer had the same cash to spend on fancy clothes. After Christmas 1387, jibes on this would lose their point.

So the two lines permit close dating for *Sir Gawain*, as well as a nearer association with Sir John Stanley (d. 1414). Born in about 1350 to a minor gentry family, Stanley shot to power in 1385 by marrying an heiress. He became courtier to Richard II and Henry IV, and even a king (of the Isle of Man). Ancestor to the present-day Earls of Derby, he founded a dynasty of national importance. One nineteenth-century earl was prime minister (thrice). As if this was not enough, Sir John Stanley was also (apparently) the *Gawain* Poet. Hence the interest of his position as de Vere's deputy in Ireland from August 1387. He perhaps wrote *Sir Gawain and the Green Knight* late that year for a festive gathering in December (which, thanks to the crisis that month, hardly took place as intended).

The implications of lines 678 and 866 are dealt with in two parts. In one, we survey what has been said on them and (more generally) on *Sir Gawain*'s dating. In the other we discuss de Vere's life and reputation. Together, we submit, they show *Sir Gawain* as a poem of 1387, and reinforce the case for John Stanley as its author.

THE DATING OF *SIR GAWAIN* AND THE GREEN KNIGHT

We begin more than a century ago in the US, with a useful summary of *Sir Gawain*'s sensational plot, including the Green Knight's decapitation (which he survives), and a bewitching chatelaine's attempts to seduce Gawain. On the matter of dating is the statement "composed at about 1370," the text supposedly being a "Garter Poem" intended to compliment Edward III (d. 1377), founder of the Garter Order.[1] Connections with Edward are now dropped, despite certain ones with the Order: its motto was added in an early hand to the manuscript, and John Stanley became a Knight of the Garter in 1405. But that was years after the text was composed. In a standard anthology is the statement "about 1350–75" for *Sir Gawain* and (slightly illogically, if they are by the same author?) "about 1375" for *Pearl*.[2]

Elsewhere is an admission on *Sir Gawain* and *Pearl* as "difficult to date," despite claims by editors that the former is of "the last quarter of the fourteenth century."[3] As for line 866, Sir Israel Gollancz (who regarded it as "difficult") proposed a translation "Verily by his appearance the spring it seemed well nigh to everyone"; his editors (Mabel Day and Mary Serjeantson) had previously remarked on the period of composition as "undetermined," if perhaps of the 1390s.[4] Gervase Matthew, in a penetrating essay, commented on illustrations in the lost original manuscript, their qualities indicated by the crude copy (from Chester?) now in the British Library. He took the vanished archetype as a deluxe production "commissioned by a magnate of wealth not much before 1390" and illuminated by an artist aware of "sophisticated French court art at the turn of the century"; all this despite the "archaic" provincial (if upper-class) language of its contents.[5] Twenty years later Mathew identified the "magnate" as perhaps John Stanley. Present analysis may vindicate him completely on dating and patronage alike (but not authorship).

There are careful remarks in an edition of *Pearl*. Features of *Sir Gawain* (dress, armor, architecture) place it in "the last quarter" of the fourteenth century; *Pearl* has more artistic "maturity" than *Cleanness* or *Patience*, and may postdate them; all four texts might thus be of the period 1360–95, with *Pearl* (and *Gawain*) "late rather than early."[6] Another scholar likewise gave "the last quarter of the fourteenth century."[7] Laura Loomis, making the fundamental observation that the poet could have been "a man of rank and wealth" (and no humble monk or clerk), proposed "between 1360 and 1400" for his floruit, with *Sir Gawain* latest in the group.[8]

In 1961 appeared remarks on the poems as of Richard II's reign (1377–1399). Significant for the context of a magnate like Stanley is reference to their politics as those of an "agrarian aristocracy." The poet hardly "questioned the aristocratic system"; he accepted its "outdated" hierarchical values, including (in *Pearl*) the "arbitrary authority" of lord over laborer in the Parable of the Vineyard. He was unlike his contemporaries Chaucer and Langland, being a reactionary (or nearly so) when they were more critical.[9] We may recall this when encountering recent comments on *Sir Gawain* as somehow "subversive."

As for dating, there is the statement "The date of the manuscript, whose author is unknown, is approximately sometime between 1360 and 1400" from Sister Hillmann.[10] A confused sentence, indicating failure to see how errors of transcription show the sole copy (of about 1400) as written some time later than the poems in it; and how the poet who composed them was not the scribe who reproduced their text. Another writer follows the Ann Arbor Middle English Dictionary for *Sir Gawain* as perhaps of about 1390 and the manuscript as of about 1400.[11] Oblivious to this was one Marxist critic, giving "1370" or so without saying why.[12] Derek Brewer contented himself with "late fourteenth century."[13] So, too, did Patricia Kean.[14]

In a famous edition is the disclaimer that "*Gawain* cannot be dated precisely"; details of costume and architecture and "lavish display" may yet "imply a date towards the end of the [fourteenth] century." As for line 866, it is rendered (after a 1956 study by H. L. Savage) "the very spring it seemed to each man from his appearance."[15] The poet was then styled "an educated layman of the fourteenth century" in a sensitive analysis.[16] There is a further observation that, if *Pearl* and *Sir Gawain* were "by the same author," the two could be read "in the light of one another" with "very valuable" insights as a result.[17] Because we maintain that *Sir Gawain* is of 1387 (postdating *Patience* and *Cleanness*) and *Pearl* of 1390, implications for the poet's artistic development are obvious. On *Patience* is a verdict that "between 1360 and 1380 would seem to accord with the various probabilities" including its apparent influence on the B-text of Langland's *Piers Plowman*, completed in about 1379.[18] One can go further. If Stanley, born in about 1350, were the author of *Patience*, he would have written it in his twenties. That points to the later 1370s for *Patience*.

In another study Gordon is followed for "the period 1370–1395."[19] Similar is the comment "from the plague of 1369 to the accession of Henry IV" (in 1399).[20] That the four poems are by the same author was then proved beyond doubt.[21] Broader is "the second half of the fourteenth century," with acute remarks on the poet as an artist "surprisingly untroubled for those troubled times"; he was a "conservative" with an "unquestioning" acceptance of feudalism and orthodox Christianity; his work is "completely devoid of identifiable personal or political references."[22] We agree. The author was a keen observer of men and women. But, like a good diplomat, he knew how to keep his mouth shut.

By now readers will be accustomed to a chorus of reviewers, all saying the same thing. So, from one critic, is "the reign of Richard II (1377–1399)."[23] From others is "probably in the last quarter of the fourteenth century."[24] But another is more cautious, with "latter part of the fourteenth century," if also emphasis on the poet's familiarity with "the most sophisticated literature of the age" in English or French or Latin.[25] Then, a surprise. It "is at least possible" that Chaucer read his work, which (like Chaucer's) "was influenced by Dante, who was otherwise scarcely read in fourteenth-century England"; the *Prologue* to *The Legend of Good Women* perhaps shows that "Chaucer had read *Pearl*," while "the opening of *The Squire's Tale* makes one suspect that he had read *Sir Gawain and the Green Knight.*"[26] This paper allows modifications here. Chaucer completed his *Legend* in about 1387. He then began serious work on *The Canterbury Tales*. Conclusion: the tale of the Squire (unfinished in 1400) shows the influence of *Sir Gawain*, apparently of 1387. But Chaucer's *Prologue* to his *Legend*, of about 1387 and describing a lady appearing in a dream of the narrator, will have influenced *Pearl*, which we place after the coming of plague in 1390. Chaucer's *Legend* had the advantage of a provenance in London. Its two versions survive in a dozen manuscripts. On that basis alone, it was more likely to influence *Pearl* than vice versa. If *Pearl* is of the early 1390s, the argument is stronger. On the other hand, *Sir Gawain* influenced *The Canterbury Tales*. We have evidence for Ricardian intertextuality, then.

It can be added to the dossier of information. *Cleanness* is later than *Mandeville's Travels* (one of its sources), of about 1357; the manuscript is now said to be "not later than 1400."[27] Questions of date were nevertheless avoided by Derek Pearsall (except for the manuscript).[28] Turville-Petre similarly rejected the view that *Cleanness* is earlier than *Sir Gawain*, for it depends upon the belief ("often demonstrably false") that artists with time move "towards greater perfection."[29] Also minimalist is the comment "late fourteenth century."[30] Still more so is one on the manuscript alone, as of "the late fourteenth century."[31]

Now for another surprise. The author of *Sir Gawain* is almost unique in this period in appreciating "the dramatic possibilities of clothing." Chaucer alone compares with him. Hence the attention to the Green Knight's attire when he bursts into King Arthur's hall. More remarkable is that his garments are in the style of "the middle of the 1360s" and by 1370 would be "going out of fashion."[32] What does this mean? Hardly that *Sir Gawain* was written in 1365 or so. Instead, new light on the poet's artistry. His mysterious figure wore clothes curiously out of date. It is not difficult to think of parallels in cinema, as with (say) Count Dracula, whose archaic raiment marks him out as strange but formidable. In this matter of the Green Knight, then, details of his clothing make a subtle artistic point.

Returning to the mainstream of commentary, we find the quartet of poems placed in "the last two decades of the fourteenth century"; line 866 (in a "difficult, perhaps slightly corrupt" passage) is understood as "verily to everyone it seemed almost to be spring by his appearance."[33] In a chapter on the poems is reference to the manuscript as from "the end of the fourteenth century."[34] The poet is allocated to the "late fourteenth century."[35] And, again, "late fourteenth century."[36] Better is another analysis, undermining earlier views on *Pearl* and the like as part of a "fringe culture" in Cheshire, remote from Richard II's sophisticated entourage.[37] That brings the poet close to the court,

particularly at the time when Richard came of age (in the latter 1380s). The
idea is developed by Ad Putter.[38]

At this point came what should have been double bombshell, but has passed
unnoticed. (It was unknown to the present writer until early 2022, when the
medievalist Ros Field gave him the book cited, together with many others
from her library.) It is an example of two brilliant ideas with implications not
perceived by their instigator, who is convinced that *Sir Gawain* was written
"between 1397 and 1400" (among many dubious notions in her book). The
two points are these. First is the curious emphasis on Gawain in line 678 (*And
have dight yonder dere a duk to have worthed* or "And have had the worthy
one yonder made a duke") with the comment that "the bestowal of dukedoms
became Richard's hallmark." Second is the suggestion that line 866 (*The ver
by his uisage verayly hit semed* or "Verily by his appearance it seemed vernal
to all") alludes to Robert de Vere, Duke of Ireland, Earl of Oxford, favorite
of Richard II. The latter will have been a quiet joke on the poet's part "for
the benefit of a Cheshire audience" who knew of the earl's delight in finery.[39]

Readers should go to the book for themselves, not least for details on
de Vere's rise and fall. We need say merely that, if his new dignity as duke
is not behind line 678, and his slavery to fashion behind line 866, both of
them will be hard to explain. At a stroke, some may regard them as together
showing *Sir Gawain* to be no earlier than October 13, 1386, when Robert
de Vere was made Duke of Ireland (to the chagrin of older aristocrats); and
no later than his downfall on December 20, 1387, after which a jest on his
expensive clothes would lose topicality; while the judicial murders exacted
by the Merciless Parliament in early 1388 would therafter make a poem about
decapitation singularly inappropriate. That might explain why it survives in
a unique copy. After the crisis of 1387–1388, its author perhaps thought it fit
for private circulation only.

So: a before and after unnoticed by other scholars (including this one until
now). *Sir Gawain* surely belongs to 1387 (and perhaps late in the year, for
reasons given below). Once realized, this puts (one fears) a somewhat strange
appearance to most statements of after 1999. There is actual comment on how
Gawain dons "robes that give the appearance that spring has arrived."[40] But
nothing on *ver* and de Vere. Commoner are the following. The date of *Sir
Gawain* "is uncertain."[41] Its author wrote "some time during the second half
of the fourteenth century."[42] He was active "towards the end of the fourteenth
century."[43]

The present writer then published a paper identifying Sir John Stanley
as the *Gawain* Poet, and placing his greatest work between 1385 (when he
attained wealth and status through marriage) and 1400 (the British Library
manuscript being no later than that).[44] It coincides with a remark (after the
poet) on his Arthur as a "boyish king."[45] Richard II was born in 1367. He was

twenty at the time of writing proposed here. A writer might well then envisage Arthur as youthful, and not as a grandfatherly figure (like the late Edward III). The hypothesis will be in total contradiction to assertions by Michael Bennett and others on the lack of "a north-west Midlands court of sufficient size and wealth" to be a milieu for the poet, so that they instead regard him as writing for Richard II's household in London.[46] This despite the Chester associations of the manuscript, allusions to Cheshire, and a Cheshire-Lancashire dialect unfamiliar to Richard and his entourage. Different again is Tony Spearing, locating *Pearl* in the fourteenth century's "last quarter," and yet silent on London or Cheshire connections alike.[47] There is further evidence from dialect, where an important paper on that of the unique manuscript's scribe has the conclusion that "Staffordshire is unlikely to be the county where the poems originated."[48] That leaves the field open for Cheshire.

Sir Gawain was thereafter allocated to the "late fourteenth century" in a book with actual reference to Sir John Stanley.[49] But nothing on him as its author. However, the present writer's work on the subject was then noted (and misunderstood).[50] A further allusion followed on Stanley as writer.[51] Then a strange opinion on "the time of the *Gawain* Poet's writing" as being about 1344.[52] In the same year came out a paper on apparent references in *Pearl* to the symptoms of plague, indicating composition in the early 1390s, when Britain saw an epidemic in which many children died, owing to lack of acquired immunity.[53] Also in that year was notice of the "spectacular claim" on John Stanley as poet.[54] It was not, however, thought to warrant further attention for dating or anything else. Nor do we hear of it in a standard edition, where the poet is placed in the "late fourteenth century"; while line 866 is related to expressions on spring and personal beauty in German and Anglo-French verse.[55] So we say again that line 866 is, it seems, unique in likening an individual's clothed form to *ver* "spring." It is subtly different from the famous passage (89–92) in Chaucer's *Prologue* to *The Canterbury Tales* on the Squire, whose emboidered clothes were like a meadow of "floures white and reede," he himself being fresh "as is the monthe of May." If the line is not a joke at de Vere's expense, why is it so and not other?

We end this part with two contrasting studies. In a Marxist one *Sir Gawain* is called "the preeminent romance of the Ricardian age."[56] If its author had considered Stanley's links with it, he could say much more on capitalism and violence, the main aspects of his thesis. After that comes once more the verdict "late fourteenth century," if with comment on arguments for *Pearl* as of the early 1390s and Stanley as its author.[57] The latter are yet regarded as inconclusive, although it is not said why.

An American book of 2019 thus reflects a slight advance on another American book of 1916. The tendency has long been to place the *Gawain*

Poet within the reign of Richard II (1377–1399). That he wrote in about 1370 (during the last years of Edward III) has ceased to be the orthodoxy.

ROBERT DE VERE (1362–1392), EARL OF OXFORD

In the case for *Sir Gawain* as a work of 1387 the essential ally is Robert de Vere, ninth Earl of Oxford. He unwittingly puts *Sir Gawain* in that year, just as Chaucer's *Legend of Good Women* and the Plague of 1390–1393 together show *Pearl* as of the early 1390s. Ostentatious in his life and actions, the earl is noticed by all historians of England in the 1380s. He is noticed too (less expectedly) by historians of Ireland, which in 1385–1387 he was supposed to be governing.

So the sources concur on Robert as a flashy character in Richard II's entourage. Five years older than the king, he was "showy," "handsome and vainglorious but utterly lacking in tact and in competence. He was made Marquis of Dublin and subsequently, in 1385 [recte 1386], Duke of Ireland." His intelligence was poor. Fellow nobles regarded him with "venom," less for his political ineptitude than for the fact that he had deserted his wife for a Czech girl and (worse) that, "aristocratic lineage" notwithstanding, he reminded them of Piers Gaveston, Edward II's minion. In the crisis of 1387 de Vere raised an army in Cheshire. (So a Cheshire poet would know of him.) At Radcot Bridge, near Oxford, he was easily defeated in December of that year. He fled abroad. In the Merciless Parliament of 1388 he was sentenced to death; after he died (by a hunting accident) in 1392, his body was eventually brought back to England and reburied in state, with Richard II present (but almost none of the old nobility).[58]

That de Vere was killed by a hunted boar, which turned and ripped him with its tusks, implies a passion for the chase. If *Sir Gawain and the Green Knight* was meant to be read aloud in Chester Castle at Christmas 1387, one may yet recall that he was not expected to be there and to appreciate it. In any case, any Yuletide cheer at Chester was by then muted. England was in crisis. No time for public reading of a new Arthurian romance. Therefore, if de Vere is alluded to in line 866, his rise and fall shed light on the poem. It must predate the catastrophe of 1387. Nor is it credible, *Sir Gawain* being about decapitation, that the poet wrote it in or after 1388. If de Vere escaped a traitor's death (hanging, drawing, quartering), others did not. By then, a poem on beheading would (in current parlance) be "inappropriate." Perhaps its author lost interest in circulating copies of it.

Further detail on de Vere is easily found. He entered the royal circle in 1378 when he married a first cousin of Richard II. His fortunes prospered, although he was "a man of neither talent nor judgement." His fortunes collapsed on December 20, 1387 at the Battle of Radcot Bridge, where fog on the Upper Thames led to disaster. Robert's ostentation survived even his death (at Louvain in 1392). When, in a sumptuous ceremony, he was reburied three years later at Earl's Colne (in Essex, northeast of Braintree), the king had the coffin reopened, gazed long at the embalmed face, and clasped the "jewel-laden fingers."[59] Even when dead, Robert still appeared dressed like a fop. But his tomb has been lost, like the jewels. Although de Vere monuments at the (vanished) Benedictine Priory of Earl's Colne were in 1935 moved north of the county boundary to a chapel near Bures, Suffolk, Robert's is not among them.[60]

All the same, he possessed courage. In his *Tripartite Chronicle*, Gower described "the Boar" (Oxford's badge was a boar's head) as "the most hated of Richard's followers" and how in 1387 in the king's name he yet raised an army in Cheshire.[61] Derek Brewer showed fumbling over facts. In an otherwise lucid account, he confused Robert with his kinsman Aubrey de Vere and claimed (misled by Shakespeare's *Richard II*) that he "lost his life" for the king.[62]

Other writers offer insights, as with the campaign around Radcot Bridge, on the Thames in the far west of modern Oxfordshire.[63] Robert figures largely in the pages of Froissart, who commented on his control of Richard. Even if he said that black was white, "the king did not contradict him."[64] Significant in the context of *Gawain*, however, are remarks on his "love of magnificence" demonstrated by a "bed with its blue hangings embroidered in gold with fleurs-de-lys and with owls" valued at over 68 pounds sterling. An interesting contrast to remarks in the same book on Stanley as "patron of the *Gawain* Poet."[65] One recalls too the bed used by Gawain on his travels. It had curtains of pure silk with bright "golde hemmes" (line 854). In 1387 de Vere's bed, eloquent of his appetite for luxury, was at Chester Castle, where in 1388 it was impounded and sold to raise money for the government.

Given his peacock strutting, contempt for Oxford was general. One disobliging comment occurs in a complaint (of 1388?) on the evils of the 1380s, which opens with the words "Syng I wold" and contains a "dark joke against Jack" (who is taken as Oxford).[66] A contrast to earlier glory, when he became Marquis of Dublin, gaining precedence over earls and with Richard investing him "by girding him with a sword and placing a golden circle on his head" in the presence of lords and commons.[67] His fall was dramatic, when he became "a fugitive from the field" of Radcot Bridge, an episode narrated in brisk terms by McFarlane.[68]

As information on Oxford accumulates, it provides further insights on *Sir Gawain and the Green Knight*. Some of this concerns Ireland. On October 12, 1385, Richard announced that Oxford would be made Marquis of Dublin;

on December 1 the king granted him regal powers in Ireland. The island would be his palatinate. Yet the new marquis never visited the place. It was Sir John Stanley whom we find "acting as de Vere's deputy in Ireland."[69] So the two were closely linked. Stanley no doubt had views upon one nominally his superior, but actually his junior by twelve years. English lords similarly had opinions on him, because the title of marquis "set him apart from all the rest of the peers, except the royal dukes." On October 13, 1386 the king again defied popular feeling. At Eltham Palace (near London) he elevated de Vere "to a new dignity, to be Duke of Ireland."[70] Hence, we submit, line 678 of *Sir Gawain, And have dight yonder dere a duk to have worthed* (on making its hero "a duk"). After late 1387, dukes were a subject in the news. We can add to that. Sir John Stanley reached Ireland to take up the position of de Vere's lieutenant in August 1386. Crisis was brewing. In the English parliament that October was a "violent clash between the king and his opponents" just after Oxford was created Duke of Ireland, when he also became "justice of Chester and North Wales."[71] That puts composition of *Sir Gawain and the Green Knight* after October 13, 1386. Oxford's position as justice further underlines his association with Stanley, the dominant political force in Cheshire.

By now, the case is clear for de Vere as offering, on the basis of lines 678 and 866, a date for when *Sir Gawain and the Green Knight* was written. An allusion to Gawain's being made a duke hardly predates October 13, 1368, when de Vere became England's first ever non-royal duke. An apparent jest on de Vere and luxury garments would be out of place after December 20, 1367, with his vanquishing and flight. Remaining accounts do not change these arguments. But they do add detail. There is more on his bed. We know much about it, including its value ("excluding the mattresses, blankets, sheets, and pillows") because his property (including books) was impounded in 1388 and sold "for the war"; there is mention too of the satire on him as "Jack," now dated to 1388.[72] Another presence in English verse for de Vere. There are varied comments on him in a fifteenth-century chronicle, including his death "now desolat and pore" at Louvain in 1392.[73] Earlier was Thomas Walsingham, monk of St. Albans, who in 1377 was "rapturous" about the new king, but by the 1380s had become critical of "Richard's attachment to Robert de Vere."[74]

Fourteenth-century London was a small place. Oxford, the king's chamberlain, was hence Geoffrey Chaucer's boss. He endorsed the poet's 1385 application for a permanent position, perhaps signing the document himself.[75] Chaucer and Stanley thus had an unexpected connection, both having de Vere as their superior. He is noted elsewhere as an instance of how, for Richard II, the nobility was not an "independent body" but "an embodiment of the king's magnificence."[76] An error that cost Richard his throne and his life. Error of a different kind occurs in the statement that de Vere became Duke of Ireland in "1385."[77] Not so. In 1385 he became Marquis of Dublin. The point is vital for present arguments.

Now for some dramatic remarks on de Vere. In 1387 he began "forging links" with soldiers of the northwest, especially Sir John Stanley. In July that year the king visited Cheshire, while de Vere over the summer "ensconced himself in Chester Castle" in "some style"; his "fine furniture and tapestries at Chester were inventoried in 1388." Living with the duke was not his wife but a Bohemian girl, abducted (by William Stanley of Wirral) from Berkhamsted Castle, where she had been a lady-in-waiting of the Queen. The love-nest at Chester Castle came to an abrupt end in December, when de Vere set off with the Cheshire troops to be routed at Radcot Bridge.[78] His fall was all the greater because he began as "the poorest among the English earls" despite holding "the longest-standing noble title in fourteenth-century England," which had made his rapid rise "all the more galling among the peerage."[79] So de Vere's conspicuous behavior at Chester in the summer of 1387 (to say nothing of his lady friend's presence, the scandal being much noted at the time) offers models for the central episodes of *Sir Gawain*. It would put the poem not merely in 1387, but in its later part. An interesting year. Near its end, de Vere mustered Cheshire troops to take on the king's enemies, on their way south by "the middle of December."[80] Another scholar adds to references on it.[81] Oxford had some 4,250 men in his contingent; his opponents had between 4000 and 5000.[82] It was well for John Stanley that he was then in Ireland (or perhaps Cheshire). He might otherwise have ended up a corpse in an Oxfordshire meadow.

More recent comments add little to the above. In a monograph on John Gower, Oxford's rise is interpreted in Marxist terms as displaying "distended reciprocalist exchange patterns."[83] Lee Patterson's more lucid remark on how Richard II saw de Vere and other nobles as a mere "embodiment of the king's magnificence" is republished in his collected essays.[84]

CONCLUSION

Even though a century of scholarship between 1915 and 2019 offers rather little progress on the dates of *Sir Gawain and the Green Knight*, apart from a tendency to move it from the latter part of Edward III's reign to that of his grandson Richard II (1377–1399), it seems that evidence was (in the modern phrase) hiding in broad daylight, actually being pointed out in 1999 by Ann Astell. She yet did not see its implications. We can. Reference in line 678 to Gawain's being made a *duk* surely puts the romance after October 13, 1386, when de Vere became the first non-royal duke in English history. Tongues will have wagged, especially those of the established nobility, outranked and outraged by an insolent upstart. On the other hand, the allusion to *ver* and delicate apparel in line 866 fixes the poem to before December 20, 1387, when Robert de Vere met his Waterloo. If *Sir Gawain and the Green Knight* postdated 1387, its author's apparent ignorance of what happened to the parvenu duke would be singular.

We can go further. Sir John Stanley, himself something of an *arriviste* owing to marriage in 1385 with an heiress, had close contacts with Oxford. In the early summer of 1387, when de Vere was living grandly at Chester Castle, he would have become familiar with his ways, including his dalliance with one of Queen Anne's ladies. On that basis Stanley (or, as some may insist, a nameless talent in his circle) would have written *Sir Gawain and the Green Knight* in the latter part of 1387. If Stanley were its author, this has the surprising implication that it was written in Ireland, for which he set sail in August that year to act as de Vere's deputy. Perhaps the work was meant to be read aloud as a public entertainment for Christmas 1387?

In any case, there can be no doubt that the question merits scrutiny. The ideas presented in Ann Astell's *Political Allegory in Late Medieval England* deserve more attention. It is of course possible that future research will refute the case set out here, demonstrating (for example) that *Sir Gawain* is of the later 1390s, or that its author was of humble status, or that there is no reason to connect it with the Stanleys of Cheshire, let alone regard Sir John Stanley as its author; or a combination of these. If so, such arguments would be welcome. They would inevitably lead to deeper understanding of that strange masterpiece, *Sir Gawain and the Green Knight*, and its associated poems *Pearl, Patience, Cleanness*.

NOTES

1. Wells, *Manual*, 54, 57.

2. Sisam, *Fourteenth-Century Verse and Prose*, 44, 57.

3. Oakden, *Alliterative Poetry in Middle English: The Dialectal and Metrical Survey*, 87.

4. Gollancz, *Sir Gawain and the Green Knight*, xiii, 108.

5. Mathew, "Ideals of Knighthood in Late-Fourteenth-Century England," 356.

6. Gordon, *Pearl*, xliv.

7. Everett, *Essays*, 68.

8. Loomis, *"Sir Gawain and the Green Knight,"* 529–30.

9. Fisher, "Wyclif, Langland, Gower, and the *Pearl* Poet on the Subject of Aristocracy," 151.

10. Hillmann, *The Pearl*, xv.

11. Borroff, *"Sir Gawain and the Green Knight": A Stylistic and Metrical Study*, 218.

12. Schlauch, *Antecedents of the English Novel,* 23.

13. Brewer, "Courtesy and the *Gawain*-Poet," 54.

14. Kean, *The Pearl: An Interpretation,* vii.

15. Tolkien and Gordon, *Sir Gawain and the Green Knight,* xxv, 100.

16. Bishop, *Pearl in its Setting,* 5.

17. Woolf, *The English Religious Lyric in the Middle Ages,* 5 n. 1.

18. Anderson, *Patience,* 22.

19. Spearing, *The "Gawain" Poet,* 2.

20. Burrow, *Ricardian Poetry,* 1.

21. Vantuono, "*Patience, Cleanness, Pearl,* and *Gawain:* The Case for Common Authorship," 37–69.

22. Muscatine, *Poetry and Crisis in the Age of Chaucer,* 37, 39.

23. Medcalf, "Piers Plowman and the Ricardian Age in Literature," 654.

24. Spearing and Spearing, *Poetry in the Age of Chaucer,* 80.

25. Barron, *Sir Gawain and the Green Knight,* 3.

26. Spearing, *Medieval Dream Poetry,* 111.

27. Anderson, *Cleanness,* 1.

28. Pearsall, *Old English and Middle English Poetry,* 170.

29. Turville-Petre, *The Alliterative Revival,* 34.

30. Davenport, *The Art of the "Gawain"-Poet,* 1.

31. Andrew and Waldron, *The Poems of the "Pearl" Manuscript,* 15.

32. Newton, *Fashion in the Age of the Black Prince,* 64.

33. Silverstein, *Sir Gawain and the Green Knight,* 15, 140.

34. J. A. W. Bennett, *Middle English Literature,* 202 n.

35. Alexander and Riddy, *The Middle Ages,* 268.

36. Blanch and Wasserman, *From Pearl to Gawain,* 4.

37. Bowers, "*Pearl* in its Royal Setting," 111.

38. Putter, *"Sir Gawain and the Green Knight" and French Arthurian Romance,* 191.

39. Astell, *Political Allegory in Late Medieval England,* 123, 124, 126, 137.

40. Hodges, *Chaucer and Costume,* 72 n. 32.

41. Simpson, "Contemporary English Writers," 124.

42. Horobin and Smith, *An Introduction to Middle English,* 134.

43. Pearsall, *Arthurian Romance,* 74.

44. Breeze, "Sir John Stanley (*c.* 1350–1414) and the *Gawain*-Poet," 15–30.

45. Cooper, *The English Romance in Time,* 51.

46. Anderson, *Language and Imagination in the Gawain-Poems,* 13 n. 5.

47. Spearing, *Textual Subjectivity,* 137.

48. Putter and Stokes, "The Linguistic Atlas and the Dialect of the *Gawain*-Poems," 488.

49. Barrett, *Against All England,* 172–73.

50. Hill, *Looking Westward,* 168 n. 53.

51. Su Fang Ng and Hodges, "Saint George, Islam, and Regional Audiences," 284.

52. Ashe, "*Sir Gawain and the Green Knight* and the Limits of Chivalry," 159.

53. Breeze, "*Pearl* and the Plague of 1390–1393," 337–41.

54. Johnston, *Romance and the Gentry in Late Medieval England,* 33–34, 136–40.

55. Putter and Stokes, *The Works of the Gawain Poet*, x.

56. Wadiak, *Savage Economy*, 88.

57. Coley, *Death and the "Pearl"-Maiden*, 14–15.

58. Green, *The Later Plantagenets*, 224, 228, 229, 231.

59. McKisack, *The Fourteenth Century*, 425, 563, 476.

60. Pevsner, *The Buildings of England: Suffolk*, 112.

61. Stockton, *The Major Latin Works of John Gower*, 292, 472.

62. Brewer, *Chaucer in His Time*, 58, 60.

63. Aston, *Thomas Arundel*, 342.

64. Froissart, *Chronicles*, 317.

65. Matthew, *The Court of Richard II*, 19, 166.

66. Cottle, *The Triumph of English 1350–1400*, 134.

67. Myers, *English Historical Documents 1327–1485*, 451.

68. McFarlane, *Lancastrian Kings and Lollard Knights*, 32.

69. Lydon, *Ireland in the Later Middle Ages*, 106, 107.

70. Keen, *England in the Later Middle Ages*, 277, 278.

71. Otway-Ruthven, *A History of Medieval Ireland*, 319.

72. Coleman, *English Literature in History 1350–1400*, 18, 86, 108.

73. Lucas, *John Capgrave's Abbreuiacion*, 199, 408.

74. Taylor, *English Historical Literature in the Fourteenth Century*, 75.

75. Strohm, "Politics and Poetics," 95.

76. Patterson, "Court Politics and the Invention of Literature," 17.

77. Pearsall, *The Life of Geoffrey Chaucer*, 311.

78. M. J. Bennett, "The Historical Background," 83.

79. Wiswall, "Politics, Procedure, and the 'Non-Minority' of Edward III," 16.

80. M. J. Bennett, *Richard II and the Revolution of 1399*, 30.

81. Bowers, *The Politics of "Pearl,"* 71.

82. Rubin, *The Hollow Crown*, 130.

83. Kendall, *Lordship and Literature*, 35.

84. Patterson, *Acts of Recognition*, 68.

Chapter Five

Sir Gawain and the Green Knight Predates Pearl

Although hardly noticed, Ann W. Askell's *Political Allegory in Late Medieval England* (Ithaca, 1999) contains revolutionary insights on the *Gawain* Poet. She there relates (pp. 124, 126) allusions in *Sir Gawain and the Green Knight* to *duk* "duke" (line 678) and (of brightly-colored clothes) *ver* "spring" (line 866) to Robert de Vere (1362–1392), Duke of Ireland. They are the poet's surreptitious comments on de Vere's creation in 1386 as Duke of Ireland, and his extravagant tastes in clothes. Together, these lines put *Sir Gawain and the Green Knight* after October 13, 1386, when de Vere was created a duke, and before December 20, 1387, when his fortunes imploded on the rout of his army at Radcot Bridge, Oxfordshire. Jokes on his attire then lost their point.

If, then, *Sir Gawain and the Green Knight* was composed in 1386–1387, there are several implications. Here are four. (a) Connections with Cheshire are underlined by de Vere's (lavish) sojourn in 1387 at Chester Castle, where he worked with the Cheshire magnate Sir John Stanley (d. 1414), his deputy for the government of Ireland. The *Gawain* Poet, long associated with Stanley, perhaps composed *Sir Gawain and the Green Knight* in late 1387 as a Christmas entertainment for Chester Castle's courtiers, not knowing how political crisis that December would change events. (b) *Sir Gawain* will be older than *Pearl*, apparently of the early 1390s. (c) On that basis, Chaucer's *Squire's Tale* (of 1400) will show knowledge of *Sir Gawain* (1387); in contrast, Chaucer's *Prologue* to *The Legend of Good Women* (1386–1387) will have influenced *Pearl* (1390–1393). (d) If *Sir Gawain and the Green Knight* were written in 1387, it may confirm arguments for the *Gawain* Poet (a man at ease in a noble and even royal ambience) as Sir John Stanley himself, and not some humble clerk in his entourage.

After this abstract, the case in detail. Dating of *Sir Gawain and the Green Knight* and its related Middle English poems (*Patience*, *Cleanness*, *Pearl*) has been problematic. Yet observations of 1999 by Ann W. Astell provide a breakthrough. Her analyses of lines 678 and 866 in *Sir Gawain* seemingly date the text to 1387. In line 678 is praise of Gawain for beheading the Green Knight: *And have dight yonder dere a duk to have worthed*, or "And have had the worthy one yonder made a duke"; in line 866 is reference to Gawain's splendid new garments: *The ver by his uisage verayly hit semed*, or "Verily by his appearance it seemed vernal to all." Here *duk* "duke" and *ver* "spring" will make fuller sense as sly digs at Robert de Vere (1362–1392), Earl of Oxford and Duke of Ireland. In late 1386 he became England's first-ever non-royal duke; until his ruin in late 1387, he was notorious for flamboyant dress (with *ver-* or spring-like colours described by the poet). More precisely, the lines locate *Sir Gawain and the Green Knight* to between October 13, 1386, when de Vere was made duke (so that creation of dukedoms was in the news), and December 20, 1387, when he lost the Battle of Radcot Bridge and fled into exile. Robert (a much-hated favorite of Richard II) then had less cash for his wardrobe. Jests on it became stale overnight. *Sir Gawain and the Green Knight* is thus unlikely to postdate Robert's fall.

If *Sir Gawain and the Green Knight* can be dated to 1386–1387, and surely late in this period, there are further implications. Because de Vere spent much of 1387 in extravagant style at Chester Castle, lines 678 and 866 strengthen the poem's links with his deputy for Ireland, Sir John Stanley (d. 1414), the Cheshire and Lancashire magnate who (under Richard II and Henry IV) dominated local politics. The romance was perhaps intended to be an entertainment for Christmas 1387 at Chester Castle. There are three further points. First, *Sir Gawain and the Green Knight* will predate *Pearl*, apparently of the early 1390s (as argued in a paper of 2014). Second, the (feeble) hypothesis advanced by Jill Mann and Ad Putter on *Sir Gawain* as written for a London mercantile audience can be dismissed. Third is the sharper focus on the poet's connections with Chaucer, whose *Prologue* to *The Legend of Good Women* (of 1386–1387) will have influenced *Pearl* (of about 1391); while *Sir Gawain and the Green Knight* (of 1387) will have influenced *The Squire's Tale*, still in process of composition when Chaucer died (October 25, 1400), so that his literary executors were left with the task of recycling it.

The above can be summed up in six dates:

1. 1968: Gervase Mathew first relates the *Gawain* Poet to John Stanley, whom he regarded as the bard's employer or patron.
2. 1976: in an influential book, Tony Spearing proposes that Chaucer knew the *Gawain* Poet's work.
3. 1999: Ann Astell points out allusions in *Sir Gawain* to Robert de Vere.
4. 2002: Freidl and Kirby relate frequent mention in *Pearl* of "spots" to the Pearl Maiden's last illness. It seems that it was bubonic plague, which

in severe cases leaves skin-blemishes due to subcutaneous bleeding. The Pearl Maiden died presumably of this disease and not, for example, pneumonic plague (leaving no such marks).

5. 2004: publication of evidence (including linguistic parallels) for identification of Sir John Stanley not as the *Gawain* Poet's patron, but the poet himself. Like Sidney or Rochester or Byron, John Stanley was an English poet of exalted status. He was not some middle-class scribe.

6. 2014: publication of arguments (after Freidl and Kirby) for *Pearl* as of 1390–1393, years of plague which (as medieval chroniclers noted) killed many children and young people, who would lack acquired immunity.

Bibliographical details on all six items are set out below.

What is, however, not dealt with here (being reserved for another paper) is Stanley's relationship to Robert de Vere in 1387, when they were jointly responsible for Ireland's administration, and when William Stanley (John's kinsman) abducted from Berkhamsted Castle one of the Queen's ladies-in-waiting (a native of Bohemia) and brought her to Chester, where she lived openly with de Vere (who had tired of his wife). The present concern is the chronology of the *Gawain* Poet and Chaucer, with the conclusion that each influenced the other.

Our survey starts in the days of Queen Victoria, when Skeat remarked on *The Squire's Tale* that an "incident of a man riding into the hall" (of "Cambinskan" or Genghis Khan) was "nothing uncommon." It had equivalents in romance and ballad. The Squire's horseman greets banqueters in proper manner; even Sir Gawain, "model of courtesy in the French romances," could not fault him.[1] Curious, this juxtaposition of Gawain with a rider bursting into a royal feast. Yet implications for *Sir Gawain and the Green Knight* were long unexplored.

From the US then came statements on *Sir Gawain* as "composed at about 1370"; it was a "Garter Poem" meant to flatter Edward III (d. 1377), who founded that Order.[2] But direct links with the Garter and the ageing Edward are now dropped. Elsewhere is "about 1350–1375" for *Sir Gawain* and "about 1375" for *Pearl*.[3] One wonders. Why a twenty-five-year gap, if the poems are by the same man? As for Chaucer's Squire, he tells how Ghengis was at table with his lords when:

> In at the halle dore al sodeynley
> Ther cam a knyght upon a steede of bras

—its rider equipped with mirror, gold ring, sword—

> And up he rideth to the heighe bord.

> In al the halle ne was there spoken a word
> For merveille of this knyght. Hym to beholde,
> Ful bisily ther wayten yonge and olde.

This "strange knyghte" salutes king, queen, lords with such "heigh reverence":

> That Gawayne, with his olde curteisye.
> Though he were comen ayeyn out of Fairye,
> Ne koude hym nat amende with a word.

The thirteenth-century *Roumans de Cléomadès* is given as Chaucer's source here.[4] Nothing on similarities to *Sir Gawain*, though.

After that, an admission on *Sir Gawain* and *Pearl* as "difficult to date," although some place the former within "the last quarter of the fourteenth century."[5] We are better off with Chaucer, whose *Prologue* to *The Legend of Good Women* is dedicated to Eustace Deschamps, with thanks for a volume of his poems (brought to England in 1386).[6] So, if *Pearl* is of the early 1390s, its pearl-decked maiden in white may derive from Chaucer's pearl-decked maiden. Chaucer's *Prologue* would be a source for *Pearl*, not *Pearl* for the *Prologue*. As for *Sir Gawain*, Israel Gollancz translated the "difficult" line 866 as "Verily by his appearance the spring it seemed well nigh to everyone"; while his editors (Mabel Day and Mary Serjeantson) previously gave the date of composition as "undetermined" but perhaps of the 1390s.[7] A later discussion of the Squire's "magic horse" is yet silent on the Green Knight's steed.[8] Still more negative was this emphatic view on Chaucer: "we have no evidence whatsoever that works such as *Pearl* or *Sir Gawain and the Green Knight* ever came his way."[9]We mean to demolish this. For Chaucer, *Sir Gawain* not only "came his way," but he and the *Gawain* Poet surely knew each other.

Offering a new perspective was Gervase Matthew on the lost original manuscript of *Sir Gawain* and *Pearl*, its nature indicated by the crude copy (from Chester?) in the British Library. The vanished archetype was a deluxe volume "commissioned by a magnate of wealth not much before 1390"; its illuminations show familiarity with "sophisticated French court art at the turn of the century."[10] Nothing provincial here. A significant point. Mathew's "not much before 1390" presumably means "not earlier than 1385." In 1968, we recall, he related its contents to Stanley. This Cheshire gentleman being relatively poor until late 1385, when he acquired wealth by marriage to an heiress, that puts an expensive manuscript (and its main texts, showing familiarity with luxury) to after 1385; while "turn of the century" still allows the 1390s as a date for that lost volume. *Pearl*, composed (early?) in the plague of 1390–1393, might thus appear in it.

There is another argument. If Stanley became wealthy only in 1385, and *Sir Gawain* is (at the very least) from his circle, then the vanished archetype postdates 1385. Stanley could not previously have afforded it. Presumably *Sir Gawain*, its author at ease with court life, also postdates 1385. So there is codicological evidence for *Sir Gawain* as no earlier than 1385. That tallies with 1387 as posited year of composition, but is independent of it. One may note too how Chaucer had by 1387 moved to Greenwich, Kent, where he wrote his *Legend* using verses (coming to hand in 1386) by Deschamps on the beauty of daisies.[11]

In a classic edition of *Pearl*, *Sir Gawain* was described (from its references to costume and armour) as of between 1375 and 1400; *Pearl* was a harder case, although its "maturity of workmanship" might put it to the decade before 1395.[12] Compare a verdict on *Sir Gawain* as of "the last quarter of the fourteenth century."[13] Meanwhile, down in Greenwich, Chaucer wrote of how he "fel aslepe" and dreamt of a meadow with a "noble quene" wearing regal attire and crowned in white:

> For of o [one] perle fyn and oryental
> Hyre white coroun was ymaked al

—adornment to be kept in mind.[14] In *Pearl* is another dreamer, who in a pastoral setting encounters a second noble queen with splendid raiment and a pearly crown.

Penetrating observations on the *Gawain* Poet then appeared. Laura Loomis saw him as perhaps "a man of rank and wealth" writing "between 1360 and 1400," with *Sir Gawain* latest of his four poems.[15] John Fisher noticed other aspects. This poet hardly "questioned the aristocratic system" (unlike Chaucer or Langland), his values being the outdated ones of an "agrarian aristocracy"; which are in no way discountenanced by *Pearl*, for its Heaven is a place where everyone (line 448) "is quen other kyng."[16] Hence the Pearl Maiden's *coroune* decked with *mariorys* (or "pearls"); where the precision of the poet contrasts with the muddled "The date of the manuscript, whose author is unknown, is approximately sometime between 1360 and 1400" of one editor.[17]

Rationality comes back with "?c1390" after the Michigan *Middle English Dictionary*.[18] It is close to the 1387 proposed here. After that, a relapse with a Marxist scholar and a *Sir Gawain* of "ca 1370," echoing Wells nearly fifty years before.[19] More pertinent are remarks on how the *Gawain* Poet's sensitivity "to the nuances that lurk behind the words he selects" and how he is "not without humour: even ironic humour."[20] If there are no "nuances" and "ironic humour" in his use of *duk* and *ver* in lines 678 and 866 of *Sir Gawain*, then no case for these as jibes at Robert de Vere, Duke of Ireland. No case either for 1387 as year of composition.

Despite the "?c1390" cited above, others were cautious. So a mere "late fourteenth century" for the author of *Pearl*; which is yet accompanied by analysis indicating his reading of Dante's *Purgatorio* and *Paradiso*.[21] It is precious evidence for Italian poetry in England. It indicates high-level literary contacts, perhaps with Chaucer himself, and deserves further study. Returning to dates, we find how styles of costume and architecture (together with comment on line 866 as "difficult") indicate composition "towards the end of the century."[22] A verdict on *Pearl*, a "fourteenth-century" work that really is about "the death of a child, presumably the poet's daughter, before she was two years old" is a further call to order.[23] Because the unfortunate infant (her name "Margaret" or "Margery," and therefore a "pearl"?) survived until she was nearly two, if she died in the plague of 1390–1393, then she was perhaps (having lived beyond her first few months) one of its early victims, being born in 1388 and dying in 1390, presumably in the August mentioned in the poem (line 39), when the epidemic would be at its worst; which might indicate late 1390 or else 1391 for when her grieving father wrote *Pearl*.

Three other critics of 1968 offered discernment. One saw a connection between *Sir Gawain* and Sir John Stanley, citing the poet's mischievous allusion (lines 700–2) to the Forest of Wirral (of which Stanley was Forester, and where his brother William lived), with few inhabitants who "wyth goud hert" loved God or man.[24] For a poem intended for Chester Castle's Christmas festivities of 1387, such words would raise smiles as they would not in (say) Whitehall, London. The second commentator stressed *Pearl*'s "deep sense of personal loss" and (less obvious) relation to the Church's daily worship.[25] The third remarked in passing on how "knowledge of authorship" for *Pearl* and *Sir Gawain* would be "very valuable"; if one man wrote both, they could be read "in the light of one another."[26]

If 1387 is a date for *Sir Gawain* and 1390 one for *Pearl*, what can be said on *Patience* and *Cleanness*? The latter has a debt to the *Travels* of "Sir John Mandeville" (of about 1357); a storm-passage in the former influenced the alliterative *Siege of Jerusalem* (now, however, put some time after 1400, as stated by Pearsall in 1977). So these do not help much. However, a passage on patience and poverty in the B-text of *Piers Plowman* (written in about 1379) seems to echo *Patience*.[27] That puts the shorter poem in the (late?) 1370s, also suggesting circulation in London, where Langland wrote. It accords as well with the feeling of many that it is an earlier and less mature work than its three fellows.

Now for the 1970s, with comment useful and otherwise. Spearing accepted Gordon for all four poems as of 1360–1395.[28] We shall refine that to

1375–1390. These productive fifteen years belong to one of English poetry's "periods of florescence."[29] There was progress with proofs by Vantuomo that the four poems are by the same man.[30] Muscatine then commented (rightly) on his "unquestioning" acceptance of orthodox Christianity and feudalism, and (wrongly) on his poems as "devoid of identifiable personal or political references."[31] Ann Astell's interpretation of *duk* and *ver* in *Sir Gawain* disposes of that. It shows a certain archness as regards Robert de Vere, Duke of Ireland, an island which in 1387 he and John Stanley governed in the king's name (Stanley actually doing the work).

Just as we maintain that Chaucer in his *Squire's Tale* steals from *Sir Gawain and the Green Knight*, we note in passing how other poets felt its spell, "especially in the North" with *The Green Knight* and *Sir Gawain and the Carle of Carlisle*.[32] All the same, there may be less connection than some imagine. For a Cumberland poem of about 1425 we are warned that a relation with *Sir Gawain and the Green Knight* is "dubious."[33] Surviving in one manuscript only, *Sir Gawain* may have had few (but élite?) readers. Which leads to a major (if slightly casual) observation by Tony Spearing. *Pearl*, like Chaucer's *Prologue* to *The Legend of Good Women*, is a dream-poem wherein "the Dreamer meets a beautiful lady, crowned with a single orient pearl"; so that one might "guess that Chaucer had read *Pearl*" (just as the opening of *The Squire's Tale* suggests "that he had read *Sir Gawain and the Green Knight*"). The northern and southern poets were each "courtly"; in both can be found the influence of Dante; both show familiarity with the colour effects found in "fashionable French art" of the day.[34] Spearing's juxtaposition of these four texts prompts this chapter.

Mindful of this, we continue our survey. The alliterative *Siege of Jerusalem* is placed in about 1420.[35] So, no use for when *Patience* was written. As for *Cleanness*, the supposition that it "is a more youthful work than *Gawain*" rests upon the hazardous premise that poets tend to "greater perfection" in their verse.[36] True. It is not hard to think of poets (Wordsworth, Swinburne, T. S. Eliot, Auden, Dylan Thomas) who declined with age; if there are others (Hardy, Yeats) who improved. For *Cleanness* are two tests only. We know that *Patience* is echoed in the B-Text of *Piers Plowman*, of about 1379. *Cleanness* being, like *Patience*, a Scriptural text, that implies composition in the 1370s or early 1380s. The second test is less precise. John Stanley acquired wealth in 1385 upon marriage to the heiress of Lathom (near Ormskirk, Lancashire). The author of *Sir Gawain* and *Pearl* was expert on luxury; the author of *Patience* begins with a lament upon his poverty. If Stanley were the poet, that locates *Patience* to before 1385 and presumably also *Cleanness*, which resembles it.

On these poems are perceptions from Andrew and Waldron, quoting Chaucer's Parson:

> But trusteth wel, I am a Southren man,
> I kan nat geeste "rum, ram, ruf" by lettre

—proving that Chaucer knew of provincial alliterative modes. For the court culture shared by Chaucer and his northern contemporary, Andrew and Waldron stress John of Gaunt's connections with the North.[37] Yet John Stanley was a Northerner as Gaunt never was. As for the Squire's echoes of *Sir Gawain and the Green Knight*, these were noticed by Severs. He accepted papers of 1947 by Whiting and 1953 by Chapman on how Chaucer had *Sir Gawain* "in his mind as he wrote" this Canterbury tale.[38] The point, referred to by Spearing in 1976, repays exploration. It places *Sir Gawain* within London's sophisticated literary circles; it also helps with dating. Norman Blake, remarking that ascription of the *Squire's Tale* to the Squire was "almost certainly made by the editor" of the Hengwrt Manuscript (and not Chaucer), believed that the story was "in process of writing when Chaucer died." Hence its incompleteness and a problem for medieval literary executors.[39] If Chaucer had not finished the text in late 1400, it puts *Sir Gawain* before that. Time was needed for the London poet to encounter work by the Cheshire one.

Now, a surprise. Despite accumulated evidence for *Sir Gawain* as not pre-dating 1385, the Green Knight's tight-fitting clothing is that of "the middle of the 1360s"; by 1370 it was "going out of fashion"; by 1380, such tunics "had disappeared altogether." How can this be reconciled? Answer; the poet had (like Chaucer) a sharp eye for "the dramatic possibilities of clothing."[40] He deliberately made the Green Knight's apparel one of quality, but outmoded. It made his entrance the eerier. The device has equivalents with menacing fictional characters like Count Dracula or (as shown by the US scholar Aviva Briegel) ghosts: well-dressed, but not in today's fashions. The detail underlines the poet's art. It also underlines implications of line 866 in *Sir Gawain*, if alluding to de Vere's flashy tastes in clothes.

At this point, unexpected light on just that. When de Vere was in 1388 condemned for treason, his property was seized, including costly raiment at Chester Castle, together with his bed, "of blue camoca, embroidered with gold owls and fleurs-de-lis and valued at 68 pounds thirteen shillings and fourpence, excluding the mattresses, blankets, sheets, and pillows": a fabulous sum.[41] The bed no doubt impressed the Bohemian lady who shared it with him. Ample opportunities to *lerne of luf-talkyng*, in a phrase (line 927) of Sir Gawain's hosts. From the ostentation of this and the expensive clothes which de Vere left behind at Chester, meaning accrues for the *ver*-like textiles (line 866) of *Sir Gawain*, a Cheshire poem.

Observations of Derek Brewer gain weight from such a background. When nineteenth-century scholars established the chronology of Shakespeare's dramas, it "revolutionized criticism." *The Tempest* was his last play, not (as

Coleridge imagined) his first. So Brewer posited "a development" from *Sir Gawain* to *Pearl* in that the protagonist "is now a father, not a 'child'": where the poignancy of the latter poem "can only be fully appreciated by parents" (whereas romance is open to young and old).[42] The purpose of this paper is to vindicate Brewer, with *Pearl* composed three or more years later than *Sir Gawain*. Significant too is Fowler's comment, on alleged signs of national "crisis and uncertainty" in *Pearl* and its three associates, that he himself did "not find it so"; "through most of the poem shines the light of faith and calm reason," with no evidence that "the Age of Faith was beginning to crumble."[43] The poet was conservative, not subversive. Attitudes necessary if we place him in government circles at Chester in 1387.

While Kittredge proved *The Greene Knight* to be a popular fifteenth-century remaking of *Sir Gawain*, Silverstein yet thought the older poem "never to have been widely read" in its time; he also saw its lines 864–70 as "difficult, perhaps slightly corrupt."[44] But the horseman of *The Squire's Tale* indicates Chaucer and other readers among the London literary élite; and line 866 suggests links with a nobleman close to Richard II. Also on *The Squire's Tale*, Blake stressed that "Chaucer was working on this tale when he died" (in 1400), as implied by the "small gap" left after it in the Hengwrt Manuscript. The scribe left room for a link. But he did not expect (Chaucer being dead) "that the rest of the tale would become available."[45] If *Sir Gawain* dates from 1387, Chaucer had plenty of time to come across it.

There is a further comment in a major study. *Sir Gawain* is in some ways "more courtly than *Troilus* and the poet evidently had in mind a courtly audience."[46] A curious reflection. It would yet be less remarkable if the *Gawain* Poet enjoyed (a) a social status higher than Chaucer's; (b) a vastly greater income; (c) political power which he (a civil servant) could not dream of. Those points illuminate another statement on the northern and southern bards, that (despite the Squire's intrusive horseman in the context of *Gawain*, and the Parson's "rum, ram, ruf") suggestions that Chaucer and the *Gawain* Poet read each other's verse are not "very persuasive."[47] On the contrary. If the *Gawain* Poet were not (as most imagine) an unobtrusive provincial versifier, but a royal councillor with a princely income, he might well know Chaucer, another (if lesser) courtier. One may remember this when again being assured on *Sir Gawain* that "there is no clear indication that Chaucer knew this romance."[48] So, too, with Helen Cooper, who tries to derail arguments (of 1983 by Elizabeth Salter) for direct connections with an assertion on how "entry of mounted knights into feasts is a widespread occurrence in romances."[49] But juxtaposition of such an entry with Gawain is not. It is singular. Preferable, then, is "as Chaucer himself evidently recalled" for rider and Gawain.[50] The London poet knew work by the Cheshire one.

After old questions on horsemen thrusting their presence upon diners, a new one: the *Gawain* Poet as household clerk of Richard II, as proposed in a 1983 book by M. J. Bennett. Some will not have it. Given "the lack of royal interest in alliterative poetry," the suggestion is "highly unlikely."[51] Others have a blurred focus here. Derek Pearsall writes of *Sir Gawain* as possessing "a 'clerkly' viewpoint" and bringing court culture to a "moral and religious inquisition."[52] Little room here for its author who was a wealthy layman, married with children, a man who delighted in hunting and the rituals of court life.

The myth of a London context for *Sir Gawain* yet blundered on, acquiring Marxist baggage on the way. Citing M. J. Bennett, Jill Mann put it within a "mercantile" context as well as a "knightly" one, declaring that, with the (supposed) "absence of any local courts" in Cheshire to provide patronage, we should seek "an audience of sophisticated and wealthy merchants and knights" in the "obvious location" of Ricardian London.[53] But there was a court in Cheshire. It was at Chester Castle in 1387. Inventories of 1388 even inform on a silk bed slept in and silk garments worn by the shining ones who dwelt there. The evidence stares us in the face.

It did not stop the fantasy of Richard II as the *Gawain* Poet's patron, reaching a *ne plus ultra* with the conjecture that "run, ram, ruf" from Chaucer's Parson is the writer's "barbed reference" to a northern rival whose verse benefited from the king's "Cheshire favoritism."[54] This despite Lee Patterson's cold words on "lack of royal interest in alliterative poetry." Equally unpersuasive is the notion of Cheshire knights and merchants assembled in London to hear *Sir Gawain and the Green Knight*, as postulated by another, with the poet's knowledge of Dante taken to reinforce the hypothesis. Only in London (we hear) would "the most recent Italian literature" be "readily accessible."[55]

At this point a digression, on *St. Erkenwald*, a poem (in Cheshire dialect) about a Saxon Bishop of London whose prayers led to a miracle. While some have attributed the text to the *Gawain* Poet, this is hardly so, for its style is "less exuberant, sparer, and more concise" than his.[56] So what is the answer, the poem being an excellent one? Here is a conjecture. Literary duos and even trios (Brontës, Sitwells) are easily recalled. The Herberts (Edward, George), Vaughans (Henry, Thomas), Wesleys (John, Charles), Tennysons (Alfred, Charles), Housmans (A. E., Laurence) are pertinent: five pairs of brothers, all composing verse similar to but different from that of their sibling. On that basis, *St. Erkenwald* was not by the *Gawain* Poet, but perhaps by John Stanley's brother William, resident in the Wirral. Michael Bennett put on record how de Vere in the summer of 1387 "ensconced himself in Chester Castle" and there established "a real court" in the company of his Bohemian lover, brought to his arms by Sir William Stanley "of Wirral." He yet failed to see the allusions in *Sir Gawain* (lines 678, 866) to de Vere, the ostentatious duke, and even regarded *Sir Gawain* as of "the late 1390s."[57]

Then a bombshell, which yet passed unnoticed. Nobody (it appears) who works on *Sir Gawain* has noticed it (including this writer, who learnt of it only in early 2022, thanks to a gift of books from Dr. Rosalind Field). In 1999 Ann Astell drew attention to line 678, with praise of Gawain after he beheads the Green Knight: *And have dight yonder dere a duk to have worthed* or "And have had the worthy one yonder made a duke," and to line 866: *The ver by his uisage verayly hit semed* or "Verily by his appearance it seemed vernal to all." The latter she took as a jest on de Vere's love of showy garments; the former to him as England's first non-royal duke. She supplied much information on de Vere, but did not see the implications for dating, instead declaring "that *Sir Gawain and the Green Knight* must have been written between 1397 and 1400"; ten years and more after Robert de Vere (1362–1392) vanished from the political scene.[58] For others it will be conclusive. The romance cannot predate October 13, 1386, when Richard II made de Vere a duke on the Feast of the Confessor; it will not postdate December 20, 1387, when de Vere lost all at Radcot Bridge. Details on the fancy garments which he left behind at Chester (and were listed by official clerks) may be compared usefully with a note on clothes in *Sir Gawain*.[59]

If Ann Astell is right on seeing allusions in *Sir Gawain* to Robert de Vere, statements thereafter appear in a new light. Clearly "inoperative" is Professor Simpson's assertion that *Sir Gawain*'s date is "uncertain."[60] For de Vere (whose exact relation to *Sir Gawain* is analyzed in a previous chapter), there is a new focus. He actually figures with John Stanley on the same page of a Marxist account of *Pearl* (but with no word on any literary implications).[61] So we have a novelty. Because in 1387 they were close colleagues, *Sir Gawain* may be seen to show what his subordinate really thought of de Vere. Of interest too is an account of how de Vere and his lover Agnes were in 1387 "keeping household in Chester," and how she left behind "two new Bohemian lady's saddles and one old saddle in the Bohemian style."[62] Handsomely made, no doubt. One wonders what they looked like. As regards parallels for the Squire's uninvited horseman, instances are found in Latin, French, even Chinese.[63] But nothing on his fellow in *Sir Gawain*, despite the resemblances.

In 2002 appeared the proposition that references in *Pearl* to "spots" imply that the Maiden died of bubonic plague, which leaves marks on the skin.[64] Twelve years later it was used to date *Pearl* to the plague-years 1390–1393. In contrast to the precision of Freidl and Kirby are Horobin and Smith, with no more on the *Pearl* group than "north-west Midlands some time during the second half of the fourteenth century."[65] Equally useless for the quartet of poems is "towards the end of the fourteenth century by an unknown poet."[66] The present writer then argued that the "unknown poet" was Sir John Stanley, whose dialect and vocabulary are part of the evidence.[67] As for a remark on Arthur as a "boyish king" in *Sir Gawain and the Green Knight*, it fits the hypothesis of composition in 1387, when Richard II was 20; Stanley in the same volume is suggested as the romance's patron (not its author).[68]

Singing the same tune, John Anderson followed Michael Bennett on there being "no evidence" for a Cheshire court with the lavish resources to maintain the *Gawain* Poet; therefore, his milieu was that of Cheshire men at "the royal court of Richard II."[69] The notion is absurd. Family wealth of Lathom and Stanley, the opulence at Chester Castle in 1387, the absence of London allusions in *Sir Gawain*, all shoot this hypothesis through the heart. Better on a London connection is Jill Mann, who admits that the Squire's "strange knight riding into the king's hall during a feast" may imply Chaucer's knowledge of *Sir Gawain and the Green Knight*.[70] Present arguments vindicate her. With Tony Spearing we again enter a *myst-hakel huge* (line 2081) or "vast cloak of mist" like that into which Gawain disappeared on the road to the Green Chapel; for we know merely that the poem is of "the second half of the fourteenth century."[71]

A return to *St. Erkenwald*. Marie Borroff thought that it was by the author of *Pearl*, "a cleric" who "lost an infant daughter" and also had an "intimate knowledge" of the "knightly nobility." This she believed preferable to the alternative, of "two extraordinarily gifted men" writing in the same style, same way, same Cheshire, at the same time.[72] Not so. We recall the Herberts, Wesleys, Brontës, Sitwells. If *Jane Eyre* and *Wuthering Heights* were anonymous, would Marie Borroff have argued that they were by a single author? Perhaps so, with assertions that two "extraordinarily gifted" writers hardly existed at the same time in the same region (when we know that they existed in the same house). Her fractured logic is evident. So the search will be on for *St. Erkenwald*'s author as a kinsman of the *Gawain* Poet. Perhaps he was William Stanley of Hooton, a landowner and magistrate whose skill in local government is reflected in *St. Erkenwald*?

Returning to the *Gawain* Poet, we find a *coup de grâce* for fantasies on him as a cleric in an aside on "undoing": the huntsman's technique of disembowelling and dismembering a stag or the like after the kill. The process ("described with some gusto in *Sir Gawain and the Green Knight*") is explained too in the *Master of Game* by Edward, Duke of York (d. 1415).[73] Implication: no job for a priest or deacon, whom canon law debarred from hunting. The *Gawain* Poet was a huntsman, like Sir John Stanley, who had forests (including that of Wirral) in his charge.

If cutting-up a deer is a practical matter, so is navigating a ship. Relevant here are comments on sailors' technical terms in *Cleanness* and *Patience*, as also their *abyme* "abyss, depths of the earth (under land or sea)," then a rare word but found too in *St. Erkenwald*, and so "a further argument for the shared authorship" of the three poems.[74] Again, the assumption that an anonymous *Jane Eyre* and *Wuthering Heights* are by one writer (presumably some nineteenth-century Yorkshire clergyman).

Despite comment on regionalism and the *Gawain* Poet as seen by Michael Bennett and John Bowers, and (elsewhere) on Sir John Stanley, nothing in a study of Cheshire tradition indicates a link between the magnate and the bard.[75] Not much better is citation of the present writer for Stanley as patron.[76] He did not claim that Stanley was the *patron*. He claimed that Stanley was the *poet*. Again on *Sir Gawain*, Jill Mann repeats her opinions for "the Ricardian court, rather than the north-west of England, as the most probable context for this poem."[77] But 1387's bustle of activity at Chester Castle knocks that on the head.

Then remarks by writers who take on board an attribution of *Sir Gawain* to John Stanley, noting his international contacts, such as one with a Navarrese esquire Janico Darasso, for whom he offered sureties.[78] That being in 1399, it is too late to have influenced *Sir Gawain*. It does, however, accord with Patterson's restated observations on the poem's boyish Arthur as "meant to represent Richard," who in 1387 was twenty; despite comments on "monarch" and "metropolis," Patterson again (in our view correctly) rules out Michael Bennett's idea of the author as a royal clerk in London.[79]

Just as work of 1999 by Ann Astell offers (it appears) a firm dating for *Sir Gawain*, so does that of 2002 by Freidl and Kirby for *Pearl*. The author's curious emphasis on "spots" and "spottiness" can be explained by the skin-marks left by bubonic plague, rampant in 1390–1393. Many difficulties of the poem are removed if we accept that it is a about a girl of nearly two who in this period died of plague (like many children, lacking acquired immunity).[80] *Pearl* would therefore postdate *Sir Gawain and the Green Knight* by three to six years. The disease being most virulent in its early stages, the child died perhaps in 1390, perhaps in August, when plague would be at its height. That may account for the poet's mention of August (line 39), whether he wrote it at the time, or a year (or two) later, on her anniversary. If so, *Pearl* could be accepted as postdating *Sir Gawain and the Green Knight*. Critics (like Derek Brewer) who thought *Pearl* a more mature work than *Sir Gawain* will have been right.

In a recent edition, no notice is taken of Astell on *Sir Gawain* or Freidl and Kirby on *Pearl*. One yet agrees with its statements on the poet as from Cheshire; and disagrees with those on his having no "association with the royal court" or on his poems as circulating solely within the northwest Midlands "dialect area."[81] Similar on the last is a Marxist critic on how *Sir Gawain* influenced some poets of the northwest (but not elsewhere).[82] The implications of Freidl and Kirby's paper were, however, acknowledged in 2019.[83]

What can we infer from the above? There seem to be thirteen conclusions, some of them long agreed.

1. *Sir Gawain and the Green Knight* was composed between October 13, 1386 and December 20, 1387, between Robert de Vere's becoming a duke and his débâcle. On the first, see line 678; while line 866 points to composition before de Vere's fall and the judicial murders (by beheading) which came after.
2. *Pearl* was written in 1390–1393, and probably early in this period.
3. *Patience* predates 1379; *Cleanness* on grounds of style and subject would be of about the same time.
4. These dates tally with the career of John Stanley (1350?–1414). As a younger son, he was (relatively) poor until 1385, when he shot to power and riches by marrying a Lathom heiress. Because the author of *Patience* complains of poverty, it confims a date for it previous to 1385.
5. If he wrote *Patience* and *Cleanness*, he would then be in his twenties or so, with *Sir Gawain* (1387) and *Pearl* (1390–1391) as works of mid-life, after he had had responsible employment and started a family.
6. A date of 1387 and connections with de Vere for *Sir Gawain* also strengthen links with John Stanley. In that year he was de Vere's number two for the government of Ireland. Hence de Vere's lavish sojourn that summer in Chester Castle (the nearest he got to the island in his charge).
7. *Sir Gawain* was perhaps written for Chester Castle's Christmas celebrations of 1387, when de Vere would (but for sudden insurrection) have been in London with the King.
8. If *Sir Gawain* is of 1387, there is no objection to Chaucer's knowing it and its presumed author. Hence an allusion to an intruding horseman and Gawain in *The Squire's Tale* (unfinished in 1400). Two great poets of the fourteenth century borrowed from each other.
9. All conjectures on the author as a Cheshire clerk in London and/or writing for Cheshire knights and merchants in London can be dismissed. The poet was familiar with court life not because he was a household clerk, but a provincial magnate.
10. If Chaucer's *Squire's Tale* has a debt to *Sir Gawain*, *Pearl* (of the early 1390s) has a debt to the *Prologue* to *The Legend of Good Women* (1387). Chaucer's text (its two versions known from twelve manuscripts) clearly had a wider circulation than *Pearl* (surviving in one). The Northern poet's development of Chaucer's pearl-maiden is, naturally, astonishing. It shows the creative powers of a great artist.
11. If Stanley is correctly identified as the *Gawain* Poet, it casts a sharper light on many subjects: Cheshire court life *vis-à-vis* that of London; politics; local and national government and administration; moral

discrimination; architecture; clothes; hunting; religion; family life; attitudes to the dead; Italian literature.

12. It also breaks ground for *Sir Erkenwald*. It is not by the *Gawain* Poet, but is perhaps by his brother, whose style and language resembled that of his greater sibling, yet without the force and pressure of his verse. Compare (say) the poems of Laurence Housman and those of A. E. Housman, the better maker.

13. In short, Ann Astell's insights permit a real advance in our understanding of English poetry. They open doors for researchers; vindicate some critics (John Fisher, Derek Brewer, Lee Patterson); discredit others (Jill Mann, Michael Barrett, Ad Putter, James Simpson). A shoal of red herrings may now be thrown overboard.

Two final points. The great house of the Lathoms was at Lathom, where there is still a chapel of about 1500 alongside the Palladian mansion replacing the medieval hall (wrecked in the Civil Wars). However, the Lathom and Stanley dead were buried not there but nearby, at the Augustinian house of Burscough. When John Stanley died (in Ireland), his body was shipped over for interment by the canons of Burscough. Later Stanley tombs are a little way to the southwest, in Ormskirk parish church (some of them brought from Burscough after its dissolution).[84] One assumes that the Pearl Maiden's grave (Margery or Margaret Stanley's?) is still at Burscough, where little survives above ground except two giant masonry piers supporting nothing but air. Chester Castle has also changed. Its medieval apartments and great hall, where Robert de Vere and his lover cut a dash in 1387, have given way to a "powerful" Greek revival Shire Hall. But the massive Agricola's Tower, with a chapel of about 1200 on its upper floor, is still there.[85] So the people of Chester have reason to think that *Sir Gawain and the Green Knight*'s first reading was planned for their castle at Christmas 1387. Its audience would understand its jokes about Wirral folk, as also Robert de Vere, who spent a memorable summer with them. But the recitation probably never occurred. Political crisis had prompted an unexpected visit from de Vere, hastening up from London to muster forces. After his eclipse and the executions ordered by 1388's Merciless Parliament, a poem about beheading was suddenly inappropriate. That would certainly explain why after 1387 its author made almost no attempt to publish or circulate it.

NOTES

1. Skeat, *The Complete Works of Geoffrey Chaucer: Notes on the "Canterbury Tales,"* 374.

2. Wells, *A Manual of the Writings in Middle English*, 54, 57.

3. Sisam, *Fourteenth-Century Verse and Prose*, 44, 57.

4. Manly, *Canterbury Tales by Geoffrey Chaucer*, 363, 599.

5. Oakden, *Alliterative Poetry in Middle English: The Dialectal and Metrical Survey*, 87.

6. Lowes, *Geoffrey Chaucer*, 130.

7. Gollancz, *Sir Gawain and the Green Knight*, xiii, 108.

8. Jones, "The Squire's Tale," 357–76.

9. H. S. Bennett, *Chaucer and the Fifteenth Century*, 10.

10. Mathew, "Ideals of Knighthood in Late-Fourteenth-Century England," 354–62.

11. Tatlock, *The Mind and Art of Chaucer*, 72.

12. Gordon, *Pearl*, ed. E. V. Gordon, xliv.

13. Everett, *Essays on Middle English Literature*, 68.

14. Robinson, *The Works of Geoffrey Chaucer*, 487.

15. Loomis, "*Sir Gawain and the Green Knight*," 528–40.

16. J. H. Fisher, "Wyclif, Langland, Gower, and the *Pearl* Poet on the Subject of Aristocracy," 139–57.

17. Hillmann, *The Pearl*, xv, 14, 26.

18. Borroff, "*Sir Gawain and the Green Knight*": A Stylistic and Metrical Study*, 218.

19. Schlauch, *Antecedents of the English Novel 1400–1600*, 23.

20. Savage, "*Fare*, Line 694 of *Sir Gawain and the Green Knight*," 383–84.

21. Kean, *The Pearl: An Interpretation*, vii, 120–32.

22. Tolkien and Gordon, *Sir Gawain and the Green Knight*, xxv, 100.

23. Bishop, *Pearl in Its Setting*, 5.

24. Mathew, *The Court of Richard II*, 166.

25. Oakden, "The Liturgical Influence in *Pearl*," 337–53.

26. Woolf, *The English Religious Lyric in the Middle Ages*, 5 n. 1.

27. Anderson, *Patience*, 5, 20–22.

28. Spearing, *The Gawain Poet*, 2.

29. Burrow, *Ricardian Poetry*, 1.

30. Vantuono, "*Patience, Cleanness, Pearl,* and *Gawain*: The Case for Common Authorship," 37–69.

31. Muscatine, *Poetry and Crisis in the Age of Chaucer*, 37, 39.

32. Elisabeth Brewer, *From Cuchulainn to Gawain*, 4.

33. Hanna, *The Awntyrs off Arthure*, 38.

34. Spearing, *Medieval Dream-Poetry*, 111.

35. Pearsall, *Old English and Middle English Poetry*, 298.

36. Turville-Petre, *The Alliterative Revival*, 34.

37. Andrew and Waldron, *The Poems of the Pearl Manuscript*, 15.

38. Severs, "The Tales of Romance," 271–95.

39. Blake, *The Canterbury Tales*, 289.

40. Newton, *Fashion in the Age of the Black Prince*, 64.

41. Coleman, *English Literature in History 1350–1400*, 18.

42. D. S. Brewer, *English Gothic Literature*, 166.

43. Douglas, *The Bible in Middle English Literature*, 224.

44. Silverstein, *Sir Gawain and the Green Knight*, 16, 140.

45. Norman Blake, *The Textual Tradition of the Canterbury Tales*, 195.

46. J. A. W. Bennett, *Middle English Literature*, 202.

47. Paul Strohm, "The Social and Literary Scene in England," 1–18.

48. DiMarco, "The Squire's Tale," 890–5.

49. Cooper, *Oxford Guides to Chaucer: The Canterbury Tales*, 222.

50. J. H. Fisher, *The Complete Poetry and Prose of Geoffrey Chaucer*, 189.

51. Patterson, "Court Politics and the Invention of Literature," 7–41.

52. Pearsall, *The Life of Geoffrey Chaucer*, 62.

53. Mann, "Price and Value in *Sir Gawain and the Green Knight*," 119–37.

54. Bowers, "*Pearl* in its Royal Setting," 111–55.

55. Putter, *"Sir Gawain and the Green Knight" and French Arthurian Romance*, 192.

56. Burrow and Turville-Petre, *A Book of Middle English*, 201.

57. M. J. Bennett, "The Historical Background," 71–90.

58. Astell, *Political Allegory in Late Medieval England*, 123, 124, 126, 137.

59. Hodges, *Chaucer and Costume*, 61 n. 32.

60. Simpson, "Contemporary English Writers," 114–32.

61. Bowers, *The Politics of "Pearl,"* 71.

62. Morse, "Griselda Reads Philippa de Coucy," 347–92.

63. DiMarco, "The Squire's Tale," 169–209.

64. Horobin and Smith, *An Introduction to Middle English*, 134.

65. Freidl and Kirby, "The Life, Death, and Life of the Pearl Maiden," 395–98.

66. Pearsall, *Arthurian Romance*, 74.

67. Breeze, "Sir John Stanley (*c.* 1350–1414) and the *Gawain* Poet," 15–30.

68. Cooper, *The English Romance in Time*, 51, 339.

69. Anderson, *Language and Imagination in the Gawain-Poems*, 13 n. 5.

70. Mann, *The Canterbury Tales*, 943.

71. Spearing, *Textual Subjectivity*, 137.

72. Borroff, "Narrative Artistry in *St. Erkenwald* and the *Gawain*-Group," 41–76.

73. Gray, *Later Medieval English Literature*, 162–63.

74. Sobecki, *The Sea and Medieval English Literature*, 38 n. 67.

75. Barrett, *Against All England*, 134, 172–73.

76. Hill, *Looking Westward*, 168 n. 53.

77. Mann, "Courtly Aesthetics and Courtly Ethics in *Sir Gawain and the Green Knight*," 231–65.

78. Su Fang Ng and Hodges, "Saint George, Islam, and Regional Audiences," 257–94.

79. Patterson, *Acts of Recognition*, 71, 282.

80. Breeze, "*Pearl* and the Plague of 1390–1393," 337–41.

81. Putter and Stokes, *The Works of the Gawain Poet*, x.

82. Wadiak, *Savage Economy*, 93.

83. Coley, *Death and the Pearl-Maiden*, 14–15.

84. Pevsner, *The Buildings of England: North Lancashire*, 84–85, 165, 184.

85. Pevsner, *The Buildings of England: Cheshire*, 156–58.

Chapter Six

Italy, *Pearl*, *St. Erkenwald*, and the Stanleys of Cheshire

Pearl and *St. Erkenwald* are anonymous but related fourteenth-century poems from Cheshire. They have two aspects discussed here: (a) Italian influence and (b) authorship. Relevant to the first are Dante, Boccaccio, and Antonio de Romanis, a Neapolitan employed by the Cheshire grandee Sir John Stanley (d. 1414). As regards authorship, in 2004 the writer proposed not that Stanley commissioned *Pearl*, but actually wrote it (plus *Sir Gawain and the Green Knight*, *Patience*, *Cleanness*). This he now takes further. While *St. Erkenwald* is certainly not by John Stanley, it may be by his elder brother, Sir William Stanley (d. 1398). There is comparative evidence. Siblings often share literary skills (Brontës, Sitwells, Durrells). Many great English poets had brothers with a lesser gift for verse: George and Edward Herbert, Henry and Thomas Vaughan, Charles and John Wesley, Alfred and Charles Tennyson, A. E. and Laurence Housman. If, then, John Stanley wrote *Pearl*, William Stanley perhaps wrote *St. Erkenwald*. Hence the extraordinary resemblances between these texts (including Italian symptoms); and yet also the differences. If the hypothesis is sound, William would be a writer of talent; but John, one of genius.

Let us expand the above. The *Gawain* Poet has since 1968 been associated with Sir John Stanley (1350?–1414), a magnate who held sway in Lancashire and Cheshire. In 1999, Ann W. Astell reinforced those connections by analysis of *Sir Gawain and the Green Knight* (lines 678, 866), there finding mischievous references to Robert de Vere (1362–1392), Duke of Ireland and favourite of Richard II. The allusions will be to Robert as England's first non-royal duke and to his flamboyant attire. That dates the poem to between October 13, 1386, when de Vere was created duke, and December 20, 1387, when his career was ruined. Because Robert spent the summer of 1387 at Chester Castle with John Stanley (his deputy for the government of Ireland), *Sir Gawain and the Green Knight* was apparently written then. It was presumably meant for recitation at Christmas 1387 before Chester Castle's courtiers, who knew de Vere well and would notice sly digs at him.

As for *St. Erkenwald*, it is a miracle-story of a Bishop of London who died in 693. Although the text is sometimes attributed to the *Gawain* Poet, the arguments are feeble. It is surely by another. The *Erkenwald* Poet yet wrote in the same Cheshire dialect at the same time in the same upper-class milieu. In taking *Pearl* as by Sir John Stanley and *St. Erkenwald* as by his brother William, links with Italian poetry are crucial, as is residence at Chester in 1387 of Antonio de Romanis, a Neapolitan physician in the service of John Stanley. So we present the case in three parts: (a) the relation of *Pearl* and *St. Erkenwald* to Italian poetry, (b) the *Erkenwald* Poet's social identity as implied by the text, and (c) Sir William Stanley as possible author.

ITALY, *PEARL, ST. ERKENWALD*

We begin with chronology. *Pearl* was first published in 1864; *St. Erkenwald* in 1881, at Heilbronn (near Stuttgart). Italian aspects of the former were noticed as early as 1904, those of the latter not until 1986 (by G. Whatley). Facts on *St. Erkenwald* were given by Wells. It has 352 alliterative lines and is found only in London, British Library, MS Harley 2250, copied in the year 1477 and from Dunham Massey, east Cheshire. Compared with other saints' legends, this "dignified and elevated" poem shines. It begins with archaeology. In "New Troy" or London, builders at St. Paul's Cathedral uncover the tomb of a judge from pre-Christian times, whose body is yet perfectly preserved. Erkenwald is summoned, the dead man tells him of his life, the bishop weeps that the soul of a virtuous pagan should be lost. But the tears act as water of baptism; and the judge's soul is saved at the very instant that his body crumbles into dust.[1]

Oakden had remarks on *St. Erkenwald* which still merit attention, even though he considered its attribution to the *Gawain* Poet as "very convincing."[2] He thereafter set out features common to *St. Erkenwald* and (for example) *Sir Gawain and the Green Knight*, concluding that linguistic tests "appear to justify the theory" that the *Gawain* Poet wrote *St. Erkenwald*: "all five poems are indelibly stamped with the same artistic personality."[3]

As for *Pearl* and Italy, a relation was examined (and rejected) by Gordon. "The striking resemblance of the general theme of *Pearl* to Boccaccio's *Olympia* is probably only one of the strange coincidences of literary history." Boccaccio (d. 1375) wrote a Latin poem on a deceased daughter seen "in a vision, glorified in eternal life." But *Olympia* is serene in spirit ("no fever of grief, no rebellious doubt"), and Gordon asserted that no modern scholar claimed a "direct link between the two poems."[4] Another commentator, however, thought the alleged "strange coincidences" no accident, with *Pearl* showing possible debts to Dante's *Divine Comedy* and Boccaccio's *Olympia*, both "unusual reading for an Englishman" in the late fourteenth century.[5]

While its importance is indirect, an account of the *Gawain* Poet's ideology is yet significant. He was a man of the right, whose poems are "about and for the aristocracy." He had no "overt questioning" of established society, unlike Chaucer and Langland; he accepted "outdated" political values, his "garden paradise" and Hautdesert Castle alike being set in "the context of the agrarian aristocracy."[6] These comments are basic to present contentions on *Pearl* and *St. Erkenwald*, because we ascribe both to members of Cheshire's ruling class. Hence their uncompromising regard for authority.

Returning to Italy, we find Patricia Kean's detailed study of features common to Dante and *Pearl* (the Earthly Paradise, a river of jewels, maiden guides). She yet said nothing on Boccaccio, and was cautious on the *Gawain* Poet's debt to Dante, something long "a matter of dispute"; but nevertheless admitted that his use of figures "part allegorical, part humanly individual" was a probable borrowing from *The Divine Comedy*. It was hard to see where else he might find this blend of "realistical and symbolic writing."[7] Parallels set out by her are fundamental. We shall return to them. There are similar penetrating comments elsewhere: how *Olympia* "comes nearer to *Pearl*" (despite lacking the "Christian consolation" which is *Pearl*'s "driving force") than it does to *The Book of the Duchess*; or how, just as Dante's Beatrice was "a historical, Florentine girl" and not an "allegorical" abstraction (Faith or Theology or the like), so too the Pearl Maiden was a creature of flesh and blood, the poem's didactic functions notwithstanding.[8]

At this point, a further wrench into actuality. In 1968, Gervase Mathew was the first to associate *Pearl* and its siblings with Sir John Stanley, "patron of the *Gawain* Poet."[9] Mathew planted a seed which has sprouted and grown. His stress on real people may be juxtaposed with a development of Patricia Kean's observations, creations of Dante and the *Pearl* Poet now being termed "figural" rather than part-allegorical, part-human; because "there is no division of functions, such as this might imply."[10]

After people, places. Independent of dispute on his identity, if the *Pearl* Poet can be linked to the Stanleys, then the Maiden will be buried at Burscough Priory, near Ormskirk, where almost nothing remains except two massive transept piers, gesturing at the sky. Stanleys were buried there until the Reformation, their mansion (destroyed by Cromwellians) at Lathom being a mile away. When the priory was dissolved, many Stanley tombs were moved to Ormskirk parish church.[11] But the Maiden's tomb was surely too small for this. If so, Burscough will, for admirers of *Pearl*, become a site of pilgrimage, as being where the Pearl Maiden sleeps to this day.

Moving our gaze from Lancashire to Italy, we find Tony Spearing scoffing at resemblances between *Pearl* and Boccaccio's *Olympia*, dismissing them as "probably coincidental"; while, citing Larry Benson's 1965 paper rejecting the *Gawain* Poet as author of *St. Erkenwald*, he concluded (with equal complacency) that "it is difficult to understand why the connection was ever made."[12] In this paper we turn Spearing upside-down. We indicate how the author of *Pearl* might learn of Dante and Boccaccio; we propose a very close connection indeed between *Pearl* Poet and *Erkenwald* Poet.

Pearl's odd similarities to Dante kept on being noticed, as with the comparison (in lines 1093–96) of how "sodanly" the narrator saw the heavenly host, progressing like the "maynful" (or powerful) moon rising at sunset. The "abstract, almost metaphysical quality" of the simile "reminds one of Dante."[13] Also significant is a translator's review, quoting three critics. Israel Gollancz in his 1922 edition of *St. Erkenwald* attributed it to the *Gawain* Poet, even if it was "simpler" than *Patience* and *Cleanness*, and lacked "their strength and intensity"; or else it was by "some disciple who very cleverly caught the style of his master." In 1964 John Gardner preferred the first option. "The hypothesis of a clever imitator of *Sir Gawain and the Green Knight* simply will not wash." But Larry Benson in 1965 had doubts: "more certain evidence is required before the poem is finally assigned to the *Pearl* Poet." The translator still felt that a "harmony of pattern" shared by all five poems, together with the "brevity and force" of *St. Erkenwald*'s ending, supported Gollancz.[14] There is a model for procedure in a study of thematic unity, imagery, diction, analogous phrases, paraphrases for "God," methods for introducing a story, stating something as hard to describe, endings that echo beginnings. It is decisive. *Patience, Cleanness, Pearl, Sir Gawain* are by the "same" poet.[15] It provides a model for work on *St. Erkenwald*.

At this point, a note on preconceptions. First, the tendency to attribute different anonymous works to one writer. The Brontës and Sitwells show the fallacy here. Fortunately, the authorship of *Jane Eyre* and *Wuthering Heights* is known. Otherwise critics would ascribe them to one individual (probably a man). Second is *St. Erkenwald* as by the *Gawain* Poet's "disciple." But literary history suggests a different view, English "Chaucerians" like Hoccleve and Lydgate are not much like Chaucer. Third, a chronological objection, *St. Erkenwald* is contemporary with *Pearl* and *Sir Gawain*. They belong to Richard II's reign. *Gawain* Poet and *Erkenwald* Poet were of the same generation. So they were hardly master and pupil.

These aspects in mind, we turn to Stephen Medcalf, a sensitive and original critic. He thought it likely that the *Pearl* Poet knew Dante's *Commedia*. Both poems concern a man who, "lost by losing his beloved," is "transformed by his vision of her in Heaven"; both have a woman (the Pearl Maiden, the *Purgatorio*'s Matilda) seen in Paradise, "beyond the stream." Yet the only pre-nineteenth-century English poets really familiar with Dante are Chaucer and Milton, who each visited Italy. Others (like John Gower) "merely mention him." Implications: there was a Middle English translation of Dante; or the *Pearl* Poet visited Italy; or he knew of Dante from Chaucer; or a combination of these. Medcalf thought the *Pearl* Poet's friendship with Chaucer "an exciting possibility." He also, less happily, ascribed *Pearl* (after Gollancz) and *St. Erkenwald* to the Merton College logician Ralph Strode (d. 1387).[16] Strode as *Gawain* Poet: a defunct notion. On the other hand, John Stanley (whom we take as the poet) surely knew Chaucer, whose *Squire's Tale* echoes *Sir Gawain and the Green Knight* for a mounted horseman startling diners at a royal banquet. As to how Stanley might know of Dante and Boccaccio, see below.

Comments on the fame of Dante (d. 1321) are here useful. His *Divina Commedia* was "extremely popular." The first commentary was published within three years of his death; before 1340 appeared another by Jacopo della Lana, with assistance from Dante's sons Jacopo and Pietro.[17] Jacopo della Lana's story of Pope Gregory and the Emperor Trajan apparently left its mark on *St. Erkenwald*. We may recall how the *Pearl* Poet's direct reception of the *Commedia* has been termed "highly likely"; for he was "no less avant-garde" than Chaucer himself.[18] No benighted Northern provincial he.

Strode's claims to be author of *Pearl* were, however, squashed flat by Jack Bennett.[19] The poet must be sought elsewhere. Another went further. The Maiden's stern reproofs of the Dreamer resemble those of "Beatrice to Dante," with the poet's knowledge of the *Commedia* taken as certain. In contrast is *St. Erkenwald*, praised as a "splendid small-scale" item "full of awe, mystery, and sadness," even though attribution to the *Gawain* Poet is quite "flimsy."[20] Elsewhere is facile scepticism, with nothing on Dante (or Boccaccio); nor can the five Cheshire poems considered here "be dated accurately."[21] (Below, we date *Sir Gawain and the Green Knight* to 1387 and *Pearl* to 1390.) Another yet mentions Dante's *Divine Comedy* as a "dream-vision" prefiguring *Pearl*.[22] Or, again, we hear how the Dreamer is "instructed and guided" by the Maiden, as Dante was by Beatrice, and how the Poet appears in his text as Dante did in his. (But no word on literary channels between them.) For *St. Erkenwald*, there is shrewd comment on how its "style and 'feel' are different" from the *Gawain* Poet's; it is "plainer," but with "some similarities of diction." It was perhaps commissioned by Robert de Braybroke, Bishop of London 1382–1404. (But why would a poem in Cheshire dialect interest him?) In any case, one should not "over-emphasize the provinciality of alliterative poems."[23] Which is true.

Now for some dynamite, in a passage on Italian doctors in Richard II's England. "In 1387 Antonio de Romanis of Naples was the physician accompanying Sir John Stanley, Robert de Vere's deputy, to Ireland."[24] Antonio was a man of education. He had an interest in books. At the very least, he shows how knowledge of Dante's *Divina Commedia* and Jacopo della Lana's commentary on it, as also Boccaccio's *Olympia*, might reach fourteenth-century Chester. We remember how Gervase Mathew in 1968 put *Sir Gawain and the Green Knight* within Stanley's circle. So Antonio de Romanis indicates how Italian verse might influence *Pearl*, which will postdate *Sir Gawain*.

Illuminating too are words on *St. Erkenwald* as "less directly biblical than *Cleanness* or *Patience*" and (significant, this) depicting "an excited and ignorant throng."[25] The *Erkenwald* Poet, like the *Gawain* Poet, believed in order and control (attitudes made clear in 1961 by John Fisher, citing *Pearl*'s no-nonsense take on the Parable of the Vineyard). But for admirable criticism of *Pearl* we turn to a golden chapter by Jack Bennett (1911–1981). Two passages may be quoted. One is about the Dreamer's first sight of the Maiden. "The scene strikingly recalls Dante's meeting with Matilda (*Purgatorio*, xxviii) in the *Paradiso Terrestre*." The other is on the Pearl Maiden and Beatrice. The Italian and English poets perhaps both drew on "the tale of Balaam and Josaphat," a "work widely diffused" throughout medieval Europe.[26] But the presence in 1387 of Antonio de Romanis at Chester dispels any need for that.

Bennett's commentary on *Pearl* is easily understood. Not so Eugene Vance's, with statements on how, "as in Dante, grace as Word will transfigure conventional speech as an instrument of the rational soul, rather than repudiate it."[27] Whatever its merits, it says nothing on how a Chester poet might know Dante. That Cheshire identity figures too in *St. Erkenwald*, surviving in a Cheshire manuscript (from Dunham Massey, near Manchester). Its words on "London in England" are not "grossly redundant," because medieval Cheshire was a county palatine, in administrative and constitutional ways unlike the rest of England. It sent "no representatives to the national parliament and was exempt from national taxation."[28] Its author might pride himself on being from Cheshire. So, an implication that he belonged to its ruling class, who possessed unique political and financial power, plus special contacts with the monarch.

A note on physicians. Fourteenth-century ones in the service of English kings and nobles were paid "at roughly the same rate as senior household staff."[29] Antonio de Romanis therefore received ample remuneration from John Stanley. He could afford books. His presence in Chester is significant, given ideas promoted by Jill Mann and Ad Putter on supposed "mercantile and chivalric values" (his phrase) in the poems, appealing to "sophisticated and wealthy merchants and knights" (her phrase) in London. In this obeisance to the capital, Italian texts are cited as evidence: Dante's *Divina Commedia*, Boccaccio's *Olympia*, and (for *St. Erkenwald*) Jacopo della Lana's commentary on Dante. Only in London (we hear) would the *Gawain* Poet be likely to encounter "the most recent Italian literature." The alternative is to regard these parallels as "strange coincidences." In a phrase quoted from a 1986 paper by David Carlson, a "linguistically marginal English poet" in remote Cheshire could hardly know the latest Continental literary fashions.[30]

How can one reply? England's academic "golden triangle" (London, Oxford, Cambridge) here has much to answer for. Despite the opulence of his verse and an obsession with hunting, the *Gawain* Poet is assumed to be an intellectual (a clerk or cleric), not (as one might think) a wealthy and powerful landowner. He is patronized as a provincial who would hardly have read Dante and Boccaccio. If there are parallels, they are mere coincidence. Or, if he did read Italian, it must have been in London. One hopes that others (especially in the North?) will be swift in rejecting such Oxbridge smugness.

Preferable is a remark on *St. Erkenwald*'s style. It is "less exuberant, sparer, and more concise" than that of the *Gawain* Poet, effectively ruling him out as author. Of interest too is its last line, on how all the bells of London rang out at once, which is related to a passage (on Treviso Cathedral) in Boccaccio's *Decameron*.[31] Although its "concise, non-redundant expression" is unusual for alliterative verse, it still lacks "the richer and more ample texture of *Sir Gawain and the Green Knight*."[32] References to work on Dante and Boccacio and *Pearl* were then given, even if "it remains unclear" whether the *Gawain* Poet read *Olympia*.[33]

If evidence published in 1983 on an Italian at Chester in 1387 has been unnoticed, so has material of 1999 on *Sir Gawain and the Green Knight* at Chester in 1387. Perhaps no surprise. Even its author did not see the implications of her words. In a study of Chaucer and others, Ann Astell took on lines 678 and 866 in *Sir Gawain*, which seemingly date the text to 1387. In line 678, Gawain is praised for beheading the Green Knight: *And have dight yonder dere a duk to have worthed*, or "And have had the worthy one yonder made a duke"; while line 866 has comment on Gawain's fine new clothes: *The ver by his uisage verayly hit semed*, or "Verily by his appearance it seemed vernal to all." Here *duk* "duke" and *ver* "spring" are (apparently) digs at Robert de Vere (1362–1392), Earl of Oxford and Duke of Ireland. In 1386 he was created England's first-ever non-royal duke; until late 1387 (when his career was wrecked), he was a notorious dandy, in finery of *ver*-or spring-like colors.[34] So the lines put *Sir Gawain and the Green Knight* to between October 13, 1386, when de Vere became a duke, and December 20, 1387, when he lost the Battle of Radcot Bridge and fled into exile. Robert being a hated favorite of Richard II, *Sir Gawain and the Green Knight* will not postdate his downfall, when he ceased to matter. Its composition belongs to 1387 and surely its later part, after de Vere had spent a flamboyant summer at Chester Castle with his Central European mistress, as also John Stanley, his deputy for the government of Ireland.

Facts on Chester Castle, pointing to 1387 and (?) a planned recitation there of *Sir Gawain and the Green Knight* that Christmas, need no emphasis. But nobody sees Italian traces in the poem. The presence at Chester of Antonio de Romanis, a Neapolitan doctor in Stanley's employment, tells us nothing there. *Pearl* and *St. Erkenwald* are another matter. Their Italian aspects would place both after 1387, according with claims for the latter as perhaps from about 1392, when Richard II "made a visit to the tomb of St Erkenwald in St Paul's," part of a solemn reconciliation with Londoners.[35] The paper has prompted observations on Richard II's "practice of disenterring corpses after they had been entombed." *St. Erkenwald* may reflect that, indicating composition in the 1390s.

Also noticed are "cosmopolitan" Italian authors like Boccaccio known to a "sophisticated London poet such as Chaucer, as well as perhaps the *Pearl* Poet."[36] He will have been a sophisticated Cheshire poet. Scarcely noticed (despite implications for dating) is a paper on how the Pearl Maiden died of bubonic plague, which can leave blemishes on the skin, explaining the text's obsessive allusions to "spots."[37] It is a clue for researchers. It is sounder than speculation on canons "drawn from all parts of England" and serving at St. Paul's Cathedral in the 1390s, and how perhaps "one of these wrote *St Erkenwald*."[38] Not so. Nothing in *St. Erkenwald* (or the provenance of its manuscript) implies a clerical or London author. The text stresses lay (and not ecclesiastical) government.

In 2004 appeared arguments for identification of the *Gawain* Poet as Sir John Stanley.[39] It was followed by renewed emphasis on an Italian feature of *St. Erkenwald*. Its narrative "resembles very closely" a legend in Jacopo della Lana's commentary on Dante, written in about 1330. The story is of how "construction workers of [Pope] Gregory's time find some bones and a skull containing a living tongue, which, in response to an injunction by Gregory, identifies the remains as those of Trajan"; whose soul is then redeemed after Gregory prays for him.[40] To this day, few people in Cheshire read commentaries on Dante. That someone did so in Richard II's time is hence extraordinary. Yet the presence in 1387 of Antonio de Romanis among the Stanley entourage reduces surprise. Contrast, then, affirmation on how "evidence is lacking" for the *Pearl* Poet's knowledge of Dante.[41] Unhelpful too are assertions on the plausibility of "a single author" for *Pearl* and *St. Erkenwald*.[42]

A digression, on Burscough Priory as the Pearl Maiden's last resting-place, and discussion of Stanley burials at this "imposing mausoleum" until Henry VIII brought matters to a close.[43] The theological implications are echoed in an essay on *Pearl*, with a passing remark on how *St. Erkenwald* "is occasionally suggested" as being by the *Gawain* Poet.[44]

Now for a clutch of rare words: *art*, *abyme*, *skelt*, two of which are from Irish. The first means "direction" and is from *áit* "place, position."[45] The second, *abyme* or "abysm, deep, depth of the sea," is a French borrowing and occurs in *Cleanness* and *Patience*, but also *St. Erkenwald*, supposedly providing "a further argument for the shared authorship" of these poems.[46] The third means "hasten" and relates to the common Irish form *scaoil* "loosen, release, discharge."[47] This Anglo-French-Irish *mélange* is extraordinary. Yet maps of the Wirral lessen our amazement. There (as place-name dictionaries show) in the Viking age were Irish-speaking settlers at Arrow (from *áirge* "cowshed"), Liscard (*lios na carraige* "court at a rocky eminence"), and Noctorum (*cnoc tirim* "dry hill"). *St. Erkenwald* will not just be a Cheshire poem, but one of the Wirral, a district subject to banter in *Sir Gawain and the Green Knight* (line 701), and also the location of Storeton, where William Stanley built a mansion, and Hooton, from which he was generally known. Living in Wirral, he would naturally have Irish loanwords in his speech.

These inconvenient linguistic facts puncture Jill Mann's belief in *St. Erkenwald* and its four associates as meant for a high-ranking London audience; as also Lynn Stacey's belief that the *Gawain* Poet perhaps had John of Gaunt as his patron (where Jill Mann declares that to her mind "the evidence for Richard's court is stronger").[48] But Ricardian courtiers would not understand Wirralisms. They might laugh in the face of a poet foolish enough to use them. This paper will fail in its objectives if it does not vaporize almost everything said by Professor Mann on the *Gawain* Poet and Richard II's court.

After philology, singing by angels, a theme common to Dante and *Pearl*.[49] The subject deserves fuller study. Musicologists could tell us much on styles of singing, woodwind, percussion, brass, strings, occasions of performance, and how they figure in Dante and our Cheshire texts. It would break ground as another and more conventional survey of *St. Erkenwald* does not.[50]

In 2014 appeared a note on the Pearl Maiden's allusions to spots (= skin-marks due to plague, it seems). They imply that she died in the epidemic of 1390–1393, which killed many children and adolescents, lacking the immunity acquired by their elders. If so, the Maiden died probably in 1390. If she had been born after mid-1389, she would hardly have survived to be nearly two. *Pearl* may itself thus date from 1390.[51] There is an inference. When the writer there attributed *Pearl* to John Stanley, he did not know of Stanley's sojourn at Chester in 1387 or the presence there of Antonio de Romanis. Stanley presumably knew nothing of Italian poetry until he met Antonio. If he then learnt from him of Dante and Boccaccio, it tallies with the hypothesis of *Patience* and *Cleanness* as dating from the 1370s, *Sir Gawain* from 1387, and *Pearl* from 1390. Hence Italian influence on the last only. If these propositions have substance, they will modify a good deal stated in one volume.[52]

We end with two recent books. In a left-wing study of *Sir Gawain and the Green Knight* are citations of progressive authorities (David Aers, Georges Bataille, Pierre Bourdieu, Andrew Cowell, Jacques Derrida, Fredric Jameson, Jacques Lacan, Claude Lévi-Strauss, Jill Mann, Karl Marx, James Simpson), with comment on the poem as indicating "how violence becomes the sign of value that unites a community."[53] Nothing, however, on *Pearl* or *St. Erkenwald*, or questions of exact dating. Another book has a footnote-reference to "speculation" (*sic*) on John Stanley as author, and a brief mention of Dante.[54]

The latest comment at hand is from an Ohio researcher, who affirms that "The audience of *Sir Gawain*, and the three other poems in Cotton Nero A.x, is largely inaccessible."[55] On the contrary. We can say much on these auditors, who would be found in Cheshire or Lancashire. The language of the poems would bewilder anyone else. Hence the Cheshire connections of MSS Cotton Nero A.x and Harley 2250. Audiences were also élite ones. They shared the social conservatism of the two authors; they valued sophisticated descriptions of armor, clothes, jewels, the chase, dismemberment of prey, attempted seduction, paradisal landscapes; they could spot mischievous humor at the expense of Wirral folk or Robert de Vere (*Sir Gawain*, lines 701, 678, 866). Even knowing nothing else, one might postulate Chester Castle, centre of royal government, as where *Sir Gawain and the Green Knight* was meant for recitation. But few will gather this from current academic discourse. In short, little progress since 1916, where we began.

AUTHORIAL FEATURES OF *ST. ERKENWALD*

Now for a closer look at *St. Erkenwald*. Although increasingly discussed, the poem still repays scrutiny for authorial attitudes (to society, kingship, public order, clerics, Scripture, the laity, law, government, books, building). Here, then, are notes on certain lines of the poem as clues to its author's identity.

a. *At London in England* (1) has been singled out (see above) as denoting pride in Cheshire, and not in the metropolis.
b. *Augustines art* (33) refers to the saint's region (not his "authority") and is a loan from Irish. It implies a Cheshire audience. Londoners would misunderstand the word.
c. *Mony a mery mason* (39) is among several allusions in the text (40, 69) to builders, of which the poet knew much.
d. *Burgheys* and *bedels* (59) are citizens and officials. They are part of a concern with secular government (also 65, 143), not that of the Church, which (in a poem on a saint) figures less than expected.

e. *A meche mantel on lofte with menyver furrit* (81) is the dead man's "great robe above, trimmed with miniver" (or squirrel fur). The writer gave details of legal attire, as elsewhere (249–52). He consistently emphasizes the Law and its dignity (82–83).

f. *Mony a gay grete lorde was gedrid to herken hit* (134) is a further allusion to secular (not ecclesiastical) authority, in this case of nobles (also 135, 138, 142, 227).

g. *But pyne was* (141) alludes to the "crush" of ordinary folk crowding round Bishop Erkenwald, and implies a disdain (noticed by others) for the commonality. The poet was not a man of the people. His politics were conservative. He upheld without flinching the power of Church and State. We may recall similar observations of 1961 by Fisher on the *Gawain* Poet.

h. *And we have oure librarie laited* (155), on how experts "searched" among books for information on the dead man. The procedure is that of a judge or other lawyer, getting assistants to find facts.

i. *Ansuare here to my sawe, councele no trouthe!* (184) Erkenwald's warning that the corpse should "conceal" nothing is severe. His language is less that of a saint than of a magistrate.

j. *I was committid and made a mayster-mon here* (200). As for the man in the tomb, he actually was a judge, calling himself a "chief official" who (202–4, 216) sat upon cases. It is curious. In literature, the law is more often satirized (Dickens, W. S. Gilbert, many others) than praised. Lawyers exalt the majesty of the Law. Poets do not. Could *St. Erkenwald* be the work of a magistrate?

k. *And all the belles in the burgh beryd* [rang out] *at ones* (352). In miracle stories, bells often toll without human agency (see above). Yet, given Jacopo della Lana's influence on *St. Erkenwald* and (?) the presence of Antonio de Romanis at Chester in 1387, the poet perhaps took this detail direct from Boccaccio's *Decameron.*

SIR WILLIAM STANLEY

So we know something of the poet from his poem. Does it coincide with what can be gathered of Sir William Stanley, John's elder brother? The records of him indicate money and power, but contain surprises too, such as kinship with the Welsh and (more distantly) Henry VIII. Central here is his daughter's marriage to Gwilym ap Gruffudd, an astute Welsh powerbroker. Years later it advantaged William Bulkeley, Sir William's grandson. In 1442, when English colonists in North Wales sought curtailment of legal rights for the Welsh, Bulkeley (an Anglesey landowner) was exempted by name.[56] Like his brother-in-law, Gwilym Fychan, who in 1439 claimed English descent through his mother, "Joan, daughter of William Stanley, knight," Bulkeley asserted rights from having "married a woman of half-Welsh blood," Joan's daughter.[57] We learn more of Gwilym ap Gruffudd from poems of Rhys Goch Eryri, "red" bard of Snowdonia. Gwilym aimed for success. In 1396 he was Sheriff of Anglesey; after his first wife died, he wed Joan Stanley, widow of Judge Paris, Chamberlain of North Wales in 1399. Gwilym himself died in 1431 (whereupon his widow married yet again).[58]

With Gwilym's second wife began a long relationship between the Stanleys and Wales. Tudur Aled (d. 1526) praised a (Welsh) Dean of St Asaph for kinship with the "earls of Hooton."[59] Border relations had certainly improved. This we know from a letter of July 30, 1405 to Henry IV from John Stanley, supplying information from Welsh spies on Owen Glendower. From the May previous come details on his kinsman, Robert Paris, Constable of Caernarfon.[60] Robert died that year, his widow Joan (John's niece) eventually taking Gwilym ap Gruffudd as her second husband, establishing a "long and profitable connection" with her family.[61] Gwilym made a "judicious, if unpatriotic, choice of sides."[62] Joan had first been married to a Constable of Caernarfon, where the castle withstood sieges by Glendower "and his French allies in 1403 and 1404."[63] She then married a man formerly on the side of those doing the besieging. He had displayed a "fine sense of timing" in deserting Glendower, soon after John sent his intelligence report to Henry IV.[64] But John, who deserted Richard II for Henry IV, also knew about tergiversation (as did a later Sir William Stanley, deserting Richard III for Henry VII at Bosworth in 1485).

In the context of *St. Erkenwald*, Joan's first husband is significant. He was Chamberlain of Chester in 1394–1399, dying (it seems) in May 1405 as Constable of Caernarfon, his son (another Robert) then taking over. Joan, again widowed in 1431, was still alive in 1438, when she "obtained a licence from the Crown" to build a tower at Penrhyn (east of Bangor).[65] So William was rich, would have served as a magistrate, and had as his son-in-law "Judge" Paris, who in the 1390s was Chamberlain of Chester and North Wales. If William in the 1390s wrote *St. Erkenwald*, its subject of a righteous and incorruptible judge might be expected.

Constructions by Joan Stanley at Penrhyn compare with those of her father at Storeton, to this day with a "fragment" of his manor house from about 1360: "Incorporated in the farm buildings of Storeton Hall Farm are extensive remains" of it. It was of H-plan, with a great hall running north-south between two wings. The two-storey north wing has survived, together with the east wall of the hall.[66] They allow reflection. If present arguments hold, they relate to *St. Erkenwald*, a poem with much on building. In addition, when Sir

Gawain crossed the Sands of Dee from Wales into Wirral, Storeton lay on his route, in a place where few "wyth goud hert louied" God or man (*Sir Gawain,* line 702). If this is not a light-hearted brotherly jibe at Sir William Stanley, it is hard to see why it is there.

Returning from Cheshire to Wales, we re-encounter Gwilym ap Gruffudd and William Bulkeley, the first married to "one of the daughters of Sir William Stanley, Knight, who is entirely English," the second to Ellen, "English on her mother's side, that is, daughter to William Stanley, Knight."[67] Both demonstrate social ascendancy, like the "white-washed walls" of Penrhyn itself.[68] That William's activities were not always positive is shown by a record of 1369, on how, while head forester of Wirral, he "was found guilty of an attack on Thursaston Hall" (in west Wirral) together with his brother John.[69]

Another account of Gwilym brings out (from a rental of 1413) his wealth, and his betrayal in 1405 of Glendower, revealing himself as just one of his "fair-weather friends." Later on Gwilym was "parading his loyalty to the English regime by taking an Englishwoman as his second wife."[70] Elsewhere he declared himself "a loyal servant of the King" and descended "for the most part wholly from the English race" (one bard went further, tracing Gwilym's descent from Brutus and the god Jupiter).[71] He never let facts spoil his story; and his acquisition of kinsmen's estates confiscated after rebellion has been related to the departure of one of them, Owen Tudor, for the court in London, where (by his marriage to Henry V's widow) he became great-grandfather to Henry VIII.[72]

Now for England. William Stanley was a man of energy and decision. In the 1370s (or 1360s?) he was "using the profits of office to build Storeton Hall in stone." More dramatic was an incident of 1387, when he abducted from Berkhamsted "a Bohemian lady-in-waiting of Queen Anne" on behalf of Robert de Vere, Duke of Ireland (who had tired of his wife), with whom she then spent the summer in luxury at Chester Castle. Quite separate is reference to MS Harley 2250, containing *St. Erkenwald,* copied in 1477 and from Dunham Massey (southwest of Manchester). This text, in Cheshire dialect and a Cheshire manuscript, is allegedly "set firmly in the metropolis."[73] Yet Dunham Massey is here important. Sir William Stanley's mother was a Massey, born at Timperley, close to Dunham Massey, a property of her family.

For all that, William is never mentioned in a study of Cheshire's literary tradition, despite a complete chapter on the Stanleys. Nor is *St. Erkenwald.*[74] That would need revision if he wrote the poem, in Cheshire dialect and surely for Cheshire auditors. A similar survey has nothing on William, but contains mention of his father, another William (d. 1360), who compelled inhabitants of Wirral "to work on his estates in the harvest of 1346."[75] Stanleys were not to be trifled with. Joan Stanley's convenient marriage (of 1413?) to ex-rebel Gwilym ap Gruffudd, helping him "reinvent himself," underlines the point.

So too (after his death in 1431) does his widow's third marriage, to John Pykemere, a Caernarfon burgess.[76] She would then be in her 60s, and was evidently of vigorous stock, like her father.

CONCLUSION

By now a great deal of circumstantial evidence has accumulated. It does not (of course) prove that, in the last years of the fourteenth century, Sir William Stanley wrote *St. Erkenwald*. However, an ascription to him removes many difficulties (perhaps all of them). So we end with a summary of points.

1. *St. Erkenwald*, a text in Cheshire dialect, survives in a Cheshire manuscript, just as *Pearl* and its three associates, all in Cheshire dialect, appear in a manuscript related to Chester. Nothing here suggests a London audience.
2. Its author writes as a layman and uses the language of a magistrate, not a cleric. That coincides with what we know of Sir William Stanley, a man of authority with strong legal connections.
3. The vocabulary of the text resembles in minute detail that of the *Gawain* Poet. But its style and artistry are unlike, being of a somewhat lesser order. A simple explanation is that the author was the *Gawain* Poet's kinsman. The social attitudes and familiarity with court life of all five texts suggest authors of rank, not the humble scribes (in a great man's employ) of conventional literary history.
4. *St. Erkenwald* also has curious emphasis on builders, of which Sir William would know much from his official duties, and particularly Storeton Hall's construction in about 1370.
5. The masses are in the poem seen *de haut en bas*. The attitude to them is that of the ruling class to which William Stanley belonged.
6. Influence on the text of Jacopo della Lana and perhaps of Boccaccio's *Decameron* accords with the presence at Chester in 1387 of Antonio de Romanis, a Neapolitan doctor unlikely to be ignorant of Italy's greatest writers. So, no need to place *St. Erkenwald*'s author in London. Antonio was physician to Sir John Stanley, indicating how his brother William might learn of Italian writers.
7. In sum, no evidence for metropolitan knights and merchants, whether from Cheshire or elsewhere. *St. Erkenwald* belongs to Cheshire's literary history, as do *Sir Gawain and the Green Knight* and (with a further Lancashire connection) *Pearl*.

Last of all, how to take matters forward: or else to explode the thesis offered above. There are two priorities. We need to know more on Antonio de Romanis, his family, education, career, and movements in England and Ireland, above all as they concern John and William Stanley. Second and more important, work is required on William Stanley's life: his dates, activities as landowner and magistrate, possible service overseas, and his genealogy, not least as it relates via his mother Alice Massey to the Masseys of Dunham Massey (MS Harley 2250's original home). A significant episode is that of 1387, when he kidnapped de Vere's Bohemian mistress from Berkhamsted Castle. Stanley, a man of action, was yet at ease in royal society. So his familiarity with London would be natural. Of course, a man with a criminal past (as he was) raises questions for *St. Erkenwald*, eulogy of a perfect judge. But the same problem exists with Sir Thomas Malory, another convicted criminal. If there are lofty sentiments in *Le Morte Darthur*, by Sir Thomas Malory, there are the same in *St. Erkenwald* and *Sir Gawain and the Green Knight*, respectively by (it seems) the brothers Sir William and Sir John Stanley.

NOTES

1. Wells, *A Manual of the Writings in Middle English*, 310.

2. Oakden, *Alliterative Poetry in Middle English: The Dialectal and Metrical Survey*, 87.

3. Oakden, *Alliterative Poetry in Middle English: A Survey of the Traditions*, 76–78.

4. Gordon, *Pearl*, xxxv.

5. Everett, *Essays on Middle English Literature*, 69.

6. J. H. Fisher, "Wyclif, Langland, Gower, and the *Pearl* Poet on the Subject of Aristocracy," 139–57.

7. Kean, *The Pearl: An Interpretation*, 6, 120, 138.

8. Bishop, *Pearl in Its Setting*, 24, 59.

9. Mathew, *The Court of Richard II*, 166.

10. Salter, "Medieval Poetry and the Figural View of Reality," 73–92.

11. Pevsner, *The Buildings of England: North Lancashire*, 84–85, 184.

12. Spearing, *The Gawain Poet*, 17 n. 2, 33.

13. Burrow, *Ricardian Poetry*, 134.

14. Stone, *The Owl and the Nightingale: Cleanness: St Erkenwald*, 247–48.

15. Vantuono, "*Patience, Cleanness, Pearl*, and *Gawain*: The Case for Common Authorship," 37–69.

16. Medcalf, "*Piers Plowman* and the Ricardian Age in Literature," 643–96.

17. Schless, "Transformations: Chaucer's Use of Italian," 184–223.

18. Spearing, *Medieval Dream-Poetry*, 111.

19. J. A. W. Bennett, *Chaucer at Oxford and at Cambridge*, 64.

20. Pearsall, *Old English and Middle English Poetry*, 183, 176, 319.

21. Turville-Petre, *The Alliterative Revival*, 34.

22. Andrew and Waldron, *The Poems of the Pearl Manuscript*, 29, 214.

23. D. S. Brewer, *English Gothic Literature*, 168, 175.

24. Childs, "Anglo-Italian Contacts," 77.

25. Douglas, *The Bible in Middle English Literature*, 194, 224

26. J. A. W. Bennett, *Middle English Literature*, 243, 257.

27. Vance, "*Pearl*: Love and the Poetics of Participation," 131–47.

28. Burrow, "*Saint Erkenwald* Line 1," 22–23.

29. Rawcliffe, *Medicine and Society in Later Medieval England*, 110.

30. Putter, "*Sir Gawain and the Green Knight" and French Arthurian Romance*, 192.

31. Burrow and Turville-Petre, *A Book of Middle English*, 201.

32. Burrow, "Redundancy in Alliterative Verse," 119–28.

33. Neuhauser, "Sources II," 257–75.

34. Astell, *Political Allegory in Late Medieval England*, 123, 124, 126, 137.

35. Grady, "*St Erkenwald* and the Merciless Parliament," 179–211.

36. Bowers, *The Politics of "Pearl,"* 20, 83.

37. Freidl and Kirby, "The Life, Death, and Life of the Pearl Maiden," 395–98.

38. Staley, "The Man in Foul Clothes," 1–47.

39. Breeze, "Sir John Stanley (*c.* 1350–1414) and the *Gawain*-Poet," 15–30.

40. McTurk, *Chaucer and the Norse and Celtic Worlds*, 91.

41. Spearing, *Textual Subjectivity*, 172.

42. Borroff, "Narrative Artistry in *St Erkenwald* and the *Gawain*-Group," 41–76.

43. Stöber, *Late Medieval Monasteries and Their Patrons*, 133–34.

44. Bugbee, "Sight and Sound in *St Erkenwald,*" 202–21.

45. Breeze, "*Art* 'Direction' in *St Erkenwald*," 273.

46. Sobecki, *The Sea and Medieval English Literature*, 38 n. 67.

47. Breeze, "*Skelt* 'Hasten' in *Cleanness* and *St Erkenwald,*" 147–48.

48. Mann, "Courtly Aesthetics and Courtly Ethics in *Sir Gawain and the Green Knight,*" 231–65.

49. Kowalik, *Betwixt "Englaunde" and "Englene Londe,"* 178–79.

50. Stodnick, "Emerging Englishness," 496–511.

51. Breeze, "*Pearl* and the Plague of 1390–1393," 337–41.

52. Putter and Stokes, *The Works of the Gawain Poet*, ix.

53. Wadiak, *Savage Economy: The Returns of Middle English Romance*, xi.

54. Coley, *Death and the Pearl-Maiden*, 16 n. 61, 183.

55. Morrison, "Choreographic Description," 21–39.

56. E. A. Lewis, *The Mediaeval Boroughs of Snowdonia*, 264.

57. Evans, *Wales and the Wars of the Roses*, 22, 25.

58. H. Lewis, T. Roberts, I. Williams, *Cywyddau Iolo Goch ac Eraill*, 401, 402, 404.

59. T. G. Jones, *Gwaith Tudur Aled*, 135, 687.

60. Lloyd, *Owen Glendower*, 101, 130 n. 2.

61. Roberts, "Griffith of Penrhyn," 1123–26.

62. G. Williams, *The Welsh Church from Conquest to Reformation*, 249.

63. Taylor, *Caernarvon Castle and Town Walls*, 19.

64. Davies, "Owain Glyn Dŵr and the Welsh Squirarchy," 150–69.

65. G. Roberts, *Aspects of Welsh History*, 209, 210, 213.

66. Pevsner, *The Buildings of England: Cheshire*, 18, 346.

67. Rees, *Calendar of Ancient Petitions Relating to Wales*, 38, 147.

68. Davies, *Lordship and Society in the March of Wales*, 421.

69. Coward, *The Stanleys, Lords Stanley, and Earls of Derby 1385–1672*, 3.

70. Davies, *Conquest, Co-existence, and Change*, 416, 446, 457.

71. G. Williams, *Recovery, Reorganization, and Reformation*, 11, 98.

72. Walker, *Medieval Wales*, 186.

73. M. J. Bennett, "The Historical Background," 71–90.

74. Barrett, *Against All England*, 134, 171–206.

75. Hill, *Looking Westward*, 68.

76. Carr, *The Gentry of North Wales in the Later Middle Ages*, 149, 254.

Chapter Seven

Place-Names and Politics in
The Awntyrs off Arthure

The Awntyrs off Arthure "The Adventures of Arthur" is a fifteenth-century Northern poem concerned with love (royal affairs of the heart) and death (a visitor from the grave). It is set in Cumberland, and some take its unknown author as a Cumbrian (others think him a Scot). Despite powerful representations of illicit love and the supernatural, the poem was until recent decades something of a Cinderella. Its dialect is unfamilar and its text corrupt, with the four manuscripts containing many obscurities.

This chapter has three purposes. Its first part summarizes previous discussion of the poem, particularly on date, but also showing how the poem has undergone critical rehabilitation, so that it can now be recognized as one of Northern England's greatest poems. In the second part we examine the text's allusions (long problematic) to places in Cumbria and beyond. Several can be identified as lordships in fifteenth-century Scotland, Wales, and Ireland, implying that the poet was well-informed and knew people of rank. This brings us to the third section, on the text as a historical source for the Borders and their grandees (above all the Neville family) in 1424 or 1425, when it may have been recited to an élite audience at Carlisle; for it is no dream-work, but (within its frame of entertainment) a political and moral sermon, or Tract for the Times. (If *Sir Gawain and the Green Knight* was intended for recitation in 1387 at Chester Castle, the *Awntyrs* was perhaps meant for other festivities nearly forty years later at Carlisle Castle.) Besides its historical implications are literary ones. Its author has sometimes been taken as a Scot, but his point of view is consistently English. The action is Anglocentric. When a Scottish knight appears, he is a dispossessed suppliant and outsider, who is worsted in combat. England dominates Scotland, Wales, Ireland, Brittany, France, and even Italy. The poem will be part of English literature, not Scottish. It is not a candidate for *The Oxford Book of Scottish Verse*.

Our analysis begins a century ago in Connecticut, where John Edwin Wells stated that the poem is about Gawain rather than Arthur, the title being a misnomer; dated it to the middle or later fourteenth century; and gave its provenance as probably Carlisle or its region. The four manuscripts are all of the fifteenth century: the Ireland Blackburne Manuscript (now at Princeton, New Jersey); Thornton Manuscript (Lincoln, Chapter Library, MS 91, now deposited in Nottingham University Library); Oxford, Bodleian Library, MS Douce 324 (= MS 21898); and London, Lambeth Palace, MS 491. Wells also summarized the plot, which in essence is this.

Arthur leaves Carlisle to go hunting, accompanied by Gawain and Queen Guinevere. While these two are resting under a laurel, a storm breaks out. In the midst of wind and lightning appears a repulsive hag, come back from the dead. She is Guinevere's mother, in torture for a life of sin. She warns of the world's transience, asks for masses to free her soul from Purgatory, and prophesies doom for Arthur and his court, unless they abandon their life of frivolity and social oppression. The skies clear and she vanishes. The hunters rendezvous and go to supper. As they dine, a fair lady enters with Sir Galeron of Galloway, who has come to reclaim lands seized by Arthur. Gawain, to whom Arthur gave those domains, challenges him; on the following day they fight and are wounded. When Gawain is about to overpower his opponent, Guinevere (at the lady's request) induces Arthur to stop the tournament. Galeron yields his rights to Gawain, to whom Arthur grants lordships in Wales, Ireland, and Brittany. Galeron receives back his territory at Gawain's request, marries the lady, and becomes one of Arthur's knights. The poem closes with reference to masses said for the soul of Guinevere's mother. Wells praised the poet's "eye for color and glitter and show" and his vivid imagination, which together prompted early editions by John Pinkerton (1786), David Laing (1822), Sir Frederic Madden (1839), John Robson (1842), and F. J. Armours (1892–97), as also a Berlin dissertation (1883) by Hermann Lübke on its manuscripts, metre, and author.[1]

As an alliterative poem, *The Awntyrs off Arthure* gained attention from J. P. Oakden, who described the Ireland Manuscript as written in Lancashire, where it still was (in private hands) when he wrote, but the Thornton Manuscript (from East Newton, near Ampleforth, Yorkshire) as best representing the original dialect. He dated the work to "the latter part of the fourteenth century."[2] He thereafter commented on the poem's moral emphasis (condemnation of Guinevere's infidelities and Arthur's greed) and supposed poor construction, the latter yet redeemed by a gift for description. A hunt sets out, a storm breaks, a phantom appears, a banquet is interrupted by a stranger and his lady, knights fight a duel: each is presented "with minute detail and an eye for colour" throughout.[3]

In contrast was George Kane. The romance was for him among those best "described as curiosities" or "minor developments" which are distinguished "by too much talent and too little art."[4] Kane did not like the poem. John Speirs liked it too much. He praised its "exuberant and often vivid imagery" as with the "dazzling and massive impression of the Pride of Life" in the "glowing hunting-scene" which begins it, paralleling *Sir Gawain and the Green Knight* itself. A rare factual comment on "Fraunce haf ye frely with your fight wonnen" (line 274) as a comparison of Arthur with Edward III (perhaps "intended by the poet") shows that he put the work before 1377.[5]

More moderate than either Kane or Speirs was O'Loughlin. He noted the poet's apparent imitation of *Sir Gawain and the Green Knight*, which he thought placed him "after 1375" or so; a *terminus ante quem* is provided by the "five [sic] manuscripts" of the fifteenth century. O'Loughlin dismissed for linguistic reasons a link with the Clerk of Tranent (in East Lothian, Scotland) whom William Dunbar (d. 1513?) lamented as author of "the anteris of Gawane" (hardly this text), but spoke up for the poet's "vigour and realism."[6] On borrowings from *Sir Gawain and the Green Knight*, we may observe that this poem surely postdates 1375 and is perhaps (as pointed out elsewhere) of 1387.

By 1970, *The Awntyrs off Arthure* was still being described as "late fourteenth-early fifteenth century" with the rider that (supposed) influence in the opening hunting scene from *Sir Gawain and the Green Knight* is dubious. This passage is taken as perhaps independent. The complete text is however "a genuinely courtly poem" which condemns Arthur as a "covetous" land-grabber. As regards reference to places near Carlisle, these were evidently "familiar to the audience."[7] John Burrow mentioned the romance as among writings "which perhaps belong to our period 1370–1400" or the age of Chaucer and Richard II.[8] But this cannot be right. The fourteenth century is out of the question.

That this is so is thanks mainly to the publication in 1974 of a new edition based on MS Douce 324. It remains essential. Imitation in the poem of the alliterative *Morte Arthure* and (less conclusively) *Sir Gawain and the Green Knight* made its editor "very hesitant to claim a date" for it much before 1400; its appearance in the Thornton Manuscript rules out one later than about 1430. The date settled for was therefore "approximately 1400–1430" and "probably" its second decade.[9] Less satisfactory, as we shall see, are editorial attempts to identify toponyms.

The 1970s thus saw increased regard for the poem. Derek Pearsall contrasted its two parts, the second seeming "grafted onto the first" with its language being "less vigorous, more conventional" and its stanza form less effective.[10] There remained disagreement on the poet's nationality. One scholar spoke of this "strange and interesting poem" merely as "a northern

work" showing points of contact with *Sir Gawain and the Green Knight* and
other poetry of the north-west Midlands, but also (in its metre) with later
Scottish poetry.[11] Another referred to it without qualification as among many
instances of "alliterative rhymed stanzaic verse" in "Scottish poetry."[12] Jack
Bennett offered a different view again, typifying the romance as "another
product of that local North Western culture that flowered in *Sir Gawain and
the Green Knight*" (associated with Cheshire). He did not relate it to Scotland.
On literary qualities, he praised it for its eeriness and implicit questioning of
the Arthurian knightly ideal, before observing that the worst thing about it is
"its misleading title: nothing whatever happens to Arthur" at Tarn Wadling.[13]

With Rosamund Allen, who edited the text for a 1968 London doctorate,
we find serious consideration of the difficulties. She regards the poem as a
"satire on the chivalric ethos" and an attack on "aristocratic assumptions of
an automatic right" to luxurious living; notes how the phantom speaks up
for "the rights of the poor and the conquered" (while warning against "luf
peramour"); and makes the arresting claim that the romance is about not
Gawain, still less Arthur, but "the role of women in upper-class society" (with
"the vanity of human ambition" as its overarching theme). Further comments
have similar weight. The dialect of the original (Northern and "probably that
of Cumberland") is modified in all four manuscripts. Of these, Thornton
predates 1454 and is in Yorkshire dialect; Ireland-Blackburne is of the late
fifteenth century and in the Midlands dialect of south Lancashire; Douce,
of 1450 × 1475, is also in Midlands dialect, of north-east Derbyshire; and
Lambeth (its text discovered in 1890) may be as early as 1425 × 1450, but
has been recast in Southern dialect (now known as an Essex one). Further
problems for editors are created by lacunae varying from six lines in Douce
to over a hundred in Thornton. Even the common origin of all four texts, their
stemma represented technically as <Ir[D(TL)]>, was "very corrupt" (because
of oral transmission?); there is also conflation in Ireland-Blackburne and possibly Lambeth.[14]

Nine years later, Ros Allen considered the problems again. She remarked
on how "no agreement has yet been reached about the date of composition" and some take parts of the work as "written decades apart" for unlike
readerships; she maintained, however, that the poem "can be fairly exactly
plotted to match a specific political moment" (perhaps that of a "celebra-
tion"). Its words on Arthur's campaigns in France surely denote "English
conquests in France from 1415 to 1424" and there are likewise allusions to
"the Border politics of northern England" in the first quarter of the fifteenth
century, when it was "the northernmost front of the Hundred Years War"
(a point worth recalling). She related the joust of Galeron and Gawain to
tournaments of English and Scots, some of them at Carlisle. Important too

are Ralph Neville, Earl of Westmorland, who married Henry IV's half-sister (and from 1420 "wielded great power on the west march"), and James I of Scotland, who in February 1424 married Joan Beaufort, Henry IV's niece (and so Ralph's kinswoman by marriage). The poem "seems to reflect" territories which James had acquired by 1425, while "Bretayne and Burgoyne is both in your bandoun" (line 276, *bandoun* being "authority, dominion") may locate it after the English regained control of Brittany, and therefore "between spring 1423 and the signing of a treaty between Brittany and the dauphinist forces" in December 1425. The conclusion is of a work alluding to events in 1424–1425, and perhaps written "in honour of the Nevilles" by a cleric of St Mary's Priory, Carlisle. It can be understood as a "clever, almost amusing, poem" which yet has a sober message on the vanity of this world, and might be suitable for reciting at festivities (perhaps for a marriage) in 1424 or 1425.[15] She summarized her views elsewhere, again proposing composition between 1423 and 1426, and links with the Nevilles, connected by marriage with James I, who was both King of Scots and Earl of Carrick (a region mentioned in lines 419 and 679). She thinks it "almost certain" that the poet knew *Sir Gawain and the Green Knight* and, after comparison of his work with other verse and prose, visualizes its performance before lords and ladies at Carlisle, the more perceptive of whom might there find "mirrored in the ghost's physical disintegration the deterioration of the very culture being commodified in the poem" being read to them.[16]

We have come a long way from the dismissiveness of Kane and enthusiasm of Speirs. Yet older views are still repeated by Thomas Hahn, who took the romance ("with Gawain as the cement for a remarkable literary structure") as of about 1375.[17] Margaret Robson examines, if without particular conclusions, "why the decomposing corpse of Guinevere's mother should appear to her daughter and Sir Gawain."[18] Quite different is a fourth paper by Rosamund Allen. It deals with place-names, crucial for questions of date and context. Among its many points are these.

The toponyms (styled "baffling") are of four kinds: those of Galeron's confiscated estates in Scotland's southwest; those of estates later granted to Gawain; "political" forms from the Continent; and local Cumberland terms. The second of these are taken as "estates of the Duke of York" and, like the others, "link the poem to the political context" of about 1425. Naturally, they perplexed copyists, above all the scribe of the Lambeth Manuscript. (Analysis of his dialect now shows him as from Rayleigh, near Southend in Essex.) After comments on women in the romance (commissioned by Joan, Ralph Neville's countess?), Ros Allen returns to place-names. The three in lines 420 and 681 are "probably Lanark, Lennox, and possibly Lowther" (or else Lothian). *Locher* in 678 could be Lugar (near Ayr) or Lochar (near Dumfries); *Lile* in 681 may be Lady Isle, off Troon. *Criffones* in 667 is certainly

Caerphilly, South Wales. *Ulster Hall* in 668 is regarded not as Oysterlow, west of Carmarthen, but related to Ulster. *Wayford* in 669 is emended to "Warkworth" (which is preferred to Wexford, Ireland). *Waterford* in the same line is nevertheless accepted as the Irish city. As for dating, 1424–1425 was a significant period of "betrothals, marriages, and consequent land acquisition" for the Neville dynasty. Ros Allen regards it as fixing the poem's first public reading between January 1424, when James I and Joan Beaufort were about to marry, and early 1425, when Richard of York came of age, and certainly before Ralph Neville's death that October.[19] The poem is from the circle of the great. Ralph was brother-in-law of Henry IV; his daughter Cecily was wife to Richard of York and mother to Edward IV and Richard III. No surprise that our author had a sharp eye for the English nobility's ceremonies, clothes, jewels, armour, weapons, horses, lands, and dovecot morals.

Of five subsequent critics, none mentions Rosamund Allen's research on the poem. Tony Spearing instead cites papers by himself on "manifestions or significant displacements of sovereignty" perceived in it.[20] Rosalind Field calls it "an original and subversive remaking of Arthurian tradition that requires of its audience the ability to recognize a dense interweaving of reference."[21] Douglas Gray comments on how the work possesses "an impressive unity, and shows a thoughtful interest in mutability" and noble lordship, but (despite reference to Hanna, who thinks no such thing) still considers it as possibly "from the end of the fourteenth century."[22] Siân Echard typifies it as "a sermon dressed up as a romance" which alludes to the power of masses said in intercession for the dead.[23] Corinne Saunders well conveys the horror of the ghost's visit. On a fine day, darkness comes without warning (with Gawain first regarding it as an eclipse). Rain and snow begin falling; flames shoot from a nearby tarn; the apparition advances toward Gawain and Guinevere. But her conclusion ("The work provides a chilling reminder that the transformative power of the Christian supernatural may be physically corrosive as well as healing") does not materially advance understanding of the work.[24]

By now readers will have had enough of literary criticism. Yet it should be clear how *The Awntyrs off Arthure* has been more highly valued since the 1970s than at any time since the fifteenth century. In our second part we turn to names of persons and places in the poem, especially those considered as insoluble, which may yet not be mysterious at all. They are set out in order of appearance and are quoted from Fichte's recent edition, which uses Hanna's text.[25]

(1) The first form is straightforward (lines 1–2):

> In the tyme of Arthur an aunter bytydde,

By the Turne Wathelan, as the boke telles.

The place is Tarn Wadling, in Inglewood Forest. Long drained, the lake was in a hollow between fells some nine miles south–southeast of Carlisle and just east (at National Grid Reference NY 4844) of the village of High Hesket. It appears as a place of supernatural encounters in romances of Sir Percival and Sir Gawain also edited by Fichte, but its reputation for the uncanny is older, being mentioned in about 1200 by Gervase of Tilbury (see below).

> (2) When Gawain and Guinevere are addressed by her mother, she tells
> them (lines 144–45):

> > "Quene was I somewile, brighter of browes
> > Then Beryke or Brangwayn, thes burdes [=ladies] so bolde."

Who was "Beryke"? Hanna (regarding this reading in Thornton as representing "the detritus of some unrecoverable proper name") proposed emendation to "Brysen." She figures in Malory as a sorceress who tricks Lancelot, so that he sleeps with Elaine in the belief that he is with Guinevere. Fichte, misunderstanding Hanna, states "In T[hornton] findet man Brysen, den Namen der Zauberin, die Lancelot dazu verführte, mit Elaine zu schlafen." But "Brysen" is an editorial emendation, not a manuscript reading. As such there are three objections to it. First, if Brysen had been celebrated for beauty, Lancelot might have shown more interest in her. Second, Brangwayn is the confidante of Isolt or Iseut in the legend of Tristan. Her name is Celtic (as are those of Isolt and Tristan); "Beryke" may thus also be Celtic. If so, it could refer to Perwyr, a British princess of filmstar looks.[26] She lived in the sixth century and her name confused even Welsh scribes, who often wrote it *Berwevr*.[27] Third, it is hence easier to read "Beryk" as a corruption of "Berwyr" or even "Beryr," closer to the manuscript reading than "Brysen" is. It would be among the poem's many allusions to Celtic tradition, with its "k" perhaps due to scribal confusion with the name of Berwick-on-Tweed.

> (3) The spectre of Guinevere's mother prophesies doom in a battle-charge
> for Arthur's court, and death for Sir Gawain (lines 293–300).

> > "Ther shal the Rounde Table lese the renoune
> > Beside Ramsey ful rad [quickly] at a riding;
> > In Dorsetshire shal dy the doughtést of alle.
> > Gete the, Sir Gawayne,
> > The boldest of Bretayne;
> > In a slake [=hollow in mudbanks] thou shal be slayne,
> > Such ferlyes [marvels] shull falle.
> > Such ferlies shull fal, without eny fable,

Uppon Cornewayle coost with a knight kene."

This is less difficult than supposed. In discussing sources and analogues, Hanna wavers between Richborough and Romney (both in Kent) and Romsey in Hampshire, opting for the last, which he imagines the poet (with "a northern perspective") mislocated to Dorset. In his note Fichte describes Hanna as conjecturing "dass der Autor Romney mit Romsey in Hampshire verwechselt." We simplify this. The place is neither Richborough, defunct as a port since ancient times, nor Romsey (six miles from the sea), which was never one. It is Romney, Kent. Old Romney was probably silted up by 1086; its functions passed to New Romney (NGR TR 0624), two miles away, then with an excellent harbor making it one of the Cinque Ports.[28] That it is Romney is proved by Wace and his English translator, who tell how Arthur, on hearing of treachery, returned to Britain, crossing the Channel from Whitsand or Wissant (west of Calais) to *Romerel* or Old Romney.[29] The usurpers there gave him a warm reception.[30]

> As the dawn was breaking, they started fighting;
> And went on all that long day: many a man there lay dead.

Among the victims was Gawain, who died like a hero. Arthur then moved westwards, besieging Winchester and advancing through Dorset to the last battle in Cornwall. Although the alliterative fourteenth-century *Morte Arthure* makes no mention of Romney, it does describes the later campaign, with the king sorrowful but fearless.[31]

> Thane drawes he to Dorsett, and dreches [delays] no langere,
> Derefulle [full of grief] dredlesse with drowppande teris;
> Kayeris [progresses] in-to Kornewayle with kare at his herte.

So the poet's geography is exact, as proved by the *slake* "mudbank hollow" where Gawain died. There were plenty of these on Romney Marsh, where Arthur began fighting his way from Kent to Cornwall via Dorset: a campaign well understood by the poet, who possessed exceptional knowledge of Insular geography. The "Ramsey" of the text will be an error for "Romney" and cannot derive from 'Richborough'; the poet will have known of Romney after Wace and his English translator.

(4) With a chilling moan, the spirit glides away; sunlight returns; there is a sound of horns, the hunt appears, Lady Guinevere and others go to dine (lines 336–38).

> Dame Gaynour and alle,

> Rayked [went] to Rondolesette Halle
> To the suppere.

This place has caused unnecessary confusion. In 1842, John Robson with reason put it near Plumpton Wall (NY 4937), four miles south of Tarn Wadling (and alluded to in line 475). Armours, however, opted for Randalholm Hall (NY 7048), near Alston, despite logistical difficulties. The spot is fifteen miles as the crow flies from Tarn Wadling and the far side of a 1900-foot pass. Jean Jost cites these suppositions with Walkling's understanding of the place as a *hale* or temporary pavilion, a word of French origin.[32] But *hale* seems otherwise unknown in English toponymy, and it does not rhyme with *alle*. Fichte further cites Walkling on the place as Randulph Seat "auf der höchsten Erhebung am Rande des Inglewood Forest" (a notion putting it 900 feet up on moors north of Caldbeck, twelve miles west of Tarn Wadling). This windy height is, however, no place for a banquet. The royal hunt would instead dine at a point on the Roman highway (now the A6 trunk road) from Penrith to Carlisle. Medieval England had few good roads, and this one would be needed to bring furniture, awnings, utensils, food, and drink from Carlisle. Rondolesette Halle was surely at a sheltered point on the Carlisle-Penrith road, and probably somewhere on the five miles between High Hesket and Plumpton Wall. That this old military road (running through a forest that would discourage excursions to right or left) was a natural place for assembly is unexpectedly demonstrated by Hesket's very name. It is from the Norse for "race course, place where horses run in competition."[33] Rondolesette Halle would be near it.

(5) Galaron and his lady interrupt the feasting. He is a Scotsman with a grievance (lines 417–20).

> "Mi name is Sir Galaron, sans eny gile,
> The grettest of Galwey of greves and gylles [thickets and ravines],
> Of Connok, of Carrak, of Conyngham, of Kyle,
> Of Lonrik, of Lennex, of Loudan Hilles."

"Galwey" is Galloway in southwest Scotland, later Wigtownshire and the Stewartry of Kirkcudbright. "Connok" is Cumnock (NS 5619), a town fifteen miles east of Ayr. Carrick, Cunningham, and Kyle are the ancient southern, northern, and central divisions of Ayrshire.[34] "Lonrick" is certainly Lanark (NS 8843), southeast of Glasgow; "Lennox" is the region northwest of Glasgow; "Loudan" refers not to Lothian hills but those of Loudoun, near Galston (NS 5036), fourteen miles northwest of Ayr. Galaron's lost domains were all on Scotland's western side. They were correctly identified by Armours as quoted in Hanna's endnotes. Fichte believes that they lay "an der heftig umkämpften Grenze zu England" (but Ayrshire and Lanarkshire do not border England).

(6) Gawain will not renounce his claim, and matters are settled by force. Preparations are made for a tournament nearby (lines 475–76), with a palisade or enclosure "set up where no warrior on earth had fought previously":

> By that on Plumton Land a palais [enclosure] was pight,
> Were never freke opon folde had foughten biforne.

The place is by Plumpton Wall (NY 4937), five miles north of Penrith and on the road to Carlisle. Materials and equipment for the lists (line 477) and a platform for royal spectators (492) hence might readily be brought there.

(7) Arthur orders a noble retainer to attend to Galaros (lines 482–83), so that he can breakfast in his tent on "rich dayntée" and be armed, leaving his lady with Guinevere.

> The king commaunded Krudely, the erlis son of Kent:
> "Curtaysly in this case, take kepe to the knight."

Hanna (remarking that nobody "of this name appears in the Middle English Arthuriana") took him as perhaps Cradoc of Caerleon (which is in Wales, however, not Kent). Allen in 1987 thought the original irretrievable. Yet Kywryd of Kent is known in Welsh tradition as the father of Guinevere. Arthur would be speaking to his father-in-law, who (as the poem makes evident) became a widower after a difficult marriage. Fichte now remarks of "Krudely" that "In der Artusliteratur ist dieser Name unbekannt" (before quoting Hanna's conjecture on Cradoc). But it is easier to relate "Krudely of Kent" to Cywryd of Kent. "Krudely" is closer to "Cywryd" than it is to "Cradoc"; Cywryd was related to Arthur by marriage, unlike Cradoc; Cywryd was specifically linked with Kent, Cradoc was not. The implication is of a poet knowing of Cywryd not directly from Wales, but from survivals of British tradition in Cumbria, where Cumbric (a language closely related to Welsh) was spoken until about 1100.[35]

(8) When the joust ends abruptly, Arthur orders these knights to attend to the combatants (lines 654–55):

> Sir Ewayn Fiz Vrian and Arrak Fiz Lake,
> Marrake and Meneduke, that most wer of might.

The poet took their names from the alliterative *Morte Arthure*. The first is Owain ab Urien, whose father ruled Rheged (on the Upper Eden and beyond) in the late sixth century, and who is the Yvain of Chrétien de Troyes. The second is his contemporary Geraint ab Erbin, ruler of Devon and Cornwall, and hero of Chrétien's *Erec*.[36] Marrake is less familiar, but Hanna cites Malory for him as one of Arthur's commanders. He may represent King Mark (the betrothed of ill-fated Isolt), who is known as a "true pan-Celtic character of folklore" in early Wales, Brittany, and Cornwall.[37] If so, his appearance in Middle English may show influence from the Britons of Southern Scotland. As for Meneduk (also mentioned by Malory), he is perhaps Mynyddog, who in the early seventh century ruled the Gododdin of southeast Scotland.[38] He has recently been a focus of interest.[39] The knights all seem protagonists of the British Heroic Age, with Marrake and Meneduk of special interest because Malory and others knew them not from French sources, but ultimately (it appears) from Celtic ones that had passed (in Scotland and northwest England?) directly into English.

(9) Honor has been satisfied. Arthur settles the dispute with grants to Sir Gawain (lines 664–71), whom he also creates a duke.

> "Here I gif the Sir Gawayn, with gerson [treasure] and golde,
> Al the Glamergan londe with greves [thickets] so grene,
> The worship of Wales at wil and at wolde,
> With Criffones Castelles curnelled [crenelated] ful clene;
> Eke Ulstur Halle to have and to holde,
> Wayford and Waterforde, walled I wene;
> Two baronrées in Bretayne with burghes so bolde,
> That arn batailed abought and bigged ful bene [built well]."

Hanna declared how on much of this "one can only make guesses" (with "Criffones" as a reference to Crieff in Scotland or Griff Grange in Derbyshire). But Rosamund Allen in her paper of 1996 cited the reading "Cirfre Castell" from Ireland-Blackburne and proposed Caerphilly Castle, one of the biggest in Europe. Her argument was supported by a paper of 1999, citing references to Caerphilly as *Kaerfili* and *kaerffili* (which might give the corrupt reading "Cirfre"), and taking "Ulstur Halle" as the lordship of Oysterlow in West Wales, and "Wayford" as Wexford, Ireland.[40] In her paper of 2004, Dr. Allen accepted the first but not the other two, regarding "Ulstur Hall" as to do with Ulster and "Wayworth" as Warkworth Castle, Northumberland. Making no reference to any of this, Professor Fichte echoes Hanna, stating that "Glamorganshire" is a part of South Wales "mit den bedeutenden Städten Cardiff und Swansea"; "Ulstur Halle und Waterforde verweisen auf Territorien in Irland"; and "Criffones Castelles könnte auf Crieff, Perthshire, oder auf Griff Grange in Nord-Derbyshire verweisen" (although neither of these was in Wales or had a famous castle with battlements).

Let us restate the identity of these places. First, Glamorgan. The reference is to the medieval lordship, smaller than the modern county. It extended from Cardiff to Neath, but did not include Swansea, which was in the lordship of Gower, united with Glamorgan to make the modern county only under Henry VIII. In the fifteenth century Glamorgan was a possession of the Nevilles (it also had connections with Richard of York, who was Ralph Neville's ward) and Gower of the Mowbrays. To the west of them and of Carmarthen was the small (but profitable) lordship of Islwyf or Oysterlow.[41] Oysterlow is known only to specialists; Ulster is known to everybody; despite the dangers of *lectio facilior*, even professional scholars have preferred the latter, although it does not explain the second "u" of "Ulstur" or its "Hall." So let us examine a few sources for Oysterlow, which not only give early spellings of its name, but show it as territory disputed between the Crown and the Earls of Pembroke.

Letters patent in London, British Library, Charter Harley 51 H 10, of 1443, grant to William de la Pole, Earl of Suffolk, the title of Earl of Pembroke, as also lands in South Wales including that of *Estrelawe*.[42] Sir John Lloyd gave its original centre as at Llanddowror (SN 2514), ten miles west–southwest of Carmarthen, and its name as Oisterlaph, a mangling of Welsh *Ystlwyf* or Ysterlwyf. A letter of 1288 or 1289 shows the uncertainty of its spelling, with William de Valence, Earl of Pembroke, complaining how "the king's men had ejected him from the land of Osterlef" which is also called "Osterlowe" and "Osterloue" in the same document.[43] Sir Rees Davies spoke of the way that Edward I regularly "exploited any weakness in the title or position of a Marcher lord to turn the screw of royal pressure" and how the "uncertain claim of Valence to the commote of Ystlwyf" was "soon seized upon by Edward's lawyers" to put it under royal administration from Carmarthen.[44] One result of such contentions was the moving of the lordship's caput from Llanddowror to Meidrim (SN 2820), seven miles west of Carmarthen.[45] The question was (like much else) resolved by Henry VIII, with Ystlwyf confirmed as in Carmarthenshire and for all time excluded from the County of Pembroke.

Rosamund Allen on "Wayford and Waterforde, walled I wene" makes out the first as Warkworth. This will not do, for four reasons. First, in the context of centuries of Border warfare, it would have been spectacularly tactless for this English stronghold to be given to a Scot. Second, Warkworth was not "walled" but had a castle and fortified bridge only. Pevsner makes this obvious. "To give the bridge a tower was a necessity; for the village lies in a loop of the river and, once an attacker could enter it from the north, he was not separated from the Keep by any curtain wall or any other defence save a moat."[46] A photograph proves the point.[47] Third, Wexford is recorded in fifteenth-century documents as *Weysford*.[48] Warkworth, on the other hand, always appears more or less in this form from its earliest attestation (in about 1050) as *Werceworthe*.[49] The poem's "Wayford" is an easy misrendering of the first, but not the second. Fourth, a progression Caerphilly-Oysterlow-Wexford-Waterford in Arthur's (or the poet's) mind goes logically from east to west. To bring in Warkworth disrupts its order by a violent shift to the north. The passage has a fundamental implication. Arthur makes free with domains in Wales and Ireland (and Brittany), but does not give away English terrain, even to Sir Gawain.

(10) His dignity acknowledged by lands in three countries, Sir Gawain thereupon restores Galeron's lands to their rightful lord (lines 677–82):

> "Now here I gif Sir Galeron," quod Gawayn, "withouten any gile,
> Al the londes and the lithes [vassals] fro Laver to Ayre,
> Connok and Carrak, Conyngham and Kile
> (Als the chevalrous knyghte hase chalandchede als ayere [claimed as inheritance]),
> The Lother, the Lemmok, the Loynak, the Lile,
> With frethis [woods] and forestes and fosses so faire."

There are variants. For Douce's *Lauer*, Ireland-Blackburne has *Logher*. In Thornton, line 681 is "The Lebynge, the Lowpynge, Þe Leveastre Iles" (which is obviously corrupt).

Cumnock and the three parts of Ayrshire we have dealt with. As for the rest, Hanna could identify none of them, although he thought "Lemmok" and "Loynak" might both mean Lennox; alternatively, "Lemmok" might be Lemmington, Northumberland. He took "Lebynge" in Thornton as perhaps the River Leven, described as flowing "through Dumbartonshire from Loch Lomond to the Firth of Forth" (where the geography is defective; the Leven enters the Firth of Clyde). In the 1998 paper already cited, the present writer identified Laver as Lavery Burn (NX 2679), south Ayrshire. Rosamund Allen in 2004 regarded Ireland-Blackburne's *Logher* in 678 as referring to Lugar Water (NS 5821) near Cumnock or (after Armours) Lochar Water (NY 0178), east of Dumfries, and *the Lile* in 681 as perhaps Lady Isle, off Troon. Professor Fichte, making no reference to this, now states, "Die hier genannten Namen lassen sich nicht mit Sicherheit identifizieren." He follows Hanna for the Laver as Laversdale in Cumbria or one of the villages Lever, Lanes, or Laverton in Yorkshire, and closes "Soll Lother auf die Lothian Hills verweisen?"

Let us be exact. "Ayr" will mean not Ayrshire or the borough of Ayr, as Hanna supposes, but the River Ayr, giving its name to the town. "Laver" thus makes sense as another river, Lavery Burn in the far south of Ayrshire, its source less than a mile from the border with Galloway. It is also easier textually to relate Lavery to Douce's "Lauer" than Lugar to Ireland-Blackburne's "Logher." Other toponyms may at once be discarded, because they were not in Ayrshire, and Arthur would scarcely endow a Scotsman with estates in England.

As for line 681, "the" refers to geographical regions, not rivers. The *OED* entry for *the* 3b actually cites "The Lennox" and "The Merse" as designating territory. They resemble "The Garioch" (in Aberdeenshire), "The Stormont" (in Perthshire), and so on.[50] "The Lother" is thus Lauderdale (Berwickshire/ Borders), its feudal caput at Lauder (NT 5347) and the form attested as *Louueder* in 1208.[51] It was prominent as soon as Hugh de Morville (d. 1162) became lord of Lauderdale, thus gaining immense power, for he was also lord of Cunningham.[52] The family is best known from Hugh's son, another Hugh, who is notorious as one of Becket's murderers. The Honour of Lauderdale allows us to take "the Lother" as "the Lauder." It is nothing to do with Lothian.

The second term ("the Lemmok") must be the Lennox, as Hanna suggests. Lennox, documented as an earldom from about 1165 onward, is the area around Loch Lomond. In 1425 it was in the news. That year, according to the Annals of Ulster, "the Earl of Lennox was destroyed through treachery by the King of Scotland": a circumstance which helps date the poem.[53] Duncan, eighth Earl of Lennox, was arrested on James I's initiative in late 1424. With others he was eventually tried by his peers, found guilty, and hastened off to execution.[54] That was in May 1425. With the Earl of Lennox dead, his lands were free to give to another. It perhaps explains the text's allusion to the Lennox and dates it to between the early summer of 1425 and October, when Ralph Neville died. As for "the Loynak," this will not be Lennox (again) but the lordship of Lanark, in Clydesdale. It has already appeared as "Lonrik" at line 420. It is further evidence for the poet as an Englishman. Lanark Castle was held by the Scottish Crown, and a subject of the King of Scots might hesitate to represent a royal possession as given away. But that would not trouble anyone in England, notwithstanding the marriage of Ralph Neville's niece to James, King of Scots.

As regards "the Lile," this is another Scottish lordship. It cannot be Lady Isle (NS 2729), three miles off Troon. Lady Isle is a "desolate rocky island with a lighthouse."[55] Lacking revenues, it had no interest for medieval magnates. Because rhyme and alliteration fix the form, the reference will instead be to the Lyle or Lyell family of Duchal (NS 3567), between Greenock and Paisley. The fifteenth century saw them reach their zenith. In 1444, Robert Lyle of Duchal was claiming lands on Deeside by descent from Isabel, Countess of Mar; in 1452, Alexander, Lord Lyle of Duchal, was rewarded by James II for support against the Earl of Crawford.[56] So "the Lile" apparently signifies estates of a powerful Renfrewshire dynasty.

(11) A line in the final stanza locates its action (709):

> This ferely [marvel] bifelle in Engelwode Forest.

Ingelwood Forest, with residual woodlands, is still marked on Ordnance Survey maps. It was a royal domain of varying bounds. In about 1250 it extended from the River Eden west to the Forest of Allerdale, itself reaching to the Cumbrian coast.[57] But Hesket, with Skelton and Hutton-in-the-Forest south of it, was at its core. That the region north of Penrith was once heavily wooded is a reminder of local difficulties in communication. The Roman road to Carlisle was vital in war and peace alike.

Now for our third part and some conclusions. There is no need to restate the implications of the romance's lordships in Scotland, Wales, and Ireland for Ralph Neville (d. 1425), Earl of Westmorland, and his son-in-law Richard (1411–1460), Duke of York. They were set out in detail by Rosamund Allen (with her arguments modified in the present writer's 1999 *Arthuriana* paper). Thanks to them, the poem provides focus on the Northern nobility in the middle months of 1425. It was an interesting period. Anglo-Scottish relations were amicable. After years of captivity in England, James I (d. 1437) was released in December 1424. Two months later he married the younger Joan or Jane Beaufort (Joan Neville's niece) in what is now Southwark Cathedral, a memorial of their courtship being *The Kingis Quair*, written by James himself.[58] Like *The Awntyrs off Arthure*, it is a poem written in 1424–25 at a period of Anglo-Scottish *rapprochement*.

Coming from a period of *détente* for English relations with France and Scotland, *The Awntyrs off Arthure* also contains a theory of imperialism (as Jean Jost observes in her article of 2012). When Arthur does justice, he does not do so at the expense of English territory, but by disposing freely of lands in Scotland, Wales, Ireland, and Brittany. That is why we can be sure that the poet was an Englishman (if one who desires justice for Scotland). The unknown English poet was, nevertheless, familiar with traditions of British kings and heroes. Cumbria was seemingly rich in legends of them, even after the Cumbric language became extinct in the early twelfth century.

Three final points. The *Awntyrs* poet is thought to have known another Northern romance, *Sir Gawain and the Green Knight*, which mentions Cheshire places and is surely the work of a Cheshire magnate who was expert on hunting and armour, as also the sophistication and luxuries of Richard II's court.[59] The poem will be of 1387, while *Pearl*, by the same author, is of 1390.[60] The relationship between the Cheshire poem and the Cumberland one would repay comprehensive analysis, but we can make a first point immediately. *Sir Gawain and the Green Knight* is in the Midland dialect of Cheshire, differing sharply from that of the *Awntyrs* poet, which is Northern. If he knew the earlier poem so well that he based his own work upon it, the notion of there being "no evidence" for its circulation "outside this dialect area" (of the northwest Midlands) is disproved.[61]

As for Tarn Wadling, its links with mystery long predate the fifteenth century. So much is proved by Gervase of Tilbury (active around 1200), who described it thus.

> In Great Britain there is a forest, rich in many kinds of game, which looks down on the city of Carlisle. Roughly in the middle of this forest there is a valley surrounded by hills near a public highway. In this valley, I say, every day at seven in the morning a gently-sounding peal of bells is heard; and so the locals have given that lonely place the name of Laikibrais *in idiomate Wallico* or the "Welsh" tongue.[62]

Now, Gervase's editors derive *Laikibrais* from the Old French for "lake that cries." It is hard to see why. Gervase gives the form as Welsh (or, better, Cumbric), not French. The standard reading is also inferior to his variant *Laikibrait*, according with the editors' citation of "in lacu de Terwathelan qui dicitur Laykebrayt" from *Pleas of the Forest of Inglewood* for 1290–1291. It is perhaps explained from the Welsh place-name forms *llech* "rock, slab" and *brad* "treachery."[63] Like Braydon Forest in Wiltshire (above which took place in 493 the siege of Mount "Bradon"), the place was perhaps the haunt of thieves. Hence a link with Welsh *brad* "betrayal." Less uncertain are folklore connections. In setting out sources and analogues, Hanna cited Joseph Ritson (1752–1803) for local legends of a castle or city under the lake, relating it "to some Celtic descriptions of the Other World" from which troublesome visitors might come. Early Welsh traditions of drowned cities are on record.[64] So, too, are accounts of Irish lakes as supernatural exits and entrances.[65] They are hence a further Celtic element in our Northern romance.

Last of all, the question of patronage. Examination of events in 1424 and 1425 might indicate more precisely when, where, and for whom such a poem was recited. In this context two points may be noted. By his two wives Ralph Neville had twenty-three children, twenty of whom survived infancy. Weddings were a frequent occurrence in the Neville household. So, too, were betrothals, including that of Ralph's youngest daughter, Cicely, to Richard of York (1411–1460). Ralph was already negotiating for it in 1423.[66] It leaves us with a choice. Rosamund Allen regards the poem as no earlier than the marriage in February 1424 of James I and Joan Beaufort the younger, when good relations between England and Scotland were secured, and no later than Ralph's death in October 1425. If we knew when Richard and Cicely were formally betrothed, this would be a suitable occasion for the poem, which has marriage and faithfulness in marriage among its themes. If its allusions to the

Lennox were topical, we could restrict it still further, to later than May 25, 1425, when "after a perfunctory trial" the Duke of Albany, two of his sons, and "his father-in-law, the aged Earl of Lennox" were executed at Stirling.[67]

On the subject of patronage, there is a further point about the Nevilles. Ralph, Earl of Westmorland, was a strenuous builder; Joan, Countess of Westmorland, preferred books. There are links with Chaucer (d. 1400), Hoccleve (d. 1426), Richard Rolle (d. 1349), and Walter Hilton (d. 1396). First, Chaucer. Cambridge, Corpus Christi College, MS 61 contains his *Troilus and Criseyde* and is a deluxe edition, with a famous illumination of Chaucer addressing an audience of high-ranking people. Among marginalia is the name "Anne neuyll." She has long been identified as a daughter of Ralph (by his second wife), who married Humphrey, Duke of Buckingham (d. 1460). Brusendorff inferred with what he thought "a fair degree of probability" that Anne's mother "had the Corpus manuscript transcribed from a family copy" of Chaucer's poem, "originally executed for her father John of Gaunt" in the 1380s.[68] Another writer is still more fanciful, imagining how Anne heard "family accounts of Chaucer reading before the court of Richard II" before "she secured a copy of a family manuscript to preserve in a book of her own" the love-poem by her grandmother's brother-in-law.[69] Others are colder. They merely date the volume to 1400 × 1425 and give its first known owner as John Shirley (d. 1456), London bookdealer and publisher.[70] Derek Pearsall then regarded it as of "about 1420" and supplied bibliography on its origins.[71]

As for Hoccleve, he addressed an envoy or final stanza to Joan Neville. It begins "Go, smal book, to the noble excellence / Of my lady of Westmerland and seye. . . . " The "smal book" (with these lines in Hoccleve's autograph) still exists. It is now Durham, University Library, MS Cosin V.iii.9.[72] Joan Neville was therefore one of Hoccleve's many patrons, who included the Prince of Wales, four dukes, a duchess, and a lord chancellor.[73] Thanks to this, she figures regularly in accounts of medieval literary patronage.[74] Hoccleve's links with her are even used for speculation on the Corpus manuscript's picture of Chaucer and the one in London, British Library, MS Harley 4866, containing Hoccleve's *De Regimine Principum.*[75] The Cosin manuscript has itself been subject to expert attention.[76] Its importance as "written by Hoccleve himself" for presentation to the Countess is obvious.[77] It is proof of her willingness to finance poets. It has also prompted the remark that England then "was neither a paradise nor a level playing-field for women of letters."[78] A curious claim, given that Joan possessed royal blood and quasi-regal wealth. The dedication to "my lady of westmerland" comes with material wherein the poet "broods with increasing bitterness upon the wiles of women," stirring another critic to wonder what she made of it.[79] More to the point is the way that these contacts with London poets show Joan Neville as interested in verse. They strengthen the case for her as patron of *The Awntyrs of Arthure*.

After poetry, religion. Joan Neville finds herself written into the autobiography of Margery Kempe (d. 1438?), who supposedly tried to persuade Lady Westmorland's daughter to leave her husband, and had to explain herself before the Archbishop of York, who yet treated her mildly.[80] Margery's interview with Joan took place in 1413 at Raby, the Neville's seat, near Durham. More significant is Joan's interest in the English mystics. It was shared by her youngest daughter Cicely (d. 1495), Duchess of York. She had Hilton's writings on Active and Contemplative Life read at her table, in addition to works by Continental female saints in "rather a highbrow collection."[81] It includes several texts printed at an early date. Joan herself possessed a copy of Rolle's *Meditations on the Passion*. It is now Cambridge, University Library, MS Additional 3042 and bears the inscription *Johanna unfortunata Westmerlandiae Cowntes*. She also, like her daughter, had special interest in Walter Hilton's *Scale of Perfection* and *Mixed Life*.[82]

We may conclude thus. What began as a commentary on place-name cruxes in a Northern poem ends by relating it to the Nevilles and events in England, Scotland, and France during 1424–1425. Further research on their literary interests may reinforce those connections. It may even be that investigation of the family's movements in those months, particularly for a festive occurrence in Carlisle (the betrothal of Cecily and Richard of York?), will allow us to suggest the exact day when *The Awntyrs off Arthure* was recited to its original audience.

NOTES

1. Wells, Manual, 61–62, 771.
2. Oakden, *Alliterative Poetry in Middle English: The Dialectal and Metrical Survey*, 113–14.
3. Oakden, *Alliterative Poetry in Middle English: A Survey of the Traditions*, 47–48.
4. Kane, *Middle English Literature*, 52–53.
5. Speirs, *Medieval English Poetry: The Non-Chaucerian Tradition*, 252–62.
6. O'Loughlin, "The English Alliterative Romances," 520–27.
7. D. J. Williams, "Alliterative Poetry in the Fourteenth and Fifteen Centuries," 107–58.
8. Burrow, *Ricardian Poetry*, 65.
9. Hanna, *The Awntyrs off Arthure at the Terne Wathelyn*, 50–52.
10. Pearsall, *Old English and Middle English Poetry*, 186.
11. Turville-Petre, *The Alliterative Revival*, 35.
12. Kratzmann, *Anglo-Scottish Literary Relations 1430–1550*, 8.

13. J. A. W. Bennett, *Middle English Literature*, 176–78.

14. Allen, "The Editing of *The Awntyrs off Arthure*," 6–25.

15. Allen, "*The Awntyrs off Arthure*: Jests and Jousts," 149–62.

16. Allen, "*The Awntyrs off Arthure*," 150–55.

17. Hahn, "Gawain and Popular Chivalric Romance in Britain," 218–34.

18. Robson, "Darkness at Noon in *The Awntyrs off Arthure*," 219–36.

19. Allen, "Place-Names," 181–98.

20. Spearing, *Textual Subjectivity*, 201.

21. Rosalind Field, "Subjects of Translation: Romance," 296–331.

22. Gray, *Later Medieval English Literature*, 386.

23. Echard, "Insular Romance," 160–80.

24. Saunders, *Magic and the Supernatural in Medieval English Romance*, 223.

25. Fichte, "*The Awntyrs off Arthure*," 135–200.

26. Bromwich, *Trioedd Ynys Prydein*, 492.

27. Breeze, "The Lady Beryke," 281–85.

28. Beresford and St. Joseph, *Medieval England: An Aerial Survey*, 205–7.

29. Brook, *Selections from La3amon's "Brut,"* 113–14.

30. Allen, *Brut*, 361.

31. Brock, *Morte Arthure*, 119.

32. Jost, "Marshy Spaces in the Middle English *Awntyrs off Arthure*," 589–606.

33. Watts, *The Cambridge Dictionary of English Place-Names*, 299.

34. Barrow, *The Anglo-Norman Era in Scottish History*, 59.

35. Fraser, *From Caledonia to Pictland: Scotland to 795*, 124–33.

36. Bromwich and Evans, *Culhwch and Olwen*, 80–81.

37. Padel, "The Cornish Background of the Tristan Stories," 53–81.

38. Jackson, *Gododdin*, 4, 12–13.

39. Koch, "Waiting for the Gododdin," 177–204.

40. Breeze, "*The Awntyrs off Arthure*, Caerphilly, Oysterlow, and Wexford," 63–68.

41. Rees, *An Historical Atlas of Wales*, plates 28, 36, 41, 43, 56.

42. Owen, *A Catalogue of the Manuscripts Relating to Wales in the British Museum*, 543.

43. Lloyd, A History of Wales, 266, 542.

44. Davies, *Lordship and Society in the March of Wales 1282–1400*, 263.

45. Anon., "Ystlwyf," 982.

46. Pevsner, *The Buildings of England: Northumberland*, 313.

47. Beresford & St. Joseph, *Medieval England*, 253.

48. Field, *Place-Names of Great Britain and Ireland*, 187.

49. Mills, *A Book of English Place-Names*, 346.

50. Watson, *The History of the Celtic Place-Names of Scotland*, 118, 120.

51. Room, *Dictionary of Place-Names in the British Isles*, 207.

52. Duncan, *Scotland: The Making of the Kingdom*, 135–36.

53. Jackson, *Gaelic Notes*, 104.

54. Dickinson, *Scotland from the Earliest Times to 1603*, 215.

55. Anon., "Lady Isle," 207.

56. McGladdery, *James II*, 22, 79.

57. Poole, *From Domesday Book to Magna Carta*, 28.

58. Norton-Smith, *The Kingis Quair*, xxii.

59. Breeze, "Sir John Stanley," 15–30.

60. Breeze, "*Pearl* and the Plague of 1390–1393," 337–41.

61. Putter and Stokes, *The Works of the Gawain Poet*, xi.

62. Banks and Binns, *Otia Imperialia*, 690–93.

63. Thomas, *Enwau Afonydd a Nentydd Cymru*, 4, 15.

64. Bromwich, "Cantre'r Gwaelod and Ker-Is," 215–41.

65. Sims-Williams, *Irish Influence on Medieval Welsh Literature*, 235, 242.

66. McFarlane, *The Nobility of Later Medieval England*, 87.

67. Root, "History," 13–26.

68. Brusendorff, *The Chaucer Tradition*, 21–23.

69. Giffin, *Studies on Chaucer and His Audience*, 18–19.

70. Marks and Morgan, *The Golden Age of English Manuscript Painting*, 112–13.

71. Pearsall, *The Life of Geoffrey Chaucer*, 179, 331.

72. Furnivall and Gollancz, *Hoccleve's Works: The Minor Poems*, 242.

73. H. S. Bennett, *Chaucer and the Fifteenth Century*, 149.

74. Mathew, *The Court of Richard II*, 57.

75. Mitchell, *Thomas Hoccleve*, 115.

76. Doyle and Parkes, "The Production of Copies of the *Canterbury Tales* and the *Confessio Amantis* in the Early Fifteenth Century," 163–210.

77. Seymour, *Selections from Hoccleve*, 135.

78. Phillips, "Contexts of Translation," 45–69.

79. Patterson, *Acts of Recognition*, 115.

80. Pantin, *The English Church*, 260.

81. Pantin, "Instructions," 398–422.

82. Hughes, *Pastors and Visionaries*, 91, 100, 102.

Bibliography

Alcock, Leslie. 1971. *Arthur's Britain*. London: Allen Lane.

———. 1972. *"By South Cadbury is That Camelot . . . "*: *Excavations at Cadbury Castle 1966–70*. London: Thames and Hudson.

———. 1995. *Cadbury Castle, Somerset: The Early Medieval Archaeology*. Cardiff: University of Wales Press.

Alexander, Michael, & Felicity Riddy. 1989. *Macmillan Anthologies of English Literature: The Middle Ages*. London: Macmillan.

Allen, Rosamund. 1987. "The Editing of *The Awntyrs off Arthure*." In *Manuscripts and Texts*. Edited by Derek Pearsall. Cambridge: D. S. Brewer. 6–25.

———, tr. 1992. *Brut*. London: J. M. Dent.

———. 1996. "*The Awntyrs off Arthure*: Jests and Jousts." In *Romance Reading on the Book*. Edited by Jennifer Fellows, Rosalind Field, Gillian Rogers, & Judith Weiss. Cardiff: University of Wales Press. 129–42.

———. 1999. "*The Awntyrs off Arthure*." In *The Arthur of the English*. Edited by W. R. J. Barron. Cardiff: University of Wales Press. 150–55.

———. 2004. "Place-Names in *The Awntyrs off Arthure*: Corruption, Conjecture, Coincidence." In *Arthurian Studies in Honour of P. J. C. Field*. Edited by Bonnie Wheeler. Cambridge: D. S. Brewer. 181–98.

Anderson, J. J., ed. 1969. *Patience*. Manchester: Manchester University Press.

———, ed. 1977. *Cleanness*. Manchester: Manchester University Press.

———. 2005. *Language and Imagination in the "Gawain" Poems*. Manchester: Manchester University Press.

Andrew, M. R., & R. A. Waldron, eds. 1978. *The Poems of the "Pearl" Manuscript*. London: Edward Arnold.

Anon. 1977. "Lady Isle." In *The New Shell Guide to Scotland*. Edited by D. L. Macnie. London: Ebury Press. 207.

———. 2008. "Dux Britanniarum." In *The Welsh Academy Encyclopaedia of Wales*. Edited by John Davies, Nigel Jenkins, Menna Baines, & Peredur Lynch. Cardiff: University of Wales Press. 228.

———. 2008. "Ystlwyf." In *The Welsh Academy Encyclopaedia of Wales*. Edited by John Davies, Nigel Jenkins, Menna Baines, & P. I. Lynch. Cardiff: University of Wales Press: 2008. 982.

Ashe, Geoffrey. 1957. *King Arthur's Avalon*. London: Collins.

————. 1968. "The Arthurian Fact." In *The Quest for Arthur's Britain*. Edited by Geoffrey Ashe. London: Pall Mall Press. 27–57.

Ashe, Laura. 2010. "*Sir Gawain and the Green Knight* and the Limits of Chivalry." In *The Exploitations of Medieval Romance*. Edited by Laura Ashe, Ivana Djordjevic, & Judith Weiss. Cambridge: D. S. Brewer. 159–72.

Astell, Ann W. 1999. *Political Allegory in Late Medieval England*. Ithaca: Cornell University Press.

Aston, Margaret. 1967. *Thomas Arundel*. Oxford: Clarendon.

Aurell, Martin. 2007. *La Légende du roi Arthur*. Paris: Perrin.

Banks, S. E., & J. W. Binns, eds. 2002. *Otia Imperialia*. Oxford: Clarendon.

Barrett, R. W. 2009. *Against All England*. Notre Dame: University of Notre Dame Press.

Barron, W. R. J., ed. 1974. *Sir Gawain and the Green Knight*. Manchester: Manchester University Press.

————. 1981. "Knighthood on Trial: The Acid Test of Irony." In *Knighthood in Medieval Literature*. Edited by W. H. Jackson. Woodbridge: D. S. Brewer. 89–105.

————. 1999. "*Sir Gawain and the Green Knight*." In *The Arthur of the English*. Edited by W. R. J. Barron. Cardiff: University of Wales Press. 164–83.

Barrow, G. W. S. 1980. *The Anglo-Norman Era in Scottish History*. Oxford: Clarendon.

Bennett, H. S. 1947. *Chaucer and the Fifteenth Century*. Oxford: Clarendon.

Bennett, J. A. W. 1974. *Chaucer at Oxford and at Cambridge*. Oxford: Clarendon.

————. 1986. *Middle English Literature*. Oxford: Clarendon.

Bennett, M. J. 1997. "The Historical Background." In *A Companion to the Gawain-Poet*. Edited by D. S. Brewer & Jonathan Gibson. Woodbridge: D. S. Brewer. 71–90.

————. 1999. *Richard II and the Revolution of 1399*. Stroud: Sutton.

Benson, L. D. 1968. "Art and Tradition in *Sir Gawain and the Green Knight*." In *Twentieth-Century Interpretations of "Sir Gawain and the Green Knight.*" Edited by Denton Fox. Englewood Cliffs: Prentice Hall. 23–34.

Beresford, M. W., & J. K. S. St. Joseph. 1979. *Medieval England: An Aerial Survey*, 2nd edn. Cambridge: Cambridge University Press.

Bishop, Ian. 1968. *Pearl in Its Setting*. Oxford: Blackwell.

Blanch, R. J., & J. N. Wasserman. 1995. *From Pearl to Gawain*. Gainesville: University Press of Florida.

Blake, Norman, ed. 1980. *The Canterbury Tales*. London: Edward Arnold.

————. 1985. *The Textual Tradition of the "Canterbury Tales.*" London: Edward Arnold.

Borroff, Marie. 1962. *"Sir Gawain and the Green Knight": A Stylistic and Metrical Study*. New Haven: Yale University Press.

————. 2006. "Narrative Artistry in *St. Erkenwald* and the *Gawain*-Group." *Studies in the Age of Chaucer*, vol. 28, 41–76.

Bowers, J. M. 1995. "*Pearl* in its Royal Setting." *Studies in the Age of Chaucer*, vol. 17, 111–55.

———. 2001. *The Politics of "Pearl."* Cambridge: D. S. Brewer.

Breeze, A. 1998. *"The Awntyrs off Arthure*, Cywryd of Kent, and Lavery Burn." *Notes and Queries*, vol. 245, 431–32.

———. 1999. *"The Awntyrs off Arthure*, Caerphilly, Oysterlow, and Wexford." *Arthuriana*, vol. 9, no. 4, 63–68.

———. 2000. "The Lady Beryke and Sir Meneduke in *The Awntyrs off Arthure.*" *Transactions of the Cumberland and Westmorland Antiquarian and Archaeological Society*, vol. 100, 281–85.

———. 2004. "Sir John Stanley (*c.* 1350–1414) and the *Gawain*-Poet." *Arthuriana*, vol. 14, no. 1, 15–30.

———. 2008. *"Art* 'Direction' in *St. Erkenwald.*" *Notes and Queries*, vol. 253, 273.

———. 2009. *"Skelt* 'Hasten' in *Cleanness* and *St. Erkenwald.*" *Leeds Studies in English*, n.s. vol. 40, 147–48.

———. 2014. *"Pearl* and the Plague of 1390–1393." *Neophilologus*, vol. 98, 337–41.

———. 2015. "The Historical Arthur and Sixth-Century Scotland." *Northern History*, vol. 52, 58–81.

———. 2016. "Arthur's Battles and the Volcanic Winter of 536–537." *Northern History*, vol. 53, 161–72.

———. 2019. "King Arthur *Dux Bellorum*: Welsh *Penteulu* 'Chief of the Royal Host.'" *Revue de Traduction et Langues*, vol. 18, 51–76.

———. 2020. *British Battles 493–937: Mount Badon to Brunanburh.* London: Anthem Press.

Brewer, D. S. 1963. *Chaucer in His Time.* London: Nelson.

———. 1966. "Courtesy and the *Gawain*-Poet." In *Patterns of Love and Courtesy: Essays in Memory of C. S. Lewis.* Edited by John Lawlor. London: Edward Arnold. 54–85.

———. 1980. *Symbolic Stories.* Cambridge: D. S. Brewer.

———. 1983. *English Gothic Literature.* London: Macmillan.

Brewer, Elisabeth. 1973. *From Cuchulainn to Gawain.* Cambridge: D. S. Brewer.

Brock, Edmund, ed. 1871. *Morte Arthure*, 2nd edn. London: N. Truebner.

Bromwich, Rachel. 1950. "Cantre'r Gwaelod and Ker-Is." In *The Early Cultures of North-West Europe.* Edited by Cyril Fox & Bruce Dickens. Cambridge: Cambridge University Press. 215–41.

———. 1954. "The Character of the Early Welsh Tradition." In *Studies in Early British History.* Edited by Nora K. Chadwick. Cambridge: Cambridge University Press. 83–136

———. 1978. *Trioedd Ynys Prydein*, 2nd edn. Cardiff: University of Wales Press.

———, & D. Simon Evans, eds. 1992. *Culhwch and Olwen.* Cardiff: University of Wales Press.

Brook, G. L., ed. 1963. *Selections from La3amon's "Brut."* Oxford: Clarendon Press.

Brusendorff, Aage. *The Chaucer Tradition.* Copenhagen: Branner, 1925.

Bugbee, John. 2008. "Sight and Sound in *St. Erkenwald." Medium Aevum*, vol. 77, 202–21.

Burrow, J. A. 1965. *A Reading of "Sir Gawain and the Green Knight."* London: Routledge.

————. 1971. *Ricardian Poetry: Chaucer, Gower, Langland, and the "Gawain" Poet*. London: Routledge.

————. 1984. *Essays on Medieval Literature*. Oxford: Clarendon.

————. 1993. "*Saint Erkenwald* Line I." *Notes and Queries*, vol. 238, 22–23.

————. 1997. "Redundancy in Alliterative Verse." In *Individuality and Achievement in Middle English Poetry.* Edited by. O. S. Pickering. Woodbridge: D. S. Brewer. 119–28.

Burrow, J. A., & Thorlac Turville-Petre. 1996. *A Book of Middle English*, 2nd edn. Oxford: Blackwell.

Campbell, James. 1982. "The Lost Centuries." In *The Anglo-Saxons*. Edited by James Campbell. Oxford: Phaidon. 20–44.

Carr, A. D. 2017. *The Gentry of North Wales in the Later Middle Ages.* Cardiff: University of Wales Press.

Chadwick, H. M., & N. K. Chadwick. 1932. *The Growth of Literature: The Ancient Literatures of Europe.* Cambridge: Cambridge University Press.

Chambers, E. K. 1927. *Arthur of Britain.* London: Sidgwick & Jackson.

Charles-Edwards, T. M. 2013. *Wales and the Britons 350–1064*. Oxford: Oxford University Press.

Childs, Wendy. 1983. "Anglo-Italian Contacts." In *Chaucer and the Italian Trecento*. Edited by Piero Boitani. Cambridge: Cambridge University Press. 65–87.

Churchill, Winston S. 1956. *The History of the English-Speaking Peoples: The Birth of Britain*. London: Cassell.

Clarkson, Tim. *Scotland's Merlin.* Edinburgh: John Donald.

Coleman, J. 1981. *English Literature in History 1350–1400*. London: Hutchinson.

Coley, D. K. 2019. *Death and the Pearl-Maiden*. Columbus, Ohio State University Press.

Collingwood, R. G., & J. N. L. Myers. 1937. *Roman Britain and the English Settlements*, 2nd edn. Oxford: Clarendon.

Collins, Rob, 2013. "Military Communities and Transformation of the Frontier from the Fourth to the Sixth Centuries." In *Early Medieval Northumbria*. Edited by David Petts & Sam Turner. Turnhout: Brepols. 16–34.

Cooper, Helen. 2000. "Introduction: The Poet." In *Sir Gawain and the Green Knight*. Translated by Keith Harrison. Oxford: Oxford University Press.

————. 2004. *The English Romance in Time.* Oxford, Oxford University Press.

Cottle, Basil. 1969. *The Triumph of English 1350–1400*. London: Batsford.

Cummins, W. A. 1992. *King Arthur's Place in Prehistory.* Stroud: Sutton.

Coward, Barry. 1983. *The Stanleys, Lords Stanley, and Earls of Derby 1385–1672*. Manchester: Manchester University Press.

Daniel, Iestyn. 2019. *Llythyr Gildas a Dinistr Prydain*. Bangor: Dalen Newydd.

Dark, K. R. 1994. *Civitas to Kingdom.* Leicester: Leicester University Press.

————, 2000. "A Famous Arthur in the Sixth Century?" *Reading Medieval Studies*, vol. 26, 77–95.

Davenport, W. A. 1978. *The Art of the "Gawain"-Poet*. London, Athlone.

Davies, R. R. 1969. "Owain Glyn Dwr and the Welsh Squirarchy." *Transactions of the Honourable Society of Cymmrodorion: Session 1968*. 150–69.

———. *Lordship and Society in the March of Wales 1282–1400.* 1978. Oxford: Clarendon.

———. *Conquest, Co-existence, and Change: Wales 1063–1415.* Oxford: Oxford University Press.

Davies, Wendy. 1982. *Wales in the Early Middle Ages.* Leicester: Leicester University Press.

Dickinson, W. Croft. 1977. *Scotland from the Earliest Times to 1603,* 3rd edn. Oxford: Clarendon.

DiMarco, V. J. 1987. "The Squire's Tale." In *The Riverside Chaucer.* Edited by L. D. Benson. Boston: Houghton Mifflin. 890–95.

———. 2002. "The Squire's Tale." In *Sources and Analogues of the Canterbury Tales.* Edited by R. M. Correale & Mary Hamel. Cambridge: D. S. Brewer. 169–209.

Dodgson, J. McN. 1963. "Sir Gawain's Arrival in Wirral." In *Early English and Norse Studies Presented to Hugh Smith.* Edited by Arthur Brown & Peter Foote. London: Methuen. 19–25.

Doyle, A. I., & M. B. Parkes. 1978. "The Production of Copies of the *Canterbury Tales* and the *Confessio Amantis* in the Early Fifteenth Century." In *Medieval Scribes, Manuscripts, and Libraries.* Edited by M. B. Parkes and A. G. Watson. London: Scolar Press. 163–210.

Drake, S. J. 2019. *Cornwall, Connectivity, and Identity in the Fourteenth Century.* Woodbridge: Boydell.

Dumville, D. N. 1977. "Sub-Roman Britain: History and Legend." *History,* vol. 62, 173–92.

Duncan, A. A. M. 1975. *Scotland: The Making of the Kingdom.* Edinburgh: Oliver & Boyd.

Echard, Siân. 2010. "Insular Romance." In *The Oxford Handbook of Medieval Literature in English.* Edited by Elaine Treharne & Greg Walker. Oxford: Oxford University Press. 160–80.

Edwards, J. Goronwy. 1935. *Calendar of Ancient Correspondence Concerning Wales.* Cardiff: University of Wales Press.

Evans, H. T. 1915. *Wales and the Wars of the Roses.* Cambridge: Cambridge University Press.

Everett, Dorothy. 1955. *Essays on Middle English Literature.* Oxford: Clarendon.

Favero, Piero. 2012. *La Dea Veneta.* Udine: privately published.

———. 2017. *King Arthur's Tribe.* Udine: privately published.

Fichte, Jörg O. 2014. "*The Awntyrs off Arthure.*" In *Mittelenglische Artusromanzen.* Edited by Jörg O. Fichte. Stuttgart: S. Hirzel Verlag. 135–200.

Field, John. 1980. *Place-Names of Great Britain and Ireland.* Newton Abbot: David & Charles.

Field, Peter. 2022. "King Arthur: Hero or Legend?" In *The Arthurian World.* Edited by Victoria Coldham-Fussell, Miriam Edlich-Mutt, & Renée Ward. London: Routledge. 25–34.

Field, Rosalind. 2008. "Subjects of Translation: Romance." In *The Oxford History of Literary Translation in English: To 1550*. Edited by Roger Ellis. Oxford: Oxford University Press. 296–331.

Fisher, J. H. 1961. "Wyclif, Langland, Gower, and the *Pearl* Poet on the Subject of Aristocracy." In *Studies in Medieval Literature in Honor of Professor Albert Croll Baugh*. Edited by MacEdward Leach. Philadelphia, University of Pennsylvania Press. 139–57.

———, ed. 1989. *The Complete Poetry and Prose of Geoffrey Chaucer*, 2nd edn. New York: Holt, Rinehart, & Winston.

Fisher, Sheila. 2000. "Women and Men in Late Medieval English Romance." In *The Cambridge Companion to Medieval Romance*. Edited by R. L. Krueger. Cambridge: Cambridge University Press. 150–64.

Fletcher, D. 1997. "The Lancastrian Collar of Essex." In *The Age of Richard II*. Edited by J. L. Gillespie. Stroud: Sutton.

Fowler, David C. 1984. *The Bible in Middle English Literature*. Seattle, University of Washington Press.

Fraser, J. E. 2009. *From Caledonia to Pictland: Scotland to 795*. Edinburgh: Edinburgh University Press.

Freidl, J.-P., & Ian J. Kirby. 2002. "The Life, Death, and Life of the *Pearl* Maiden." *Neuphilologische Mitteilungen*, vol. 13, 395–98.

Frere, Sheppard. 1967. *Britannia*. London: Routledge.

Froissart, Jean. 1968. *Chronicles*. Translated by Geoffrey Brereton. Harmondsworth: Penguin.

Fulton, Helen. 2019. "Britons and Saxons: The Earliest Writing in Welsh." In *The Cambridge History of Welsh Literature*. Edited by Geraint Evans & Helen Fulton. Cambridge: Cambridge University Press, 26–51.

Furnivall, F. J., & Israel Gollancz, eds. 1925. *Hoccleve's Works: The Minor Poems*. London: Oxford University Press.

Giffin, Mary. 1956. *Studies on Chaucer and His Audience*. Hull: L'Éclair.

Gollancz, I., ed. 1940. *Sir Gawain and the Green Knight*. London: Oxford University Press.

Gordon, E. V., ed. 1953. *Pearl*. Oxford: Clarendon.

Gradon, Pamela. 1971. *Form and Style in Early English Literature*. London: Methuen.

Grady, Frank. 2000. "*St. Erkenwald* and the Merciless Parliament." *Studies in the Age of Chaucer*, vol. 22, 179–211.

Gray, Douglas. 2006. *Later Medieval English Literature*. Oxford: Oxford University Press.

Green, V. H. H. 1955. *The Later Plantagenets*. London: Edward Arnold.

Hahn, Thomas. 2000. "Gawain and Popular Chivalric Romance in Britain." In *The Cambridge Companion to Medieval Romance*. Edited by Roberta L. Krueger. Cambridge: Cambridge University Press. 218–34.

Halsall, Guy. 2013. *Worlds of Arthur*. Oxford: Oxford University Press.

Hanna, Ralph, ed. 1974. *The Awntyrs off Arthure at the Terne Wathelyn*. Manchester: Manchester University Press.

Harding, Stephen. 2002. *Viking Mersey*. Birkenhead: Countyvise.

Higham, N. J. 2002. *King Arthur: Myth-Making and History.* London: Routledge.

———. 2011. "The Chroniclers of Early Britain." In *The Arthur of Medieval Latin Literature.* Edited by Siân Echard. Cardiff: University of Wales Press. 9–25

———. 2018. *King Arthur: The Making of the Legend.* New Haven: Yale University Press.

Hill, Ordelle G. 2009. *Looking Westward.* Newark: University of Delaware Press.

Hillmann, M. V., ed. 1961. *The Pearl.* Notre Dame: University of Notre Dame Press.

Hodges, Laura E. 2000. *Chaucer and Costume.* Cambridge: D. S. Brewer.

Horobin, Simon, & Jeremy Smith, eds. 2002. *An Introduction to Middle English.* Edinburgh: Edinburgh University Press.

Hughes, Jonathan. 1988. *Pastors and Visionaries: Religion and Secular Life in Late Medieval Yorkshire.* Woodbridge: Boydell.

Hunter Blair, Peter. 1977. *An Introduction to Anglo-Saxon England,* 2nd edn. Cambridge: Cambridge University Press.

Jackson, K. H. 1953. *Language and History in Early Britain.* Edinburgh: Edinburgh University Press.

———. 1955. "The Britons in Southern Scotland." *Antiquity,* vol. 29, 77–88.

———. 1959. "The Arthur of History." In *Arthurian Literature in the Middle Ages.* Edited by R. S. Loomis. Oxford, Clarendon. 1–11.

———. 1963. "Angles and Britons in Northumbria and Cumbria." In *Angles and Britons: O'Donnell Lectures.* Cardiff: University of Wales Press. 60–84.

———. 1969. *The Gododdin: The Oldest Scottish Poem.* Edinburgh: Edinburgh University Press.

———. 1972. *The Gaelic Notes in the Book of Deer.* Cambridge: Cambridge University Press.

Jackson, Robert. 1984. *Dark-Age Britain.* London: Stephens.

Jacobs, Nicolas. 1978. "Y Traddodiad Arwrol Hen Saesneg." In *Astudiaethau ar yr Hengerdd.* Edited by Rachel Bromwich & R. Brinley Jones. Caerdydd: Gwasg Prifysgol Cymru. 165–78.

Jarman, A. O. H., ed. 1982. *Llyfr Du Caerfyrddin.* Caerdydd: Gwasg Prifysgol Cymru.

Johnson, Flint F. 2014. *Evidence of Arthur.* Jefferson: McFarland.

Johnson, Stephen. 1980. *Later Roman Britain.* London: Routledge.

Johnston, Michael. 2014. *Romance and the Gentry in Late Medieval England.* Oxford: Oxford University Press.

Jones, H. S. V. 1941. "The Squire's Tale." In *Sources and Analogues of Chaucer's Canterbury Tales.* Edited by W. F. Bryan & Germaine Dempster. Chicago: Chicago University Press. 357–76.

Jones, Owen, Edward Williams, & W. O. Pughe, eds. 1870. *The Myvyrian Archaiology of Wales,* 2nd edn. Denbigh: T. Gee.

Jones Pierce, T. 1972. *Medieval Welsh Society.* Cardiff: University of Wales Press.

Jones, T. Gwynn, ed. 1926. *Gwaith Tudur Aled.* Caerdydd: Gwasg Prifysgol Cymru.

Joyce, Stephen J. 2022. *The Legacy of Gildas.* Woodbridge: Boydell.

Jost, Jean E. 2012. "Marshy Spaces in the Middle English *Awntyrs off Arthure.*" In *Rural Space in the Middle Ages and Early Modern Age.* Edited by Albrecht Classen. Berlin: De Gruyter. 589–606.

Kane, George. 1951. *Middle English Literature*. London: Methuen.

Kean, P. M. 1967. *The Pearl: An Interpretation*. London: Routledge.

Keen, M. H. 1977. *England in the Later Middle Ages*. London: Methuen.

Kendall, Elliot. 2008. *Lordship and Literature*. Oxford: Clarendon.

Koch, John T. 2013. "Waiting for Gododdin." In *Beyond the Gododdin*. Edited by Alex Woolf. St. Andrews: University Committee for Dark Age Studies. 177–204.

Kowalik, Barbara. 2010. *Betwixt "Englaunde" and "Englene Londe."* Frankfurt: Peter Lang.

Kratzmann, Gregory. 1980. *Anglo-Scottish Literary Relations 1430–1550*. Cambridge: Cambridge University Press.

Lawton, David. 2000. "Englishing the Bible 1066–1549." In *The Cambridge History of Medieval English Literature*. Edited by David Lawton. Cambridge: Cambridge University Press.

Lewis, C. S. 1962. "The Anthropological Approach." In *English and Medieval Studies Presented to J. R. R. Tolkien*. Edited by Norman Davis & C. L. Wrenn. London: Allen & Unwin.

Lewis, E. A. 1912. *The Mediaeval Boroughs of Snowdonia*. London: H. Sotheran.

Lewis, Henry, Thomas Roberts, & Ifor Williams, eds. 1925. *Cywyddau Iolo Goch ac Eraill*. Bangor: Evan Thomas.

Liebhard, Kurt. 2016. *Suche nach dem historischen Arthur*. Weissenthurm: Cardamina Verlag.

Lloyd, J. E. 1911. *A History of Wales*. London: Longman.

———. 1931. *Owen Glendower*. Oxford: Clarendon.

Lloyd-Morgan, Ceridwen, & Erich Poppe. 2019. "Introduction." In *Arthur in the Celtic Languages*. Edited by Ceridwen Lloyd-Morgan & Erich Poppe. Cardiff: University of Wales Press. 1–10.

Loomis, Laura H. 1959. "*Gawain and the Green Knight*." In *Arthurian Literature in the Middle Ages*. Edited by R. S. Loomis. Oxford: Clarendon. 528–40.

Lowes, J. L. 1934. *Geoffrey Chaucer*. Oxford: Clarendon.

Lucas, Peter J., ed. 1983. *John Capgrave's Abbreuiacion of Cronicles*. Oxford: Oxford University Press.

Lydon, James. 1973. *Ireland in the Later Middle Ages.* Dublin: Gill & Macmillan.

Mac Cana, Proinsias. 1980. *The Learned Tales of Medieval Ireland.* Dublin: Dublin Institute for Advanced Studies.

Manly, J. M., ed. 1928. *Canterbury Tales by Geoffrey Chaucer*. New York: Holt.

Mann, Jill. 1993. "Price and Value in *Sir Gawain and the Green Knight*." In *Medieval English Poetry*. Edited by Stephanie Trigg. London: Longman. 119–37.

———, ed. 2005. *The Canterbury Tales*. London: Penguin.

———. 2009. "Courtly Aesthetics and Courtly Ethics in *Sir Gawain and the Green Knight*." *Studies in the Age of Chaucer*, vol. 31, 231–65.

Marks, Richard & Nigel Morgan. 1981. *The Golden Age of English Manuscript Painting*. London: Chatto & Windus.

Mathew, Gervase. 1948. "Ideals of Knighthood in Late-Fourteenth-Century England." In *Studies in Medieval History Presented to Frederick Maurice Powicke*. Edited by R. W. Hunt, W. A. Pantin, & R. W. Southern. Oxford: Clarendon. 354–62.

———. 1968. *The Court of Richard II*. London: John Murray.

McFarlane, K. B. 1972. *Lancastrian Kings and Lollard Knights*. Oxford: Clarendon.

———. 1973. *The Nobility of Later Medieval England*. Oxford: Clarendon.

McGladdery, Christine. 1990. *James II*. Edinburgh: John Donald.

McKisack. May. 1959. *The Fourteenth Century*, Oxford: Clarendon.

McTurk, Rory. 2005. *Chaucer and the Norse and Celtic Worlds*. Aldershot: Ashgate.

Mills, A. D. 1991. *A Dictionary of English Place-Names*. Oxford: Oxford University Press.

Mitchell, Jerome. 1968. *Thomas Hoccleve*. Urbana: University of Illinois Press.

Medcalf, Stephen. 1973. "*Piers Plowman* and the Ricardian Age in Literature." In *The Mediaeval World*. Edited by David Daiches & Anthony Thorlby. London: Aldus. 643–96.

Moorman, John. 1966. "Myth and Mediaeval Literature." In *Sir Gawain and Pearl: Critical Essays*. Edited by R. J. Blanch. Bloomington: Indiana University Press.

Morris, John. 1973. *The Age of Arthur*. London: Weidenfeld & Nicolson.

———, tr. 1980. *British History and the Welsh Annals*. Chichester: Phillimore.

———. 1982. *Londinium*. London: Weidenfeld & Nicolson.

Morse, Charlotte C. 2001. "Griselda Reads Philippa de Coucy." In *Speaking Images*. Edited by R. F. Yeager. Asheville: Pegasus Press. 347–92.

Muscatine, Charles. 1972. *Poetry and Crisis in the Age of Chaucer*. Notre Dame: University of Notre Dame Press.

Myers, A. R., ed. 1969. *English Historical Documents 1327–1485*. London: Eyre & Spottiswoode.

Naismith, Rory. 2021. *Early Medieval Britain*. Cambridge: Cambridge University Press.

Neuhauser, Richard. 1997. "Sources II." In *A Companion to the Gawain-Poet*. Edited by D. S. Brewer & Jonathan Gibson. Woodbridge: D. S. Brewer. 257–75.

Newton, Stella Mary. 1980. *Fashion in the Age of the Black Prince*. Woodbridge: Boydell.

Norton-Smith, John, ed. 1971. *The Kingis Quair*. Oxford: Clarendon.

Oakden, J. P. 1930. *Alliterative Poetry in Middle English: The Dialectal and Metrical Survey*. Manchester: Manchester University Press.

Oakden, J. P. 1935. *Alliterative Poetry in Middle English: A Survey of the Traditions*. Manchester: Manchester University Press.

Oakden, J. P. 1968. "The Liturgical Influence in *Pearl*." In *Chaucer und Seine Zeit: Symposium für Walter F. Schirmer*. Edited by Arno Esch. Tübingen: Max Niemeyer. 336–53.

O'Loughlin, J. L. N. 1959. "The English Alliterative Romances." In *Arthurian Literature in the Middle Ages*. Edited by R. S. Loomis. Oxford: Clarendon. 520–27.

Otway-Ruthven, A. J. 1980. *A History of Medieval Ireland*, 2nd edn. London: Benn.

Owen, Edward. 1900–22. *A Catalogue of the Manuscripts Relating to Wales in the British Museum*. London: Honourable Society of Cymmrodorion.

Owen, Morfydd E. 2007. "Some Points of Comparison and Contrast Between Early Irish and Welsh Law." In *Ireland and Wales in the Middle Ages*. Edited by Karen Jankulak & J. M. Wooding. Dublin: Four Courts. 180–200.

Padel, O. J. 1981. "The Cornish Background of the Tristan Stories." *Cambridge Medieval Celtic Studies*, vol. 1, 53–81.

———. 1994. "The Nature of Arthur." *Cambrian Medieval Celtic Studies*, vol. 27, 1–31.

———. 1999. "Arthur." In *The Blackwell Encyclopedia of Anglo-Saxon England*. Edited by Michael Lapidge, John Blair, Simon Keynes, & Donald Scragg. Oxford: Blackwell. 48.

———. 2000. *Arthur in Medieval Welsh Literature*. Cardiff: University of Wales Press.

———. 2013. *Arthur in Medieval Welsh Literature*, 2nd edn. Cardiff: University of Wales Press.

Panton, W. A. 1955. *The English Church in the Fourteenth Century*. Cambridge: Cambridge University Press.

———. 1976. "Instructions for a Devout and Literate Layman." In *Medieval Literature and Learning*. Edited by J. J. G. Alexander & M. T. Gibson. Oxford: Clarendon Press. 398–422.

Patterson, Lee. 1992. "Court Politics and the Invention of Literature." In *Culture and History 1350–1600*. Edited by David Aers. Hemel Hempstead: Harvester Wheatsheaf. 7–41.

———. 2010. *Acts of Recognition*. Notre Dame: University of Notre Dame Press.

Pearsall, D. A. 1977. *Old English and Middle English Poetry*. London: Routledge.

———. 1992. *The Life of Geoffrey Chaucer*. Oxford: Blackwell.

———. 2003. *Arthurian Romance*. Oxford: Blackwell.

Pérez, Karen. 2014. *The Myth of Morgan la Fey*. Basingstoke: Palgrave Macmillan.

Pevsner, Nikolaus. 1957. *The Buildings of England: Northumberland*. Harmondsworth: Penguin.

———. 1961. *The Buildings of England: Suffolk*. Harmondsworth: Penguin.

———. 1969. *The Buildings of England: North Lancashire*. Harmondsworth: Penguin.

———. 1971. *The Buildings of England: Cheshire*. Harmondsworth: Penguin.

Phillips, Helen. 2008. "Contexts of Translation: Nation, Region, Class, and Gender." In *The Oxford History of Literary Translation into English*. Edited by Roger Ellis. Oxford: Oxford University Press. 45–69.

Poole, A. L. 1955. *From Domesday Book to Magna Carta*, 2nd edn. Oxford: Clarendon.

Putter, Ad. 1995. *"Sir Gawain and the Green Knight" and French Arthurian Romance*. Oxford: Clarendon.

———, & Myra Stokes. 2007. "The Linguistic Atlas and the Dialect of the *Gawain*-Poems." *Journal of English and Germanic Philology*, vol. 106, 468–91.

———, eds. 2014. *The Works of the Gawain Poet*. London: Penguin.

Rawcliffe, Carole. 1995. *Medicine and Society in Later Medieval England*. Stroud: Sutton.

Rees, William. 1924. *South Wales and the March 1284–1415*. London: Oxford University Press.

———. 1951. *An Historical Atlas of Wales*. London: Faber.

———. 1975. *Calendar of Ancient Petitions Relating to Wales*. Cardiff: University of Wales Press.

Rhŷs, John. 1904. *Celtic Britain*, 3rd edn. London: SPCK.

Richards, Melville, ed. 1948. *Breudwyt Ronabwy*. Caerdydd: Gwasg Prifysgol Cymru.

———, tr. 1954. *The Laws of Hywel Dda*. Liverpool: Liverpool University Press.

Roberts, Glyn. 1959. "Griffith of Penrhyn." In *The Dictionary of Welsh Biography*. London: Honourable Society of Cymmrodorion. 1123–26.

———. 1969. *Aspects of Welsh History*. Cardiff: University of Wales Press.

Robinson, F. N., ed. 1957. *The Works of Geoffrey Chaucer*, 2nd edn. Boston: Houghton Mifflin.

Robson, Margaret. 2000. "Darkness at Noon in *The Awntyrs off Arthure*." In *The Spirit of Medieval English Popular Romance*. Edited by Ad Putter & Jane Gilbert. New York: Pearson Education. 219–36.

Room, Adrian. 1988. *Dictionary of Place-Names in the British Isles*. London: Bloomsbury.

Root, Margaret. 1948. "History." In *Stirling Castle*. By J. S. Richardson and Margaret Root. Edinburgh: HMSO. 13–26.

Rowland, Jenny. 1990. *Early Welsh Saga Poetry*. Cambridge: D. S. Brewer.

Rubin, Miri. 2005. *The Hollow Crown*. London: Penguin.

Salter, Elizabeth. 1968. "Medieval Poetry and the Figural View of Reality." *Proceedings of the British Academy*, vol. 54, 73–92.

Salway, Peter. 1981. *Roman Britain*. Oxford: Oxford University Press.

Saunders, Corinne. 2010. *Magic and the Supernatural in Medieval English Romance*. Cambridge: D. S. Brewer.

Savage, H. L. 1966. "*Fare*, Line 694 of *Sir Gawain and the Green Knight*." In *Studies in Language and Literature in Honour of Margaret Schlauch*. Edited by Mieczysław Brahmer, Stanisław Helsztyński, & Julian Krzyżanowski. Warszawa: Panstwowe Wydawnictwo Naukowe. 383–84.

Schlauch, Margaret. 1963. *Antecedents of the English Novel 1400–1600*, Warszawa: Panstwowe Wydawnictwo Naukowe.

Schless, Howard. 1974. "Transformations: Chaucer's Use of Italian." In *Writers and Their Background: Geoffrey Chaucer*. Edited by Derek Brewer. London: Bell. 184–223.

Severs, J. Burke. 1979. "The Tales of Romance." In *Companion to Chaucer Studies*. Edited by Beryl Rowland, rev. edn. New York: Oxford University Press. 271–95.

Seymour, M. C., ed. 1981. *Selections from Hoccleve*. Oxford: Clarendon.

Silverstein, Theodore, ed. 1984. *Sir Gawain and the Green Knight*. Chicago: University of Chicago Press.

Simpson, James. 2000. "Contemporary English Writers." In *A Companion to Chaucer*. Edited by Peter Brown. Oxford: Blackwell. 114–32.

Sims-Williams, Patrick. 2011. *Irish Influence on Medieval Welsh Literature*. Oxford: Oxford University Press.

Sisam, Kenneth, ed. 1921. *Fourteenth-Century Verse and Prose*. Oxford: Oxford University Press.

Skeat, W. W., ed. 1900. *The Complete Works of Geoffrey Chaucer: Notes on the "Canterbury Tales,"* 2nd edn. Oxford: Clarendon.

Sobecki, Sebastian. 2008. *The Sea and Medieval English Literature.* Cambridge: D. S. Brewer.

Spearing, A. C. 1970. *The Gawain-Poet.* Cambridge: Cambridge University Press.

———. 1972. *Criticism and Medieval Poetry*, 2nd edn. London: Edward Arnold.

———. 1976. *Medieval Dream Poetry*, Cambridge: Cambridge University Press.

———. 1987. *Readings in Medieval Poetry*. Cambridge: Cambridge University Press.

———. 2005. *Textual Subjectivity*. Oxford: Oxford University Press.

———, & J. E. Spearing, eds. 1974. *Poetry of the Age of Chaucer*. London: Edward Arnold.

Speirs, John. 1957. *Medieval English Poetry*. London, Faber.

Staley, Lynn. 2002. "The Man in Foul Clothes." *Studies in the Age of Chaucer*, vol. 24, 1–47.

Stenton, F. M. 1971. *Anglo-Saxon England*, 3rd edn. Oxford: Clarendon.

Stöber, Karen. 2007. *Late Medieval Monasteries and Their Patrons*. Woodbridge: Boydell.

Stockton, E. W., tr. 1962. *The Major Latin Works of John Gower*. Seattle: University of Washington Press.

Stodnick, Jacqueline. 2010. "Emerging Englishness." In *The Oxford Handbook of Medieval Literature in English*. Edited by Elaine Treharne & Greg Walker. Oxford: Oxford University Press. 496–511.

Stone, Brian, tr. 1971. *The Owl and the Nightingale: Cleanness: St. Erkenwald*. Harmondsworth: Penguin.

Strickland, Matthew. 2020. "Undying Glory by the Sword's Edge. " In *Writing Battles*. Edited by Rory Naismith, Máire Ní Mhaonaigh, & Elizabeth Ashman Rowe. London: Bloomsbury Academic. 39–75.

Strohm, Paul. 1990. "Politics and Poetics." In *Literary Practise and Social Change in Britain, 1390–1530*. Edited by Lee Patterson. Berkeley: University of California Press. 83–112.

Su Fang Ng & Kenneth Hodges. 2010. "Saint George, Islam, and Regional Audiences." *Studies in the Age of Chaucer*, vol. 32, 257–94.

Tatlock, J. S. P. 1950. *The Mind and Art of Chaucer*. Syracuse: Syracuse University Press.

Taylor, A. J. 1964. *Caernarvon Castle and Town Walls*, rev. edn. London: HMSO.

Taylor, John. 1987. *English Historical Literature in the Fourteenth Century*. Oxford: Clarendon.

Thomas, Charles. 1971. *Britain and Ireland in Early Christian Times.* London: Thames & Hudson.

———. 1981. *Christianity in Roman Britain*. Berkeley: University of California Press.

Thomas, Rebecca. 2022. *History and Identity in Early Medieval Wales*. Cambridge: D. S. Brewer.

Thomas, R. J. 1938. *Enwau Afonydd a Nentydd Cymru*. Caerdydd: Gwasg Prifysgol Cymru.

Tolkien, J. R. R., & E. V. Gordon, eds. 1967. *Sir Gawain and the Green Knight*, 2nd edn. Oxford: Clarendon.

Tolstoy, Nikolai. 1960–62. "Nennius, Chapter Fifty-Six." *The Bulletin of the Board of Celtic Studies*, vol. 19, 118–62.

Turville-Petre, Thorlac. 1977. *The Alliterative Revival*. Cambridge: D. S. Brewer.

———. 2008. "The Green Chapel." In *A Commodity of Good Names*. Edited by O. J. Padel & D. N. Parsons. Donnington: Shaun Tyas. 320–29.

———. 2010. "Places of the Imagination." In *The Oxford Handbook of Medieval English Literature*. Edited by Elaine Treharne & Greg Walker. Oxford: Oxford University Press. 594–608.

Vance, Eugene. 1991. "*Pearl*: Love and the Poetics of Participation." In *Poetics: Theory and Practice in Medieval English Literature*. Edited by Piero Boitani & Anna Torti. Cambridge: D. S. Brewer. 131–47.

Vantuono, William. 1971. "*Patience, Cleanness, Pearl*, and *Gawain*: The Case for Common Authorship." *Annuale Mediaevale*, vol. 12, 37–69.

Wadiak, Walter. 2017. *Savage Economy: The Returns of Middle English Romance*. Notre Dame: University of Notre Dame Press.

Walker, David. 1990. *Medieval Wales*. Cambridge: Cambridge University Press.

Watson, W. J. 1926. *The History of the Celtic Place-Names of Scotland*. Edinburgh: William Blackwood and Sons.

Watts, Victor, ed. 2004. *The Cambridge Dictionary of English Place-Names*. Cambridge: Cambridge University Press.

Wells, J. E. 1916. *A Manual of the Writings in Middle English*. New Haven: Connecticut Academy of Arts and Sciences.

Wiliam, Aled Rhys, ed. 1960. *Llyfr Iorwerth*. Caerdydd: Gwasg Prifysgol Cymru.

Williams, A. H. 1941. *An Introduction to the History of Wales: Prehistoric Times to 1063*. Cardiff: University of Wales Press.

Williams, D. J. 1970. "Alliterative Poetry in the Fourteenth and Fifteen Centuries." In *The Middle Ages*. Edited by W. F. Bolton. London: Sphere. 107–58.

Williams, Glanmor. 1962. *The Welsh Church from Conquest to Reformation*. Cardiff: University of Wales Press.

———. 1987. *Recovery, Reorganization, and Reformation: Wales c. 1415–1642*. Oxford: Clarendon.

Williams, Hugh. 1912. *Christianity in Early Britain*. Oxford: Clarendon.

Williams, Ifor, ed. 1930. *Pedeir Keinc y Mabinogi*. Caerdydd: Gwasg Prifysgol Cymru.

———, ed. 1938. *Canu Aneirin*. Caerdydd: Gwasg Prifysgol Cymru.

———. 1944. *Lectures on Early Welsh Poetry*. Dublin: Dublin Institute for Advanced Studies.

———. 1972. *The Beginnings of Welsh Poetry*. Cardiff: University of Wales Press.

Williams, Stephen J., & J. Enoch Powell, eds. 1942. *Cyfreithiau Hywel Dda yn ôl Llyfr Blegywryd*. Caerdydd: Gwasg Prifysgol Cymru.

Wiswall, F. L. 1997. "Politics, Procedure, and the 'Non-Minority' of Edward III." In *The Age of Richard II*. Edited by J. L. Gillespie. Stroud: Sutton. 7–25.

Wood, Ian. 1984. "The End of Roman Britain." In *Gildas: New Approaches*. Edited by Michael Lapidge and David Dumville. Woodbridge: Boydell. 1–25

Woods, David. 2010. "Gildas and the Mystery Cloud of 536–7." *Journal of Theological Studies*, vol. 61, 246–34.

Woolf, Rosemary. 1968. *The English Religious Lyric in the Middle Ages*. Oxford: Clarendon.

Index

About the Author

Andrew Breeze (b. 1954), FSA, FRHistS, was educated in Sandwich (at Sir Roger Manwood's School) and then at the universities of Oxford and Cambridge. Married with six children, he has taught since 1987 at the University of Navarre, Pamplona. Amongst his books are the controversial *Medieval Welsh Literature* (1997), *The Mary of the Celts* (2008), *The Origins of the* Four Branches of the Mabinogi (2009), and *British Battles 493–937: Mount Badon to Brunanburh* (2020).